The Origins of the English Civil War

Each volume in the 'Problems in Focus' series is designed to make available to students important new work on key historical problems and periods that they encounter in their courses. Each volume is devoted to a central topic or theme, and the most important aspects of this are dealt with by specially commissioned essays from scholars in the relevant field. The editorial Introduction reviews the problem or period as a whole, and each essay provides an assessment of the particular aspect, pointing out the areas of development and controversy, and indicating where conclusions can be drawn or where further work is necessary. An annotated bibliography serves as a guide for further reading.

TITLES IN PRINT

FURTHER TITLES ARE IN PREPARATION

The Origins of the English Civil War

EDITED BY
CONRAD RUSSELL

MACMILLAN

First published 1973 by
MACMILLAN EDUCATION LTD
Houndmills, Basingstoke, Hampshire RG21 2XS
and London
Companies and representatives
throughout the world

ISBN 0–333–12400–6

Printed in Hong Kong

Reprinted 1983, 1985, 1987, 1989, 1991, 1992

Contents

Table of Events

1633   Laud appointed Archbishop of Canterbury

1634   First Ship Money writs

1637   Enforcement of new Scottish Prayer Book; rebellion in Scotland

1638   Decision in Hampden's Case: 7 judges rule in King's favour, 5 against

1639   First Bishops' War; failure to fight Scots; pacification of Berwick

1640   April–May   Parliament summoned: the 'Short Parliament'
       May onwards   Taxpayers' 'strike'
       August   Second Bishops' War; Scots invade England, and win battle of Newburn
       September   Treaty of Ripon: Scots to be paid £850 a day until conclusion of peace treaty
       November   Parliament meets: the 'Long Parliament'

1640–1   Nov.–April   Unsuccessful negotiations for a settlement; Triennial Act

1641   May   Death of Bedford; execution of Strafford; Crowds demonstrate outside House of Lords; unsuccessful plans for use of force against Parliament
       June   King forms intention of making separate peace with the Scots
       August   King leaves London for Edinburgh
       September   Treaty with Scots concluded; departure of Scottish army

1641   October   Irish rebellion
       November   King returns to London; publication of Grand Remonstrance begins open pamphlet war for popular support
       December   Parliamentarians gain control of City Common Council; King considers use of force; riots outside House of Lords

1642   January   Attempt to arrest the Five Members; Parliament takes refuge in the City; Parliamentarians gain control of City militia; King leaves London; Parliament returns to Westminster; passage of Militia Ordinance
       January–August   'The paper war': Remonstrances and Counter-Remonstrances
       April   Sir John Hotham shuts the gates of Hull against the King
       June   The Nineteen Propositions
       August   King raises his standard at Nottingham: the Civil War formally begun.

Preface

THE relations of authors and publishers, like those of men and women, rest on a mixture of mutual need, desire and incomprehension. An editor, then becomes a sort of marriage counsellor, devoted to the task of explaining the outlook of each party to the other. My greatest debt then is to the parties, for allowing themselves to be guided to the marriage now solemnised by the printers. My thanks are due to Mr. Derick Mirfin, of Macmillan, for his patience, understanding and perceptive suggestions and particularly for his tolerance of a lateness on delivery dates which authors share only with the shipping industry. My thanks are due to my contributors for their kindness and forbearance in adapting their work to the needs of the volume. In particular, I would like to thank Professor Lamar Hill and Mr. Michael Mendle for contributing at very short notice and Professor J. H. Elliott for writing his concluding review chapter at high speed during the 1972 power cuts.

Since publishers, like early Stuart kings, are suffering severely from the effects of inflation, we have found it necessary to accept a number of economies which have helped me to understand the unpopularity of Lord Treasurer Cranfield. There has been severe pressure on the length of the book, and even more pressure to reduce the number of footnotes. The editorial ruling has been that footnotes must be kept for verbatim quotations, and for research discoveries. The chief casualties, then, have necessarily been those courteous bibliographical footnotes in which one acknowledges the use of a colleague's work. We hope that any colleagues who find their work drawn on in this volume will appreciate that our gratitude is none the less because we have been unable to express it in a footnote. Spelling has been modernised throughout.

I would like to thank Professor G. E. Aylmer, Mr. J. P. Cooper, Mr. Derek Hirst, Mr. Horace Sanders and Mr. David Thomas for reading parts of the manuscript, and making a number of helpful suggestions and corrections, and Penelope Corfield for a number of stimulating debates which have helped to enrich the introduction and for reading most of the proofs. For any errors which remain, we alone are responsible. I would like to thank the Trustees of the Bedford Settled Estates for permission to quote from manuscripts in their possession, and Messrs. C. J. Sawyer & Co. of Grafton Street, for permission to quote from one of their sale catalogues. I would like to thank the librarians and archivists who have helped in the preparation of this book, and especially Mrs. M. P. G. Draper, of the Bedford Settled Estates, Mr. A. Andrews of Birmingham Reference Library, and Mr. P. J. Locke, of Huntingdon County Record Office. I would like to thank Mrs Audrey Cornwall, Miss Winifred Close and Miss Brenda Johnstone for their care, speed and accuracy in typing parts of this book. I would like to thank the Central Research Fund of the University of London for a grant towards the cost of work on the papers of the Earl of Bedford. Above all, I would like to thank my wife for her continued generosity in allowing me to pick her brains: she is the source of far more of the best ideas in this book than anyone except I will ever realise. In addition to inspiration, she has provided patient and detailed advice at all stages, and deserves more credit for the finished product than I can persuade her to admit.

CONRAD RUSSELL

Introduction

CONRAD RUSSELL

I

BEFORE attempting explanations, it is worth knowing what we are attempting to explain. Uncertainty on this point has accounted for much of the confusion which has pervaded accounts of the origins of the Civil War. In the first place, we cannot fully understand why the Civil War broke out until we understand better how it broke out. We can describe with some precision the discontents created by Charles I's government, and we can describe the measures wanted by most M.P.s to remedy these discontents. But between the thought and the action, between the discontent and the resort to arms, there is a gulf. By what political processes the reforming intentions with which Long Parliament M.P.s came to Westminster were translated into a desire to fight, we do not yet know. It is clear from a wealth of contemporary newsletters that in the autumn of 1640, when the Long Parliament met, contemporaries did not expect the crisis to come to war: they expected some sort of settlement to be patched up. For most observers, the realisation that war was a practical possibility dates from some time between November 1641, when they heard the news of the Irish rebellion, and January 1642, when the attempt on the Five Members was followed by the King's departure from London.

If, as royalist writers sometimes suspected, the Parliamentary leaders came to Westminster intending to start a war, and waited only until they had sufficiently inflamed public feeling, then one type of explanation will be appropriate. If, on the other hand, they came to Westminster expecting to reach a settlement with the King, and were driven into war in fear and desperation because all their political plans had broken down, a quite different type of explanation will be appropriate. So far, the bulk of the evidence suggests that we are dealing with the second of these phenomena: an accidental war, growing out of the panic and confusion which followed the failure of the Parliamentary leaders' plans for a bloodless coup. If this is so, we must be looking, not for explanations of a desire for revolution, but for explanations of a state of chronic misunderstanding, terror and distrust.

Uncertainty about what we are trying to explain is deepened by the fact that the English Civil War, as much as the Russian Revolution, was two revolutions, and the aims of these two revolutions were as profoundly opposed to each other as the aims of Mensheviks and Bolsheviks. Naturally, our explanations of the Civil War will be influenced by our assumptions on the question whether it is the first or the second of these revolutions which provides the driving force of the Parliamentarian cause in 1642. Whether we think the gentry made the war in 1642, or that they were pushed into it by pressures from below, will do much to determine the type of explanation we adopt. In 1642, the supporters of both revolutions were in alliance, and the balance of power within this alliance is still uncertain. The first revolution is the one symbolised in the execution of Strafford, the legislation of the Long Parliament, the Militia Ordinance, and the outbreak of Civil War in 1642. The second is the one symbolised in the creation of the New Model Army, Pride's Purge and the execution of Charles I. The first was, in anthropologists' terms, a rebellion rather than a revolution; it was not a social revolution, but a split in the governing class: a movement by a large number of peers and gentlemen to force a change of policy and a change of ministers on Charles I. The second revolution was a revolution in the full sense of the term: it was an assault on the existing social structure, and particularly on the position of the gentry. Unlike the first rebellion, the revolution of 1647–9 was supplied by the Levellers and the Fifth Monarchists with truly revolutionary ideologies. In the face of this second revolution, the vast majority of the leaders of the original rebellion against King Charles grew so frightened of their own followers that their sympathies returned to the King. The number of members of the Long Parliament who ultimately voted for Charles's execution was no more than twenty-six. But, alas for simplicity, one cannot divide the Parliamentarians into supporters of the first revolution and supporters of the second: the two movements, though socially and ideologically quite distinct, always remained politically confused. One can distinguish two types of approach: as Professor Underdown has put it:

> Broadly, and with much over-simplification, two general positions can be observed. That of the majority of the Parliamentarian gentry was that the war was fought for limited goals, mainly political and constitutional, but also including a further moderate reformation of the church, leaving the essential framework of government and society

intact. That of the minority for whom Colonel Pride was the obedient
agent was that it was fought for a total and complete reconstruction
of Church and State, and (for some) social justice, to achieve which,
all measures, even revolution, were justified. . . . The presence of
these two contradictory elements, one moderate and reformist, the
other radical and revolutionary, accounts for most of our difficulties
when we try to grasp the central meaning of the Puritan revolution.[1]

The second revolution was the revolution of the army, as the first was
the revolution of Parliament, but even after the Army, through Colonel
Pride, had purged Parliament to its liking, Parliament was so keen to
broaden the basis of its support that it admitted conformists and time-
servers in such numbers that, even after Pride's Purge, they outnumbered
the genuine revolutionaries. Even Cromwell, as Professor Underdown
has shown, was not a committed revolutionary. Cromwell's apparent
leadership of the army revolution then is an optical illusion: his real
achievement was his defeat of army radicalism, and the restoration of
the supremacy of the gentry in English political life. We have then a
political rebellion which was to a limited extent successful, and a social
revolution which, largely as a result of the gentry's unbroken control of
local government, was almost totally unsuccessful.

The brief given to contributors to this volume has been that they
should try to explain the first revolution, and not the second. This is
not because of any desire to minimise the importance of the second
revolution, but because this volume is to appear in the same series with
one on the Interregnum, edited by Professor Aylmer. Since the second
revolution happened well after the outbreak of the Civil War, the view
has been taken that its explanations are within the province of Professor
Aylmer and his contributors.

The English Civil War is perhaps the outstanding example of the
need of each generation to re-write its own history, and it is impossible
to survey its origins without surveying also the origins of the discussion
of its origins. Any such discussion must begin with Edward Hyde,
Earl of Clarendon, whose *History of the Great Rebellion*, written shortly
after the event, could draw on knowledge we may now never possess.
For Clarendon, the moralistic overtones of the story involved a collapse
in respect for established institutions: the abandonment of the text,
'fear God: honour the King'. For him, this contempt for established
authority appeared to be implicit in Puritanism, and therefore he thought
the seeds of the second revolution were necessarily contained in the

first. However, underneath his moralistic message Clarendon is telling a rather different story. This is an essentially *political* story, a story of mistaken decisions and missed opportunities. He thought it would have been possible for the King to reach a settlement with the leaders of the Long Parliament and was constantly prepared to make statements to the effect that the war would not have happened if one or another thing had happened differently. It is precisely these statements which must be denied by all the various schools that hold that an English Revolution was inevitable.

Another touchstone separating schools of historians is the date at which we begin the story. One who believes that the war was the inevitable result of deep social forces must take the story back into the sixteenth century, and diagnose long-term changes which, he claims, inevitably led to war. Such persons existed among Clarendon's contemporaries, as they have done ever since, but Clarendon observed that he was not so far-sighted as they were, and firmly began his story from the beginning of the reign of Charles I. From then on his real story, underneath the moralistic overtones, is of the steady alienation, by a series of political blunders, of men like the Earls of Bedford and Essex, who should have been instinctive supporters of the political establishment. Clarendon thought the Parliamentarians were dominated by a small aristocratic leadership, without whose backing the more widespread political and religious discontents could never have found effective expression. Recently, historians have been coming to take his political judgements, except about his own career, more seriously. Above all, his analysis of the Parliamentarian leadership is repeatedly confirmed by detailed research. For example, his picture of Bedford as much more of a friend to the church than most of the Parliamentary leaders is abundantly confirmed by an examination of Bedford's commonplace book.[2] Within the limited scope of his knowledge Clarendon deserves to be treated as a serious authority, but there are many questions we now have to answer on which Clarendon had nothing to say.

The contrary notion to Clarendon's, of the inevitability of the English Civil War, is now generally associated with Marxism and its offshoots, and yet, ironically, the notion of inevitable historical progress was established not by Marxists, but by the greatest of the Whig historians, S. R. Gardiner. Gardiner's distinctive contribution was not so much the notion of the 'Puritan Revolution', with which he is now particularly associated, as his views on the development of the English constitution. Gardiner was of the generation most heavily influenced by Darwin, and held the view of society now described by anthropologists as 'evolutionary': that society was evolving towards some predestined end, and growing nearer to perfection at each stage of its development. For Gardiner, as *homo sapiens* was the ultimate perfection of biological evolution, so the British Constitution was the ultimate perfection of political evolution. He thought that 'the Parliament of England was the noblest monument ever reared by mortal man',[3] and that the real cause of Charles's fall was his attempt to obstruct the inevitable development of the national will. Yet, though it is easy to attack some of Gardiner's interpretations, the fact remains that technically he was probably the finest scholar who has ever worked on this period. The great narrative of his *History of England* does not answer many of the questions we now wish to ask, and yet its factual accuracy is so nearly impeccable, and its scale so monumental, that as a record of events, it has stood unchallenged from 1893 to the present day. Some time, if we are to understand the story we are explaining, something must be added to Gardiner's political narrative, especially of the years 1640–42; and yet so far the task has daunted even the most foolhardy of historians.

The assumption of inevitability has been carried over from Whig to Marxist historiography. It is, indeed, time to begin to question those assumptions which nineteenth-century Whig and early twentieth-century Marxist historians have in common. Both Marxism and nineteenth-century Whiggery grew out of the same intellectual climate. Both are products of the middle of the nineteenth century, when the notion of 'progress' was at its most fashionable. Both grew out of that intellectual climate of which Darwin was both a consequence and a cause, in which history was seen moving, by a series of inevitable stages, from the worse to the better, until it reached what Jeremy Bentham called 'this age, in which knowledge is rapidly advancing towards perfection'.[4] The common assumptions of these two creeds, then, have included not only the belief in inevitability, but also the belief that the Parliamentarians, because they won, were 'progressive', and in some way stood for the future. This assumption has looked questionable, at least for the gentry who made the first revolution, ever since Brunton and Pennington for Parliament, and Professor Aylmer for the civil service, discovered that the royalists were, on average, ten years younger than the Parliamentarians, though Dr. Hill is right to stress that these figures do not apply to the radicals outside Parliament.[5] One of the aims of this volume is to show the ways in which the Parliamentarian gentry

were the conservatives, standing for the outdated values of the Elizabethan world in which many of them had grown up. It must be stressed,
however, that this picture of the Parliamentarians as the conservatives
is only meant to apply to the first revolution, the revolution of the Long
Parliament against Charles I.

Though Marxist historiography shares with the Whigs its devotion
to 'progress' and to inevitability, it differs from them in laying almost
exclusive emphasis on social and economic change as a cause of political
change. The characteristic effort of the last generation has therefore
been to explain political change in the light of preceding social and
economic change. This process began with R. H. Tawney's article, in
1941, on 'The Rise of the Gentry'. Tawney revealed the Marxist origins
of the whole idea by identifying the gentry as 'bons bourgeois', and argued
that the century from 1540 to 1640 had seen an overwhelming shift of
economic power to the gentry, and that in 1640 the gentry were trying
to achieve a political power to match their economic power.

To this argument Professor Trevor-Roper replied with his article
on the decline of the gentry. He rightly stressed that the gentry were not
bourgeois, and, by all meaningful tests, their leading members belonged
to the same class as the peerage. He then argued that many members of
the gentry were not rising but declining, and claimed that those who
were rising owed their fortunes, not to the rise of their class, but to their
success in obtaining government offices. Professor Trevor-Roper saw the
Civil War as the protest of a declining class against its loss of fortune—
a sort of martial equivalent to the reaction of the House of Lords to the
Lloyd George budget. Professor Hexter, in an article which did not at
the time secure the respect it deserved, rejected these economic
determinisms both of left and of right, and argued that neither offered
a sufficient explanation of what the Parliamentary leaders were trying
to do.

Today both these attempts at a social and economic explanation
must be regarded as having broken down, and, ironically, as having
done so as a result of advances in the study of economic history. Most
economic historians would now accept the verdict of Dr. Bowden,
writing in the *Cambridge Agrarian History*, that theories about shifts in
economic and political power as a result of inflation 'seem . . . to be
built on very uncertain foundations'.[6] The result of a vast amount of
study on the fortunes of the gentry has been to show that there were
some rising gentry and some declining gentry, but that no general
picture emerges. Mrs. Keeler, studying the members of the Long

Parliament, has also found that there is no correlation whatever between a member's wealth and his allegiance in the Civil War.[7] Moreover, it has become clear that the rise and fall of individual families of gentry owed more to biological accidents than to overall economic trends. Probably what did most to determine the fortunes of landed families was the rate of mortality among their tenants, since this determined the frequency with which they could make new leases, and so raise rents to keep pace with inflation. Neither 'the rise of the gentry' nor 'the decline of the gentry' ever happened.

These explanations did not only depend on the wrong social changes: they were also designed to explain events which did not happen. They were designed to explain a deliberate aim at revolution on the part of a class as a whole. But when the crisis came in 1640–42, the gentry did not react as a whole: they were split down the middle in ways which economics cannot easily explain. Nor is there any point in explaining why the gentry may have wished to make a deliberate revolution until it can be shown that some of them did wish to make a deliberate revolution.

The epilogue to the gentry controversy has recently appeared, in Professor Lawrence Stone's *The Crisis of the Aristocracy* (1965). Professor Stone's aim is to show that the supposed 'rise of the gentry' is largely a result of a decline of the aristocracy. Professor Stone's book will survive as a brilliant piece of social history, and his contribution to the history of such varied subjects as patronage, mining and violence will always leave us in his debt. But as an explanation of the origins of the Civil War, Professor Stone's book breaks down for the same reason as the other social change explanations: he attempts to explain events which did not happen in terms of a social change for which the evidence remains uncertain. It is hard to reconcile his 'crisis of the aristocracy' with the overwhelming evidence for the Parliamentarians' dependence on aristocratic leadership.[8]

Nor is it possible to explain the Civil War in terms of demands for political power expressed by a rising community of merchants. The number of merchants in the House of Commons was always small, and it was steadily falling. Moreover an analysis of the debates in the House of Commons suggests that the influence of merchants was even smaller than their numbers: only one merchant, Alderman Penington of London, can claim a place among the couple of dozen most important Parliamentarian leaders at the beginning of the war. Economic historians have shown us that industrial prices were rising much less fast than agricultural ones, and therefore that any rising class is more likely to have depended on the profits of agriculture than on those of trade or industry. Nor is it true to say that the leaders of the merchant community did badly out of Charles I: a study of the list of Charles I's grants passing the Great Seal may tempt one to the heretical suspicion that he was the real leader of the *bourgeois* revolution: the proportion of merchants receiving high honours and rewards is remarkably large, while the gentry were entitled to their resentment at being left out in the cold.[9] Both Mrs. Pearl, in her study of London, and Dr. Howell, in his study of Newcastle, have shown that the real split among the merchants was between the privileged oligarchy who benefited from Charles I's concessions, and the outer ring who envied the success of their more favoured rivals.

For the time being, then, social change explanations of the English Civil War must be regarded as having broken down, though it remains an undisputed fact that the economic position of the Crown and the Church had much worsened during the century before the Civil War. In this limited sense, social change remains an undoubted part of the causes of the Civil War.

It would be a great mistake, however, to go on to assume that the Civil War was not caused by social change. It is possible that a new social change explanation may hereafter be constructed.* Advances in economic history would now permit any new explanation to be based on social changes which did happen. In so far as there was a general social change in the century before the Civil War, it was not in the position of the gentry or the peerage, but in the rise of many of the upper yeomanry, a rise illustrated by the number of families who claimed to have moved up the social scale, and become entitled to the status of gentlemen. That 'the yeomanry' were rising is a statement of more precision than we can yet confidently make, but it is certainly true that many of them were rising. Malvolio, an estate steward who claimed to be a gentleman, provoked a ribaldry which such people commonly had to encounter, but Malvolio's son and grandson would probably have passed without question for gentlemen. In the light of Malvolio's Puritanism, Mr. Michael Burn's conceit of the Civil War as 'Malvolio's revenge' is not altogether far-fetched.[10] Even if the merchant class as a whole was

---

* Professor Lawrence Stone's *The Causes of the English Revolution* (Routledge & Kegan Paul, 1972) unfortunately appeared too late to be used here. It is to be noted that in discussing the English *Revolution* Professor Stone is not answering the same question as the contributors to this volume.

not rising, there were certainly many tradesmen and artificers, what Dr. Christopher Hill calls 'the industrious sort of people', who were also rising. These were the sort of people who provided much of the backbone of those truly revolutionary movements the New Model Army and the Leveller movement. These people did not belong to what were normally regarded as the political classes, but without strong support from among them, Parliament would not have been able to win its first crucial victory by frightening the King out of London in January 1642.

Any new social change explanation will have to be based on the power of these people, most of whom were rising, not so much at the expense of the gentry, as at the expense of smallholders and the labouring poor. In times of rapid inflation, their small amounts of ready capital gave them economic advantages over those below them: they could profit in a good year and survive a bad one, and often had the capital to pay the entry fine for a valuable long lease. But the mechanics of an explanation based on this type of change are far from obvious: why should the rise of those below the gentry explain a split among the gentry? Why, unless for political and religious reasons, should the gentry be divided in the face of these hungry generations below them, rather than uniting in class solidarity against them?

An introduction is not the place to answer questions as large as this, and all suggestions must be tentative. However, there is already some work to give us a solid foundation. One necessary result of the increase in the numbers of gentlemen, and of peers, was an increasingly intense competition for posts in county government, and for the majority of Stuart gentlemen, the government of their county was a far more attractive prize than the government of their country. Professor Barnes has given us a brilliant study of the effect of this competition for county power on one Parliamentary leader, Sir Robert Phelips. Phelips appeared to Gardiner to be a man of principle, dedicated to his country's liberty. To Professor Barnes, who has studied him in his local context, he appears an unprincipled opportunist, concerned only with defeating his rival, Sir John Poulett, in the contest for supremacy in Somerset. For him at least, the rise of the class below him had a crucial influence on his politics. Power in the county depended on two pillars: friends at court, and friends among the population of the county. Poulett had Phelips beaten at court, so Phelips' only recourse was to outdo Poulett in winning the support of lesser gentlemen and leading yeomen in the county. In this process county elections, the key test of local prestige, played a crucial part. Phelips was thus driven by his ambition to become the servant of his social inferiors, and to oppose the court in the process. As Poulett sourly remarked, the common people were willing to applaud those unwilling to lay burdens on them. Professor Barnes concluded: 'Phelips was not the creator of opposition: he was its creature'.[11] For how many more opposition M.P.s such remarks could be made yet remains to be discovered.

Certainly, economic change can be invoked to show why the gentry of 1640 might be more eager to please yeomen, and less eager to please the Crown, than the gentry of 1540. Professor Plumb, viewing the battle with the detached eye of an eighteenth-century specialist, has recently suggested that the growth of the electorate, as inflation brought more people within the property qualification, may have had a general influence on politics in the early seventeenth century. Certainly many other members as well as Phelips were in the habit of saying they had to take account of the views of their constituents. This may often have been a convenient excuse for refusing the King's requests for money, but James I, among others, took these protestations seriously and thought the Commons were often 'too eager for the affection of the people'.[12]

In undertaking this line of investigation, we raise questions about the relationship between the two revolutions which our knowledge of the political narrative does not yet permit us to answer. Hugh Peters, the radical clergyman, was an enthusiastic supporter of the execution of Charles I and showed a remarkable enthusiasm for using the power of the state to improve the condition of the poor. Robert Rich, Earl of Warwick, was a dedicated believer in the existing social order, and aiming at nothing more radical than a baronial *coup d'état* followed by changes in foreign and religious policy. Yet before the war Warwick and Peters were working in close alliance: what did they have to offer to each other, and what was the balance of power within the alliance? At present, we do not know.

Certainly it seems to be true that the majority of the Parliamentary leaders showed a more sympathetic attitude to those just below the rank of gentry than most of the royalists did. Whether this was because of a genuine sense of social responsibility or simply a cynical bid to win allies against the king, we do not yet know and may never know. One thing at least is clear: the leaders of 1641 did not offer patronage to their social inferiors out of any desire to change the existing social order. Even Cromwell, one of the most radical, did not champion the interests of the fenmen, or of his troops, out of any desire to change their position in the social hierarchy, as his almost hysterical reaction to the Levellers and the Fifth Monarchists makes quite clear. Cromwell was a benevolent paternalist. The same benevolent paternalistic strain was in many other Parliamentary leaders, with the conspicuous exception of Manchester, who, of them all, was the closest to the court. Twice, over Ship Money and over the Forced Loan, Lord Saye and Sele set himself up as the champion of his poorer neighbours against the exactions of the court. It is clear too that Warwick thought his claim to be the spokesman of the county was the ground for his claim to be heard at court.[13]

By contrast, Royalists and future Royalists tended to react with fear and anger to such demands from below. During the months before the war, few things so sharply distinguished future Royalists from future Parliamentarians as their attitude to the gathering of crowds of petitioners outside the Houses of Parliament. What exactly this signifies, it is hard to say. It may only indicate that the Parliamentarian leaders found the crowds had a short-term usefulness, not that they had any real sympathy with them. We know little about the organisation of the crowds, though one of the M.P.s for the City helped to collect them. Except for the well-advertised name of John Lilburne, we know little about the people who composed them. If a newsletter writer is correct that in May 1641 many of them were 'persons of fashion and quality' we may have to think again.

It is possible to argue that after May 1641, when they first learnt that the King might be prepared to use force, the Parliamentary leaders had come to the end of their resources, and had become the prisoners of their followers. Only detailed work on the history of 1641–2 can show how far this is so. We are the more completely in the dark for the fact that we do not know what the revolutionaries of 1647–9 were doing in 1641, still less what they were doing in the 1630s. Were the Parliamentarian M.P.s, as Dr. Christopher Hill would suggest, dependent from the first on a Puritan radicalism which was already hostile to that supremacy of the gentry which they were committed to preserving?

Certainly, there was a genuine social conflict in the middle of the seventeenth century. It was not, however, the conflict between royalists and Parliamentarians, but the conflict, after the war was over, between the two wings of the Parliamentarian movement. It is thus only possible, to see the original Civil War as a social conflict if it is assumed that from the beginning, the leadership of the gentry among the Parliamentarians was nominal and the driving force was provided by the radical faction. This assumption may be true, but it yet remains to be proved.

II

The task of explaining the split among the gentry, which is here attempted, has become comparatively simple. That this is so is largely to the credit of Tawney and Trevor-Roper, who, by their stimulating questions, started a flood of research on the gentry, their fortunes, their connections and their interests.

The crisis among the gentry appears to be due to the coincidence of two causes, long-term institutional, and short-term political. The first section of the book concentrates on long-term institutional causes. Long before the Civil War, the machinery of English government was beginning to break down. This fact alone would not have caused a Civil War: institutional chaos may cause irritation and even indignation, but it is not often a sufficient cause of war. Nor could political and religious hatred alone have caused the war. In the 1630s most of the fears which boiled to the surface in 1640 were already there, but the fact that government was in working order denied them any means of expression. It was not until the institutional collapse of Charles's government, when faced with the Scottish wars of 1639–40, that political discontent could find a means of expression. And in the collapse of Charles's government, the crucial part was not played by the gentry: it was played by the refusal of innumerable ordinary citizens to pay their taxes. These citizens are mostly anonymous, and will probably always remain so, but it was they who gave the discontented gentry their opportunity.

It has not been possible, in a limited number of essays, to cover all the issues which led to the crisis of the Long Parliament. To some extent, the pattern of the volume has been dictated by the availability of contributors, and to some extent by considerations of length. Two crucial issues are missing. The first is Scotland and Ireland and the second is foreign policy. Though the Civil War is often known as 'the English Revolution' it was not the English who started it, but the Scots and the Irish who gave them their opportunity. It was the Scots' army which Charles I failed so ignominiously to defeat, and which until September 1641 endowed the leaders of the Long Parliament with almost all the bargaining strength they possessed. The Scots' religious grievances against the new Prayer Book and Canons imposed by the English and Scottish bishops are well known. But behind these grievances there were others. Many of the Scottish nobility who allied with Puritan

ministers against Charles were not really Puritans at all. For them, there
was an issue of Scottish dignity and independence: a protest against
reduction to the status of a neglected frontier province. There was a
demand for a voice in foreign policy, expressed in the demand that
neither England nor Scotland should make war without consent from
the other, and probably a desire to enter the Thirty Years' War on the
French, or Protestant, side. There were economic demands, including
one for the right to trade with English colonies. There was the issue of
arbitrary taxation, as there was in England, and an assertion of the
privileges of the nobility, threatened by Charles's attack on the inheritance of Scottish offices. All these demands coalesced in the demand
that Charles should spend a part of each year in Scotland. Had he done
so before 1640, his regime might have survived.

The moment, in September 1641, when the Scottish army disbanded
and went home was the moment of most acute danger the Parliamentary
leaders faced. The Irish rebellion, at the end of October 1641, was the
most fortunate thing that happened to the Parliamentary leaders, since
it meant that Charles again needed an army, and when he needed an
army, he needed a Parliament to pay it. Much of the background to the
Irish rebellion is described in Dr. Hawkins' chapter. Since the time of
James I, and to some extent earlier, the English had been trying to
carry through the Anglicisation of Ireland, and its conversion to
Protestantism (two processes they often regarded as synonymous)
through the 'plantation' of English and Scottish settlers. When Strafford's
strong rule was removed, Ireland burst into a rebellion which was both
nationalist and Catholic, and, in the process, roused the fears and suspicions of English Protestants to boiling point. Without the Irish
rebellion, as much as without the Scottish, Charles I would have
overcome opposition, and stayed in power.

The other conspicuous issue missing from this volume is foreign
policy, a subject which has not been adequately investigated since
Gardiner's work. In the light of Dr. Clifton's suggestion that foreign
policy crises were crucial to the raising of Popish Plot scares, it seems
that foreign policy may be of central importance. From 1618 to 1648,
Europe was involved in the Thirty Years' War, and though the war
was not primarily a religious war, the majority of English Puritans
thought it was. In the face of a crisis in which they thought the very
survival of Protestantism was at stake, many of them suspected that
Charles I's sympathies, if they were anywhere, were on the wrong side,
that of Spain. During the 1620s, the tortuous and so far unexplained

foreign policy of Buckingham had created a widespread, and justified, belief that foreign affairs were too important to be left to the government. In the years 1639 to 1642, when the English Civil War was breaking out, the crisis between France and Spain on the continent was at the point of resolution. As far back as the 1620s, the Tuscan ambassador had pointed out that there was a strong correlation between Parliamentary Puritanism and political support for the French against the Spaniards. It was therefore in France's interest that Parliament, and France's old ally Scotland, should defeat Charles, and conversely, it was in the Spanish interest that Charles should defeat all his enemies. What influence this fact may have had on the struggle yet remains to be discovered, but within the Privy Council it is probably not a coincidence that its pro-French members, such as Holland, Pembroke and Northumberland, tended to side with the Parliament, while its pro-Spanish members, among whom Strafford was the most prominent, gave unfailing loyalty to Charles.*

Even if there had been no ground for political conflict at all, the Tudor system of government would have needed to be replaced at some time during the seventeenth century. The essence of this system had been the sharing of effective power between the Crown and the dominant elements among the propertied classes. The symbolic expressions of this partnership had been Parliament and the notion of the rule of law, though in practice these two came to the same thing, since the highest law-making authority was Parliament. When Charles I's opponents demanded that he hold frequent Parliaments and that he abide by the rule of law, they were demanding that he resume the Tudor political partnership with the county gentry. Charles I's occasional threats to dispense with Parliament were taken to indicate a real desire to hold a power unfettered by this need for co-operation.

Whatever Parliament may have feared, there is no reason to suspect Charles of *wanting* to dissolve the Tudor system of government: the threat to it was not from the intentions of individuals, but from the pressure of events. The system was most seriously threatened by inflation. The cornerstone of Tudor government was not in fact Parliament, but the conduct of local government by unpaid county gentry. If these gentry were to do all the government's hard work in the counties, they expected there to be something in it for them. They expected, and under Elizabeth were allowed, to be able to return

* I am grateful to Professor J. H. Elliott for a number of helpful discussions of this subject.

dishonest valuations when their friends' estates were assessed for taxation. Above all, they expected that their exercise of power on behalf of the central government should contribute to their standing in their own communities.

The authority of the central government was thus always likely to break down if it offered too effective a challenge to local vested interests, and the need to increase its income in step with inflation was constantly forcing the Crown to issue just such a challenge. Dr. Hawkins' chapter shows, in a variety of contexts, the limitations on the central government's power. At the same time as inflation caused the Crown to demand more taxation, it created an ever more intense resistance to taxation among 'the industrious sort of people'. In 1627, when Essex, Warwick, Saye and Lincoln were sacked from their local Commissions of the Peace for opposing the Forced Loan,[14] they probably improved, rather than worsened, their standing among their neighbours. In this situation, the financial exactions of the 1630s were the last straw. In 1640, even those who were later the king's supporters were unanimous that local government could not be conducted under this sort of pressure. The unanimity of opposition to Charles in 1640 reflected the collapse of the system of government, as the division of 1642 represented the failure to replace it by anything else.

Tudor government had also depended heavily on the exercise of royal patronage: those who were to serve the Crown loyally would have to be rewarded. Under Henry VIII, and to a lesser extent under Elizabeth, this had been done at the expense of the Church. Yet even before Charles I decided to reverse the trend of a century by restoring the material position of the Church, this source was running dry, and had been increasingly neglected by James I. At the same time as inflation was eroding the Crown's collection of possible rewards, the gentry, also under pressure from inflation, were becoming more greedy in their demands for royal patronage. The situation was illustrated in 1610, when the Commons complained of James I's lavish giving, and James replied that most of them had either had a share in his gifts, or had asked to do so. As Dr. Hawkins argues, the patronage problem was probably insoluble: there was not enough to create a Walpolean class of government dependants.

Caught in this dilemma, the government steadily resorted to more and more undignified forms of patronage, which in turn increased its unpopularity. The symbolic issue here is monopolies. One story will illustrate the sort of odium they might create for the government. The task of maintaining the vital lighthouse at Dungeness was given to a group of monopolists, who duly collected their rewards in the form of tolls on all shipping passing Dungeness. But instead of a lighthouse, they provided only one candle, which, as the sailors reasonably pointed out, could not be seen until ships were already in acute danger. This story took up much of the time of the Parliament of 1621, but it is typical of the inertia of early Stuart government that the same story came before the Long Parliament twenty years later. The ultimate absurdity in matters of patronage was reached in the 1630s, in the fines Charles I levied on those who had encroached on the Forest of Dean. He granted, as a piece of patronage to one offender, the right to collect the fine imposed on another offender.[15] Such things may be in themselves small issues, but they do as much to bring a government into hatred and contempt as issues which are much more far-reaching.

Throughout the period from 1610 to 1625, it was these financial and administrative grievances, rather than broad issues of principle, which were the staple of complaint in the House of Commons. But though such matters might put men in a fever of indignation, they did not put them in fear for their lives or their souls: they were not the material of which war is made. As Dr. Tyacke shows, while the Church was under the effective control of Archbishop Abbot, religious opposition was no real threat to the Crown. Many of the opposition leaders of this period, indeed, were not Puritans at all. Sir Edwin Sandys had sympathies with Arminianism, and Sir Dudley Digges claimed, as late as 1626, that 'no clergy in Christendom is clearer from badness than the body of the church of England'.[16] It is not a coincidence that these two were among the opposition leaders who ultimately made their peace with the Crown. Professor Elton is right: James I's reign, though it witnessed the collapse of a system of government, was not 'a high road to Civil War'.[17]

This situation had changed abruptly within a few months of Charles I's accession to the throne. In the Oxford session of the 1625 Parliament, when the opposition leaders first prepared to impeach the royal favourite Buckingham, they were issuing, even if with backing from within the Council, a revolutionary challenge to the king of a type which had been unknown throughout James's reign. Why such a sudden change? There are some superficial reasons. One is the descent of Buckingham as favourite from father to son: what may have been tolerable when it could be hoped that the next king would reverse it may have been intolerable when it continued into a new reign. Another is the character of Charles, who differed from James as Neville Chamberlain did from Stanley Baldwin. He had no knack for smoothing over crises with ambiguities, and above all, he had not the saving laziness of James I. Even if the system of government had broken down, it was not easy to credit James with a grand design for altering it: if he started such a design, he would never finish it. By about 1626, however, such opposition leaders as Bedford were taking Charles I's threats to dispense with Parliament seriously.[18] The Grand Remonstrance, when it claimed that there was a great conspiracy to change the government and religion of England, dated this conspiracy from the beginning of the reign of Charles I. Charles did not have a grand conspiracy to change the system of government, but he did have a deliberate intention of reversing the political and religious traditions of the Elizabethan establishment: those very traditions in which his older opponents had grown up.

In foreign policy this reversal extended back into the reign of James. It had been one of the most successful, and most difficult, achievements of Elizabethan government propaganda to convince people that Spain, and not France, was the natural enemy, and the people for whom this achievement was most successful were those who were children during the Elizabethan war with Spain, and members of Parliament in the 1620's. In 1624, it seemed that Buckingham and Charles were likely to reverse James's policy of friendship with Spain, but by August 1625, it was apparent to careful observers that they were more likely to fight France. The actual event, that Buckingham went to war with both at once, was so incredible that it was impossible to believe that the man who did it could be trusted with power in any form.

This reversal of policy by Charles I is the theme of the second section of the book, the chapters by Dr. Tyacke, Dr. Clifton and Dr. Thomas. The most important way in which Charles reversed the traditions of the Elizabethan political establishment was his decision to open an assault on the main stream of English moderate Puritanism. In stating this point, one must avoid stating it in the way M.P.s did. Charles did not reverse the traditions of Queen Elizabeth, who would have had more sympathy with him than with most of his opponents. What he did reverse was the traditions of Elizabeth's Puritan Councillors. In the 1580s, it had been possible to be a Puritan (at least as Charles and Laud defined the term) and at the same time an Anglican and a loyal member of the political establishment. As Professor Barnes has said, in Somerset in 1625 what the Laudians called Puritanism was not disloyal, but 'the established faith practised in the established church'.[19]

religion used as political eg. Holland.

Puritan extremism in the 1580s had been more revolutionary than it, ever was in the 1630s. The leading opposition families of Hampden, Knightley, Rich and Russell had been more vehemently Puritan in the 1580s than they were in the 1630s. In the 1580s Field, Cartwright and Travers had wanted to overthrow the whole hierarchy of the church in a way few leaders of the 1630s did. But even these extreme Puritans of the 1580s had had friends at court: they had had channels of communication with the government, and had not been forced into the outsider's status which makes a revolutionary. Leicester had been prepared to take such men as his chaplains to the Netherlands, and Burghley to employ them in writing propaganda against the Spanish Armada. Even the extremist Puritans of the 1580s knew that in foreign affairs Sir Francis Walsingham's heart was in the right place, and that Sir Walter Mildmay, Chancellor of the Exchequer, was using his profits of office to finance the training of godly preachers at Emmanuel College, Cambridge. In contrast, the more moderate Puritans of Charles's reign were forced out of the political establishment by the extent of the King's hostility to them: Bedford was disqualified from office by his opinions, while his more Puritan grandfather had been a loyal and effective Privy Councillor.

Whatever bishops might say, Puritan gentlemen were not instinctive enemies of authority, and in Scotland they could provide it with very powerful support. In Holland, it was Calvinists who were supporters of the authority of the Prince of Orange, and Arminians who were thought potential revolutionaries. If religious divisions were likely to lead to revolution, this was not primarily because of any particular characteristic of the religions concerned. It was because it was almost unanimously assumed by the governing class that it was one of the first purposes of government to achieve unity of religion. It was therefore governments' duty to inflict religious persecution on their opponents. It was fear of persecution, combined with the desire to inflict it in return, which made religious dissidents revolutionary. So long as religious division existed in a society which thought it its duty to enforce religious unity, revolution was always a possibility. The story of events after the Civil War broke out suggests that this religious unity creed was largely a creed of the governing class: true religion was the way to keep the people in due obedience. Yet even if it was a creed of a governing class, it was also one which, by leading to the persecution of some of its members, could drive them into rebellion. If holders of two conflicting creeds both tried to enforce religious unity, the result could only be war. In classifying as 'Puritans' many who in the previous reign would have been bishops, and some who already were bishops, the Caroline government made potential rebels of many natural supporters of the political establishment.

Explanations of the Civil War are thus led back to Puritanism. Recent work has given us a much better understanding of the context in which Puritanism appealed to so many people. Puritanism was the heir of all the disappointed hopes raised by the Reformation. If there was one thing more central to the Reformation than anything else, it was the desire to dispel superstition and ignorance. Dr. Keith Thomas, in his book on *Religion and the Decline of Magic*, has shown how much there was to provoke this desire. Much popular religion before the Reformation amounted to little more than a set of magical charms, endowed with the partial and sometimes reluctant blessing of the Church. Even a parish priest could suggest that whooping cough could be cured by drinking three times from the Communion chalice. Bishop Jewel was attacking a real target when he asked how an Agnus Dei could preserve its wearer from being struck by lightning, and so was Bishop Pilkington when he claimed that the use of St. Agatha's letters to protect burning houses, or of consecrated bells for protection against thunderstorms, were mere 'witchcrafts'. Ignorance was an equally real target, as shown by the story of the regular churchgoer who was asked what he thought of God, and

He answers that he was a good old man; and what of Christ, that he was a towardly young youth; and of his soul, that it was a great bone in his body; and what should become of his soul after he was dead, that if he had done well he should be put into a pleasant green meadow.[20]

The aim of the early Protestants, and of the Puritans after them, was to substitute a genuine understanding of Christianity for this mixture of magic and ignorance. This was the point of the insistence on Justification by Faith rather than Justification by Works. Works, such as the sprinkling of holy water, could be performed in a way not far removed from magic, but faith demanded that people understand what their beliefs were about. It was this demand for understanding which explained the early Protestant, and Puritan, insistence on preaching. Any minister could make the sign of the cross in baptism, but only a preaching minister could make the parents understand what baptism was really about.

One of the things which did most to create the ferment leading to the Reformation was the demand for an adequate ministry in the parishes: the complaints about the ignorance of the parish clergy before the Reformation command widespread sympathy from modern readers. But all these complaints were equally true, and equally deserving of sympathy, a hundred years after the Reformation. Dr. Christopher Hill, in his book on *Economic Problems of the Church*, has shown why this was so; the money available in the church was never channelled to a preaching ministry in the parishes. The early Protestants had wanted a preaching ministry, but they had not got one. The Puritans of the seventeenth century still thought this demand might be satisfied, and believed, as Stephen Marshall put it in 1640, that preaching was the chariot on which salvation came riding into the hearts of men. If they could not satisfy it in the official church, they would satisfy it by lecture-ships with the added advantage of lay control. But to many of the Laud-ian bishops, preaching was potentially subversive. It is hard now to imagine the shock to the most moderate of Puritans when the Laudian Bishop of Bath and Wells tried to stop ministers expounding the Catechism on the ground that it was 'as bad as preaching'.[21] Perhaps the nearest parallel is the shock which would be created now if a Chief Education Officer should congratulate himself on reducing the number of teachers in his area.

The Laudian attack on preaching was not particularly powerful or effective, but it did enough to convince moderate men that the sympath-ies of Charles and Laud were on the wrong side, and did much to increase the militancy of the preachers.[22] Such sermons as the Laudians did encourage were preached in an ornate and witty style designed to tickle the ears of courtiers, and not in the plain style for ordinary people in which Puritans believed.

The Laudians' worst offence was their attack on Predestination. Dr. Keith Thomas has suggested that Puritans, not having abolished the emotional needs met by magic, created their own substitute for it. He stresses the doctrine, beloved of Oliver Cromwell, that each event was the mark of God's providence. But perhaps the most important Puritan charm against evil was the doctrine of Predestination, stressing that a man who had once become Elect could never fall from grace. This doctrine, as the Thirty-Nine Articles said, was 'full of sweet, pleasant and unspeakable comfort' to those who believed they were predestined to salvation. On this point, the Puritans of Charles I's reign, as Dr. Tyacke has shown, were in line with the main tradition

of the Anglican church, and indeed believed they were the true Anglicans
In Bedford's commonplace book, many of the strongest reflections on
Arminians, who tried to take away the comfort of Predestination, are in
the section headed 'heretics'.[23]

Dr. Tyacke's chapter shows very clearly the departure of the Laudians
from the traditions of Elizabethan orthodoxy. This took many other
forms as well as the theological. The attempt to restore the beauty of
holiness looked to many like an attempt to restore the delusions of
magic: the Separatist who said the sacraments were used as sorceries
was making a valid observation of many people's behaviour. With the
return to magic went an emphasis on the dignity of the magician: a
determined attempt to increase the wealth of the church and the
dignity of the priesthood: to reverse the trend of the whole century
since the Reformation. Indeed, for many Protestants, the very word
'priest' signified one with magical powers, and until Laud's day it was
almost unused in the Anglican church. As late as 1625, a Wiltshire
vicar got a conviction for slander against one of his neighbours for calling
him a priest. For many moderate men, the Laudians' habit of calling
the clergy a priesthood was a symbol of all their complaints. The
Laudians were not Roman Catholics, but they did reverse many of the
traditions of the Reformation. Indeed, as Dr. Tyacke has said, they were
a Counter-Reforming movement in the Church of England, for whom
'the Reformation itself was becoming an embarrassment.'[24]

In this atmosphere, the terror of Popish plots described by Dr.
Clifton could become a fatal reality. Even if the government were not
Popish, it could not be trusted to defend the country against the danger:
it did not have the awareness of Rome's evil and conspiratorial nature
which had informed the intelligence work of Sir Francis Walsingham.
At the crisis of the Thirty Years' War, when the survival of European
Protestantism as a whole was in the balance, such terrors were all the
more acute. To appeal to Charles I's government for protection against
them was as vain as appealing to Neville Chamberlain for protection
against Fascism. In most of the issues which Puritans regarded as
crucial in dividing Protestants from Catholics, the Laudians, unlike
the Elizabethan bishops, were on the wrong side. In the fog of fear and
misunderstanding which prevented settlement in 1641, the fear of
Popish plots, confirmed by the knowledge of Strafford's intrigues
for armed help from Spain and the Queen's intrigues for armed
help from France, contributed as much as anything else. How far these
fears were encouraged by the Parliamentary leaders is uncertain,

and in a sense irrelevant. The point is that rumours were readily believed.

Puritanism was mainly an assault on magic, superstition and ignorance. But was Puritanism also a revolutionary force? Was there anything in the essence of Puritanism which made it *necessarily* an enemy of authority? If the question is phrased in this strict form, the answer must be 'no'. In Massachusetts, Governor Winthrop did much to meet the Puritan ideal of the 'godly prince', while at the same time developing a doctrine of his prerogative almost as high-flown as that of James I. Governor Winthrop, it is true, got into some trouble for this doctrine, but his troubles were not comparable to those of Charles I in England: Winthrop did not offend the central belief of Puritanism (or of any strongly held religion) that God must be obeyed. However, Massachusetts is something of a special case: the new Israel, like the old one, was surrounded by hostile and infidel tribes, which provided a powerful incentive to unity.

Puritanism, it is true, inherited what Dr. Christopher Hill calls 'the built-in anarchy of Protestantism'.[25] Protestants took over from Roman Catholics the belief in the unity of the church, and the belief that this unity must be secured by persecution. At the same time, by rejecting the Pope, they had thrown over the only practical machinery for securing this unity. The Protestant bishops had thrown over the Pope because his doctrines were contrary to Scripture, and if bishops then found their followers throwing over their own doctrines for the same reason, they had no logical weapon with which to meet them. As early as 1567, the bishops were being faced by congregations who rejected their own services on the same ground as the bishops had rejected the papists' services, because they were contrary to the Word of God. All the High Commission could find to say to these people was to ask them whom they would have to be judge of the Word of God, only to meet the crippling reply, 'why, that was the saying of the Papists in Queen Mary's days'.[26] The church hierarchy had introduced a cult of the Bible as the final authority, without managing to endow themselves with any claim to have special authority in interpreting the Bible. Perhaps, then, we should be discussing, not the revolutionary character of Puritanism, but the inherent weaknesses of the Church of England.

Moreover, disciplinarian bishops seem to have not only lacked any other doctrine of authority than the power of the state, but also to have failed to capture popular imagination as effectively as either Puritanism or Roman Catholicism. John Selden's remark that the clergy enjoyed less respect among Anglicans than among Puritans or Catholics was very much to the point. For example, when faced by the psychiatric disturbances classified as possession by devils, Roman Catholics could use exorcism, and Puritans could use prayer and fasting, but people like Archbishop Bancroft could do little. They did not reject the doctrine of exorcism, but after 1604 they decided, with a typical readiness to fall back on legal authority, that it could only be done by those who were legally licensed to do it—and such licences were not given.

The failure of the Church of England to maintain religious unity, and the chaos caused by the disappearance of religious unity in a society which believed it could not survive without it, were then inevitable. In matters of religion, as in matters of money, there was a situation which was bound to end in some form of crisis.

But though a crisis was inevitable, it can only be regarded as a coincidence that the crisis took the form it did at the time it did. The history of the 1650's and of 1688, show that High Anglicanism, as well as Puritanism, was capable of becoming a revolutionary force when the weight of authority was turned against it. Moreover it can only be regarded as a matter of coincidence that Charles I chose to make a personal commitment to the doctrines of Arminianism. In doing this, he bound himself to try to cast out of the church the whole generation of Puritan Anglicans—including most of the people in the Church of England who had done anything to capture the popular imagination. Laud's notion that he could improve respect for his clergy by beautifying churches and increasing the wealth of the clergy appears to have been totally erroneous. In attacking Predestination, however, Laud does appear to have been able to call on some popular feeling, as the later history of the sects shows. The Arminianism of many members of the sects also shows, as Dr. Tyacke has pointed out, that there are. 'reasons . . . against there being any necessary link between anti-Calvinist theology and special emphasis on the prerogative of kings In practice it is true that during the personal rule of Charles I the two became closely associated, but this was largely because the supreme magistrate chose to support the Arminians.'[27]

Thus the connection between Puritanism and revolution was largely of Charles I's making. The Puritan Anglicans whom he alienated were not natural enemies of authority. Men like Pym and Bedford held most of the same political theories as the later royalists. They believed in the Divine Right of kings. They believed in the Great Chain of Being, the doctrine which guaranteed the hierarchical ordering of society. They believed in the privileges and dignity of the aristocracy. But, like all Christians, they also had to believe in the supremacy of truth. As a result, they were forced into alliance with a radical Puritanism which was very different from their own beliefs, and for which Bedford at least had a profound contempt.

This alliance was not a natural one, and after the Civil War it split down the middle. Its creation can only be regarded as a feat of incompetence by Charles and Laud. It is when this alliance was forged that the conjunction of 'Puritanism and Revolution' became a reality. For there were forces in Puritanism which, once they were taken out of the control of the gentry, could become genuinely revolutionary. One of these was its sense of priorities. The duty to serve God was so all-embracing that it could easily blot out other duties. Most Puritans also held a very strict doctrine of Providence, believing that every event in the world fell out because God had so decreed it, that, as Calvin put it, it was certain that not a drop of rain fell without the express command of God. This doctrine of Providence enabled Puritans to construct a somewhat unusual doctrine of political expediency. Sin, they thought, was punished by God on this earth, as well as in the after life. God's people, like the Israelites of old, would succeed if they kept God's worship pure, and fail if they did not. This doctrine was not confined to Puritans (the Emperor Charles V held it, for example), but Puritans provided many of those who took it most seriously. The sort of compromises which most politicians make in order to ensure success thus appeared to them likely to ensure failure, because they would prevent the Lord from going out with their armies. This doctrine of Providence, as well as leading to a rejection of expediency, also carried an assurance of success. Stephen Marshall told the Long Parliament:

> Mark this, all ye wise men, and great politicians of the world, that dare drive designs against the cause of God and his church, write it down, and say your unworthy minister taught you this day from God, though ye take counsel together it shall come to naught, though ye speak the word it shall not stand, for God is with us.

God's adversaries, he said, 'though they may carry the ball long at their foot, they can never win the goal'. Such beliefs, then as now, tended to lead to success.

Another potentially revolutionary belief, which was added to Puritanism by the great Cambridge Puritan William Perkins, was that it was possible to know who the people were who were predestined to salva-

EG. hystorical.

tion. They might, as Puritan preachers often said, be mean men, rather than the great ones of this world. As Marshall said, 'they have little countenance from men, few of them are wise, noble or mighty, but they are the foolish, weak and base ones of this world'. In the hands of Marshall, who was securely dependent on his aristocratic patrons, such doctrines were not necessarily subversive. A good Puritan sermon, like a good horror film, was meant to make the flesh creep: William Perkins, for example, had been said to be able to pronounce the word 'damn' so that his whole audience shuddered at it. When Marshall told the Lords and Commons that 'I speak to an assembly of Gods, but I speak in the name of a great God, before whom you are but as so many grasshoppers, his potsherds, his poor sinful creatures', he was merely telling his audience what they wanted to hear.[28]

Nevertheless it comes as no surprise to find complaints that Marshall's sermons later promoted unduly radical sentiments among Parliamentary soldiers. In the hands of another preacher, the doctrine that the Saints, the Elect, were an identifiable community of people might be a much more revolutionary force than it was for Marshall. On the same day as this sermon by Marshall, the Long Parliament heard a sermon by Jeremiah Burroughes which was much more genuinely revolutionary in content. Marshall had spent the 1630s sheltering comfortably in an Essex vicarage under the protection of the Earl of Warwick, while Burroughes had preached to a congregation in the poor and radical suburb of Stepney, and finally had been forced into exile in Holland. Though Burroughes, in common with almost all of the Long Parliament's preachers, was prepared to accept the patronage of the Earl of Warwick, his experiences had left him with a radicalism very different from Warwick's respectable views. When Burroughes talked of 'the saints', or 'Israel' he genuinely meant the people to whom he liked to preach. His message to the Lords and Commons was clear: if they wished to join in a godly reformation, they were welcome, but if not, it would go ahead without them. 'Antichrist shall never prevail again as he hath done: God will give, yea he hath given such a spirit to his saints, as they will never be brought to bow their backs again'. He called explicitly, as Marshall had not, for the abolition of bishops, saying that they were the men of whom God had said 'I will spew them out of my mouth'. 'There wants but the putting of the finger into the throat, and they are gone. . . . They have slighted the people, the vulgar, as if their very souls were made to lie under them for them to trample upon, but they shall be ashamed for their envy at the people'. When he said that God's people were Israel escaping from the bondage of Egypt, the old Biblical image had the force it has along the Suez Canal today.

The biggest issue raised by Burroughes was in his claim that the Long Parliament had to thank the Saints for the fact that they were sitting at all:

> If none had been willing to have ventured themselves to have suffered, in denying illegal taxations, in refusing superstitious innovations, what had become of us by this time, and who were they who principally suffered in vindicating the liberties of the subject, and resisting innovations in religion, but such as did it out of conscience, such as were the mourners in Sion, for the evil that was upon us, and that hung over us. . . . Therefore these who have borne the brunt who have suffered much for you, and that out of conscience of their duty to God for their country and their posterity: these, I say, ought now to be comforted by you.

From Burroughes, this was not only an entreaty: it was a threat.[29]

Whether Puritanism played as big a part in the tax refusals of 1640 as Burroughes would have liked to think is an open question. However, it is certainly true that the Long Parliament owed its opportunity to meet to the refusal of its social inferiors to pay their taxes during the summer of 1640. How far this resistance was encouraged or inspired by the gentry, or how far it depended on the fact that the 1630s had only seen one good harvest in ten years, remain open questions. However, even if the gentry encouraged the tax refusals of the summer of 1640, they did not encourage the series of mutinies among the troops which prevented Charles from effectively fighting the Scots. These mutinies expressed a wave of class hostility. When troops from Devon rioted, and murdered some of their Catholic officers, Nathaniel Fiennes, one of the inner ring of the Parliamentary leadership, was profoundly shocked: for him, the fact that the officers were gentlemen was more important than the fact that they were Popish.[30] Bedford, the Lord Lieutenant of Devon, took the same view, and willingly co-operated in hanging the leading offenders.

These outbursts of hostility to authority among the lower classes had happened before, and Dr. Christopher Hill is undoubtedly right in arguing that they were always capable of becoming a major political force. This type of discontent was associated with bad economic years, and it is impossible to understand the years 1640–42 without remembering that they were bad years in the cloth industry. Unemployment did

much to provide the riotous crowds of these years, and the poverty
created by the slump probably did much to prevent even those willing
to pay taxes from doing so.

Two things distinguished the outbursts of 1640 from those of, for
example, 1597. One was religion. The odd mixture of religious and
social discontent in the army mutinies is shown by the story of one officer
who managed to get his troops to obey him. He had to do two things to
win their trust: to sing Psalms with them, and to give them 'stinking
tobacco at 6d. a pound'.[31] For many soldiers, class and religious hatred
were merged in assaults on Popish officers.

The other thing which distinguished the lower class discontent of
1640 from that of 1597 was the fact that the gentry were not willing to
help the Crown to suppress it. Normally these social crises were not
dangerous to the government because the gentry, feeling as threatened
as the Crown, would rally round and suppress the rebels. Against the
combined forces of Crown and gentry, lower class discontent could
achieve nothing. In 1640, many gentry sympathised with the discontents, and many others, having no sympathy with the Scottish war which
had triggered them off, were prepared to stand aside and let the King get
out of trouble unaided. The last time this had happened was in 1525,
when the trouble was also caused by very heavy taxation for an unpopular foreign war. In 1525, Henry VIII, when he found that the
gentry would not help him against the tax refusers, prudently changed
his policy, stopped the war and withdrew the tax. This was the only
practical course open to Charles I in the summer of 1640, but, having
more obstinate pride than Henry VIII, he would not take it, and summoned the Long Parliament instead.

Thus Charles I created the second of the two major coincidences
which led to the Civil War: the union between the discontents of the
Parliamentary gentry and those of their social inferiors. The two forces
which held this alliance together were Puritanism and resistance to
arbitrary taxation. The alliance was never a natural one: victory dissolved it immediately, and it took all the incompetence of Charles
to hold it together until the outbreak of war in 1642.

When Charles I called the Long Parliament, in November 1640,
he was unable to collect taxes from his English subjects, and was maintaining an uneasy truce with a powerful army of his Scottish subjects,
which he was unable to suppress. This was the situation within which
both Charles and the Parliamentary leaders had to manoeuvre. It is
most unlikely that either side intended this situation to come to the

ideology in time of depression

point of Civil War, and the outbreak of Civil War two years later represents the failure of the political manoeuvres of both sides.

The chief Parliamentarian strategist until his death in May 1641 was Bedford, who, in Clarendon's words, 'only intended to make himself and his friends great at court, not at all to lessen the court it self'.[32] The aim of the Parliamentary leaders was to get themselves taken into office, and thereby to force radical changes of foreign and religious policy on Charles I, without substantially changing the existing constitution. They were prepared to use constitutional change as a way of winning power, but Bedford at least did not particularly want it for its own sake. Bedford's constitutional ideas, as expressed in his commonplace book, might, as his opponents alleged, have reduced Charles to the status of a Doge of Venice. But they would have subordinated him, not to his Parliament, but to his Privy Council.[33]

The Parliamentary leaders were, from the beginning, operating in a revolutionary situation. From October 1640 to September 1641, there were two armies in the kingdom, and the Parliamentarians knew well that it was only their alliance with the Scottish army that gave them any power to extort concessions from Charles. By concessions they did not mean Acts of Parliament. They had already, in the Petition of Right of 1628, obtained much of what they wanted on paper, only to find that Charles maintained that the Petition of Right was not an Act of Parliament, and that it did not mean what it said. They knew that any paper concessions embodied in nothing more forcible than an Act of Parliament could be taken away as soon as Parliament was dissolved. As they constantly said, good laws were no use if they were not executed. Like their medieval predecessors, they wanted a grip on the machinery of government so secure that they could not be dislodged.

Since Charles obviously had no wish to give them this grip, they could only obtain it by power, and power meant two things: arms and money. Dependence on the Scots' arms, and the promise to solve Charles's financial difficulties were their main bargaining weapons. At first this strategy seemed to be on the point of success. On May 7, 1641, Secretary Vane said that he expected to be able to report within the week that the King had accepted the Parliamentary leaders' terms, 'there being in truth no other [course] left'. It is still not entirely clear what happened during May and June 1641 to prevent this settlement from being concluded.

However, it soon became clear that it was not going to be concluded. By June 18, 1641, Sir Henry Vane was reporting in very different terms, saying that nothing had happened in Parliament worth repeating: 'we are here still in the labyrinth, and cannot get out'.[34] By this time, the Parliamentary leaders knew of the army plots, and of the Queen's attempts to gain armed help in France: they knew in short that Charles would rather fight, even with foreign help, than grant their terms. It was also becoming common knowledge that the King intended to go to Edinburgh and conclude a treaty with the Scots.[35] It was this decision to make peace with the Scots which transferred the political initiative from Parliament to the King.* Without the Scottish army, the Parliamentary leaders would have little or no bargaining power, and the adviser who thought Charles would be able to dissolve Parliament in the autumn of 1641, as soon as he returned from Scotland, was not being over-optimistic. If Charles had the military power to dissolve Parliament, the Act against Dissolution would not restrain him. The Parliamentary leaders had committed themselves too far to draw back, and, if they allowed Charles to dissolve Parliament, they could expect to be tried and convicted for treason. Moreover their escape route was cut off when their colony of Providence Island was conquered by the Spaniards in the autumn of 1641.

In this situation, they became more heavily dependent on the support of the London crowds, which, as one of Charles's advisers reported, 'is their anchor-hold and only interest'. Their hope no doubt was that if Charles dissolved Parliament, popular discontent would again prevent him from collecting his taxes. It was also in response to this situation that they raised their terms, from a mere demand that they should be appointed to office to the demand that Parliament should elect the great officers.[36] The more apparent it became that Charles was unwilling to trust them, the more powerful were the means they needed to force him to do so.

The original deadlock was restored at the beginning of November 1641, when the Irish rebellion made Charles again dependent on Parliament for the raising of an army. Parliament were not prepared to let Charles have this army, since they had the very reasonable fear that he might use it against themselves rather than against the Irish. From this time onwards, disputes increasingly concentrated on three issues: the winning of a majority in the House of Lords, control of the militia and control of the London streets. Of these, it was probably the third which was of most immediate importance.

* I am grateful to Mr. Michael Mendle for his help in understanding the events of these months.

It was in the battle for control of the London streets that it came to be of crucial importance that Charles had alienated a large body of substantial London merchants who were not members of the privileged inner ring. For, whatever Royalists might say, the crowds were not simply 'rabble'. Many of them no doubt were unemployed men or labourers, but the organisers, and many of the members of the crowds, were substantial City merchants. It was these substantial men, and not 'rabble', who organised the key Parliamentarian coup: the capture of the City Common Council in the elections of December 1641. This happened at a crucial time for the Parliamentary leaders, for it was at the same time that Charles seems to have finally decided to break the deadlock by using force: he had changed the Lieutenant of the Tower, and was busy stocking it with arms. It was this new Common Council, in collaboration with the Commons, who completed a constitutional revolution in the City by setting up a Committee of Safety, and securing for it control of the City militia. On January 5, 1642, on the same day on which Charles came to the City hoping to arrest the Five Members, the City trained bands were placed under the command of the leading Parliamentary Puritans in the City. This was the event which gave the Parliamentarians military control of the capital, and this which was perhaps the greatest victory of the whole Civil War.

Five days later, Charles left London, and the story of the Civil War is the story of his attempt to fight his way back there. This crucial victory had not been won by the Parliamentary peers and gentry. Unlike medieval barons, the peers of 1641 had no armies of their own. Finally, in accepting the protection of the radical Puritans of the City, they accepted the protection of a military force which was not under their control. To regard this force as representing any one class would be misleading. Puritanism in the City seems to have cut across classes, and in the alliance which gained control of the City trained bands, employers and employees seem to have worked in harmony.

Nevertheless this acceptance of the protection of the City trained bands represented something very different from the comfortable political settlement which Bedford had envisaged in the autumn of 1640. It could help Parliament to fight a war, but it could not help them to reach a settlement with the King. The Civil War then broke out because, in the two years which led up to it, the political strategy of both sides ended in defeat. Parliament failed to reach a settlement with the King, who retained the sole power to choose the holders of the major executive offices, and refused to exercise it to their advantage. The King, equally, failed to create a situation in which he could send Parliament home and revert to his normal methods of governing the country.

In explaining this deadlock, one must put much weight on the peculiar obstinacy of the personalities on both sides. The political crisis of 1640–42 could have had many possible results, and among them, a Civil War, with the two parties equally balanced, had originally seemed one of the least likely.

Yet, though the Civil War was far from an inevitable result of the political crisis, some form of crisis was inevitable. At some time, the royal finances were bound to collapse in the face of inflation. Any new settlement of the royal finances was bound to disturb the balance of power between King and Parliament, but it was not inevitable that it should disturb it in the particular way it did. At some time, the attempt to enforce unity of religion was bound to fail, and its failure was bound to lead to some confusion. It was not inevitable, however, that this crisis should coincide with the financial one. Nor was it inevitable that when it came, it should come in the form of a clash between Puritan and Arminian, with the King on the Arminian side and most defenders of the Elizabethan church on the Puritan side. It was perhaps inevitable that some government should have trouble with the slum-dwellers of the London suburbs, but it was not inevitable that a substantial minority of the City Aldermen should be found at the head of the crowds. The particular situation which produced the Civil War was the result of two coincidences. The first, in 1625, was the decision of the King to challenge the religious orthodoxy of the Parliamentary classes at the moment when the need to settle his finances had become desperate. The second, in 1640, was the alliance of discontent among the gentry with two separate social discontents, that of the poor and that of substantial merchants who were not members of the privileged group. Without these coincidences there would have been some form of political crisis during the century, but it would have been a very different crisis from the one which actually happened.

Section One

1. The Government: Its Role and Its Aims

MICHAEL HAWKINS

I

BY the summer of 1641 Charles I had lost the first 'Civil War' without firing a shot. In the first few months of the Long Parliament, the men, measures and administrative machinery of royal government, as Charles understood it, had been destroyed with no more than token royal resistance. The parliamentary triumph left problems which plagued successive regimes during the next twenty years, and were left unsolved at the Restoration; but within its negative limits it was complete. This 'Civil War' was bloodless because the king had no party; the Civil War as we know it was made possible by the growth of royalist support and the collapse of parliamentary unity. This realignment gave the King a chance to attempt an independent policy again. Why it occurred and how deep-rooted were the reasons for it are disputed, but this debate is peripheral to the purpose of this chapter.

Charles I was merely the legatee of parliamentary splits. More for our purpose is to explain how he contrived to create such an extraordinary degree of unanimity against him that, as in 1688, the Crown lost without a fight.

The old 'Whig' account, in which the House of Commons was cast as defender of liberal virtues against an unfettered and potentially tyrannical government, has long been attacked by both right and left. Tories and Marxists have agreed in seeing the parliamentary classes' defence of their interests as essentially selfish, and their triumph as opening the way to an irresponsible society based either on big property-owners, on an individualist free-for-all, or an ill-defined combination of the two. Tories with an organic view of society have stressed what was lost by the destruction of a royal government which was claimed to have had a wider sense of social responsibility than the avaricious gentry and merchants in the Commons. Marxists have rejected, quite properly, the notion that a government can act in the interests of the whole of society. 'Is it supposed absolute monarchy existed anywhere without a social basis, or that it is a form of state without a ruling class ?' asked Manning. But his own statement that the 'fundamental characteristic (of absolute monarchy) is the continued domination of the big land-owners' has been variously described as 'odd', 'unhelpful', and 'curious'.[1] Whatever hesitations may be felt about its relevance to continental conditions, in England it seems to beg the questions of the nature of the post-Restoration state, and of whether, in Marxist terms, it was feudal or capitalist property which the absolute monarchy existed to defend. Marxists have had some difficulty in deciding whether the Tudor and early Stuart state was feudal, capitalist, or represented a peculiar hybrid transitional stage, since the regime appeared to be suspicious of both feudal war-lords and capitalist enclosers. But the last possibility savour-ed too much of gradualism in the historical process and was too dangerous a threat to the dialectic. Dr. Christopher Hill has assured us that in Russian eyes the Middle Ages ended in 1640, and he has sub-sequently written that 'the destruction of the royal bureaucracy in 1640-1 can be regarded as the most decisive single event in the whole of British history'.[2] The Great Rebellion is preserved as a bourgeois revolution, and absolutism is safely, if vaguely, defined as feudalism reorganised.

Influential members of the government and many rank and file office-holders were recruited from the same social groups as those who were influential locally, and they naturally shared many preconceptions. But it is necessary to restate the distinct interests of government: that they overlap, but are not and cannot be co-terminous with the interests of any particular group or class in society; that office-holding modifies the policies and attitudes of members of a government, even if they are recruited from a particular class or if a particular class has seized power; and that clashes of interests arise and are no less significant (that is, likely to lead to political action) for not having a class basis. Whatever their other errors, the liberal historians did not equate the interests of government and subject, even a particular class of subjects. Trevor-Roper's argument that the political upheavals in mid-seventeenth century Europe represented a crisis ' of the relation of the state to society' is not, as Elliott claimed, a truism.[3] It is an assertion, correct or not, that the structure and working of government had become a major, even the key, political issue of the time. This is *not* the case in every political conflict, and it does not necessarily reflect or conceal a 'deeper' class struggle.

Only a pluralistic view of classes and groups can do justice to the complexity of early Stuart society. The processes of class differentiation and division are normally as active as those of class cohesion, and the polarisation of classes on which Marxists concentrate was as transient a phenomenon in the English Revolution as in any other. Men's interests as individuals and as members of families, localities, classes and nations may coincide or conflict and may or may not be mutually reinforcing. Occasionally their interests as members of an economic class—their relation to the system of production—may be dominant. It is not lastingly so, and the achievement, or non-achievement, of specific class ends may bring other interests to the fore. These points apply also to government servants, who have some of the characteristics of a 'class' in sharing a common relationship, partly parasitic, partly functional, to the economic system. Government officials and the assorted lawyers, clergy, monopolists, favourites, patent-hunters and general hangers-on of Trevor-Roper's 'Court' had conflicting interests as individuals and as members of departments, professions, companies or clientage networks. If society was pluralistic, so too was its government. This competitiveness, which is underestimated in Trevor-Roper's 'Court-Country' polarity, could override the clash of interest between 'government' and 'opposition'.

The fact that government was a congeries of conflicting individuals and groups meant that officials might be in opposition on some or many of the issues of 1640–1. It also meant that the 'aims' of the government are difficult to discover. Policy-makers were subject to a host of conflicting pressures and interests, apart from those which they themselves represented. Again, to have aims implies a degree of freedom of manoeuvre. Given the financial problems of the early Stuart government, the realisation of ambitious aims was unlikely; 'aims' were often confined to seeking a degree of financial independence which would provide manoeuvrability in other fields. Historians have often implied an intention to transform society or government, whether by the introduction of continental absolutism, the application of the vague principles of 'Thorough', or otherwise. The idea that a government should actually wish to do something, beyond merely maintaining its existence, is particularly associated with modern reforming or revolutionary regimes, and for most of them existence quickly becomes most important. Governments find it easier to react to events than to control them, especially governments as deprived of information as those of the *ancien régime*. Of course the early Stuart government made plans – to get back the Palatinate by a Spanish Match, to finance a fleet by Ship

Money – which, whether realised or not, were an element in the situation. But we must not impose on the government an unrealistic degree of consistency, coherence or long-term planning. The height of its ineptitude was to give influential people the impression it was changing the basis of political life without intending to or in fact doing much about it. This impression mattered more than the reality. In any case, whether the government had such aims is not significant in the last resort: by the summer of 1641 it had failed in a more basic test; it had failed to survive.

II

To be more precise, what had been removed from the political scene were certain key figures, and certain institutions and practices which the Commons had come to regard as innovatory. Preserved were those institutions and powers of the Crown which had been legitimised by time and were not, in the eyes of the Commons, corrupted: gone were those modifications and extensions which many members of the government, in Church and State, had believed necessary to make the system work. It is unsurprising that the 'political nation', possessing great social and economic influence, should regard 'innovation' or 'novelty' as the greatest political sin. But how did they become convinced that the government was innovatory and how were they able to destroy it so easily?

The difference between government and opposition did not reflect radically different political philosophies, or views about the way society should be organised. The problem was essentially one of political management, though none the less serious for that. In Professor Fisher's words, 'The famous Civil War was the result less of a major social conflict than of the breakdown of a clumsy political machine in the hands of a remarkably inefficient operator'.[4] We must look for destabilising elements, and inelasticities in the political system, which prevented such elements from being successfully dealt with. In the first place, the agreement on fundamentals was dangerous, since it was expressed in such generalities that it left the way open for widely divergent practical applications, and concealed a host of differences about the specific distribution of powers in the State. In his book, *The Stuart Constitution*, Kenyon notes that a benevolent, patriarchal and authoritarian view of the State was widely accepted in the early seventeenth century. He cites appositely the similarities between the political philosophies of Charles I, Wentworth and Pym; their concern with maintaining the 'circle of order' and 'arch of government'; and the general acceptance of an 'ancient constitution' which gave the King certain prerogatives and the subject certain rights (especially to property) and stressed the dangers of tipping this balance too far in favour of king or subject.

A hierarchic view of society was consistent with (indeed it reinforced) the notion that each rung had its duties to the commonweal; the severest condemnation was reserved for those who seemed to be using their position for undue personal gain. James I, the most noted exponent of a 'free monarchy', stressed in *Basilikon Doron*, as a Christian Prince should, a king's responsibilities to his subjects; even his *Trew Law of Free Monarchies* was subtitled *The Reciprock and Mutuall Duetie betwixt a Free King and his Naturall Subjects*. Recognition of the subjects' rights clearly distinguished an abhorrent tyranny from a God-given 'free monarchy', but James, like his contemporaries, stopped short of specifying what those rights might be. In the early seventeenth century it became clear that there was no agreement about a number of issues, some of which, like control of foreign policy, the King had every historical justification for regarding as an unquestionable part of his prerogative.

Political thinking stressed rights and duties, and attributed to men's public actions a high moral significance. But the ambiguities meant that such actions often appeared shockingly immoral to contemporaries. Of course not everything was vague. For example the Crown's earliest governmental function was as the source of justice, which, in medieval England, meant essentially encouraging the evolution of an acceptable system of land law to preserve real property and to facilitate its conveyance. James I was still able to say that 'the most part of a King's office standeth in deciding that question of *Meum* and *Tuum*, among his subjects'.[5] There had evolved a complex and sophisticated law, administered in a highly centralised fashion, which, for all the complaints it roused, survived the reformers of the Interregnum. In fact these complaints were a consequence of its development: expense and delay in suits and conveyancing followed from the detailed procedures which had evolved. Land law was the core of English common law, and there were strong tendencies to see its concepts and procedures as appropriate to the clarification of the political ambiguities referred to above. The Crown itself was seen as a piece of heritable property; so too, we shall see, were offices. Some lawyers held that an appeal to precedents was sufficient to settle disputed political questions: an error which Crown and opposition fostered by their distrust of novelty and their assumption that what had been done in the fourteenth century was relevant to contemporary problems.

There was nothing necessarily subversive of the established political order in James I's statement, 'The state of monarchy is the supremest thing on earth'. Indeed, from one point of view, it was a truism in a state which had rejected papal supremacy. It has long been established that James and Charles I acted within the common law framework of the constitution, as they saw it. The personal exercise of royal power, as in any political system of the least sophistication, had long been regularised and flowed in particular channels. Royal favourites and monopolists required letters patent authorising their grants: these were legal instruments whose authenticity and interpretation were testable in the courts. But the key phrase is 'as they saw it': others might see it differently.

If an area of especial difficulty can be defined, it was not the supremacy of statute. The legislative supremacy of King in Parliament was generally agreed, and was not crucially affected by appeals to fundamental law: James acknowledged in 1610 that 'he had no power to make laws of himself, or to exact any subsidies de jure without the consent of his three Estates.' He also wrote, 'A Parliament is the honourablest and highest judgement in the land (as being the King's head Court) if it be well used, which is by making of good laws in it'.[6] James in fact sometimes seems to claim less 'freedom' for monarchy than Sir John Eliot, the persistent opponent of the Court, was to do later in his De Jure Majestatis. But the important issue was not the supremacy of statute, but the exercise and control of the Crown's equally unquestioned executive responsibility. With parliamentary sessions dependent on the royal will, with the appointment and dismissal of ministers in the Crown's hands (apart from the cumbrous procedure of impeachment which required conviction of a crime), with growing public requirements for state intervention in economic, social and religious life, it is not surprising that the range of the government's activity and control of the proper exercise of its de facto legislative power became the key political issue. It links the notable constitutional cases from Bate to Hampden with the dispute over Convocation's power to issue canons without parliamentary approval, and the squabbles over royal grants of monopoly or billeting of troops. James's more assertive statements – 'For albeit the King makes daily statutes and ordinances, enjoining such paines thereto as he thinks meet, without any advice of Parliament or estates' – were efforts to assert an extensive freedom of executive action. But in the preceding paragraph he wrote, 'The King tak(ing) land from his lieges' at his pleasure and the 'People . . . unmak(ing) the King' are both 'unlawful, and against the ordinance of God'. On the previous page, the people are to obey '(the King's) commands in all things, except directly against God'.[7] The ambiguity reappears: the limits of disobedience are not specified and have to be decided in each instance.

The voluminous writings on political obligation in the early seventeenth century did not help the well-meaning citizen to decide how to react to the Privy Council's demand for Ship Money; what limits, if any, there should be to the Crown's power to grant monopolies; or, on a more mundane level, what was the proper level of the fees of the Clerk of the Pipe Office in the Exchequer. It was over such issues, big or small, that the substantive political disputes of the period arose. The 'political nation's' acceptance of conscientious, patriarchal kingship certainly did not mean that the Crown's views on such disputes would always be accepted. Perhaps constitutional liberties were better preserved by the cumbrous workings of the administrative machine than by more formal methods. But when doubts were raised about specific government actions, settlement was reached, if at all, by recourse to common law precedent. A legal, not a political, decision had to be reached when political philosophy offered no guidance. Equally, it is unsurprising that the judges 'were not prepared to abandon . . . case law, crabbed but certain, for the misty profundities and vague generalisations of fundamental law'.[8] Fundamental law, so prized in the political thinking of the period, offered a set of unspecific truisms from which could flow many different views. 'It was very usual in this period for judges whose real conclusions were based on the narrowest and most technical grounds to embellish their judgments with vague philosophy.'[9] This merely reflected the feeling that 'philosophy', on which all right-thinking men thought themselves in agreement, ought to be relevant. A situation in which the Crown and its opponents could accuse each other of misusing 'misty profundities' was potentially very unstable: the gap might be narrow but unbridgeable.

One final point may be made about the consequences of the belief that there were agreed spheres of rights and duties in public life and that no difficulty need arise if they were adhered to. It emphasised the personal element in politics. If the system was perfect, any strains must be due to 'evil' counsellors or 'factious' M.P.s. The tone and nuance of political utterance excited people more than its content deserved. This was most obviously so of the occasional wild clergyman – Cowell, Manwaring or Montagu – whose views, on close analysis, were rarely as revolutionary as their tone. In any case none of them offered the Crown a practical way of attaining that degree of independence which Parliament feared. But general agreement made tact and delicacy in political life more necessary (if the ambiguities were not to be revealed), and more unlikely. It tended to concentrate attention on the forthright men in politics – the Wentworths and Lauds – who seemed to offer neat solutions to the problems of a 'free' but responsible monarchy. (In fact they may not have been so dangerous to the political balance as the men who thought of the Ship Money as an annual tax, who jacked up wardship fines or continued to try to negotiate City loans.) It encouraged self-confidence when the political situation appeared to be quiet, and gave added weight to those in the government (not necessarily the exponents of Thorough) who advocated a rather more aggressive policy which tended to break rather than strengthen links with the politically influential. It contributed to the dangerous cultural and political isolation of the Court in the 1630s.

Men felt wrongly that their agreement on broad principles was sufficient to secure political peace. It became increasingly apparent in the 1620s and 1630s that this agreement concealed disputed views about everything of political significance. Moreover, this situation was dynamic. The suspicions it generated had their own momentum: in trying to cope with the ambiguities men were forced into postures which oversimplified their relations with each other, polarised opinion and made destruction rather than change of men and institutions seem the answer to political problems.

III

But all political systems have an uncertain distribution of power. Although the feeling of agreement on fundamentals added an extra degree of danger, we must still ask why these uncertainties became important and why peaceful compromise was impossible. First, more was asked of the government: developments at home and abroad, and society's growing aspirations and expectations, brought these uncertainties to the surface, and made a decision on some of them imperative. Second, even if agreed solutions were reached, implementation of them was very difficult amid the vested interests, privileges, franchises and liberties common to political society at the time. Third, and perhaps worst of all, many aspirations were particular and could only be satisfied at the expense of the community; to meet them alienated wider political opinion.

A full account of the origins of the English Civil War would concern itself with the many discontents and strains in English society, which became sticks with which to beat the government. Officialdom is always likely to be unpopular in periods of rapid social and economic change. If we confine ourselves to areas in which the government was thought to have, and accepted, some competence, we find a widening gap between the demands of society and the government's ability to meet them. This gap existed not because the government did not share society's aspirations, but because it did not have the institutional, intellectual or financial means to satisfy them, and because the aspirations themselves were often conflicting. Inflation necessitated some testing of the Crown's rights to new or long-disused forms of income at a time when taxpayers faced similar problems and were anxious only to reduce royal demands. Population growth, especially in London, apparently led to vagabondage and a threat to social order and property: accordingly the politically influential hammered out over two or three generations the broad outlines of a social policy which placed great responsibility on the government. But there was no parallel development of the government's administrative and financial strength. In religious policy the Crown was assumed to be ultimately responsible for an ambitious programme which ranged from moral regeneration (mostly for the lower orders) to withstanding an apparently dangerous international Catholic conspiracy. This was to be achieved without reversing the impoverishment of the Church, and while the ecclesiastical administrative structure was under attack. The introduction of a strong ideological element into the Englishman's view of foreign affairs increased public concern and restricted the government's freedom of manoeuvre without giving it the means to carry out a more effective policy. The same pattern of higher aspirations without concern for means may be seen in the growing, though often conflicting, demands for a domestic and overseas economic policy which, whatever its particular form, placed great weight on government intervention, government support, or government control.

The government showed little unwillingness to shoulder these burdens. The Middle Ages had left England with a high degree of centralisation, and reliance on the Crown to achieve desired social goals was not new. We have referred briefly to the Crown's part in the evolution of English land law. There was no reason why (in an ideal world) the

Crown should not accept the ideals of a sober God-fearing population, a learned preaching ministry, a regulated economy (the expansion of which was carefully controlled to avoid social tensions), and a foreign policy in which Englishmen played their full part in the restoration of the Palatinate and the defence of Protestantism.

It would be remarkable if it were not so, given that leading policy-makers were recruited from similar social backgrounds, received the same education, and had the same first-hand experience of social and economic conditions (often as local magistrates or as M.P.s.) as the politically influential groups as a whole. But the government was not big enough, rich enough, or sufficiently in control of its own members, to fulfil these expectations. Under pressure it became increasingly concerned with its interests *qua* government, with preservation of its rights and even with its very existence. It pushed to the fore issues which tended to be divisive and to break its links with the political nation, so that even policies which might have been acceptable (such as much of Laud's reforming programme) appeared to be examples of bureaucratic or clerical tyranny.

To take the question of size first. It has often been pointed out that the English monarchy lacked a standing army or any extensive local bureaucracy with which to back its interventionist aims. This was a drawback, but we must be careful in analysing what sort of drawback it was. There is no simple correlation between big government and successful government. Too often it is assumed that the English monarchy was a pale shadow of the French, but, as we have stressed, its strength rested on its close sympathies with the locally influential. Extension of the central government influence meant higher taxes and less local independence. As the experience of parliamentary and army rule in the 1640s and 1650s showed, it was a destabilising feature which raised political tension. In fact England was a much-governed country locally, with an extensive judicial and administrative system ranging from Lords Lieutenant down to petty constables (omitting the lively ecclesiastical courts and the surviving private manorial jurisdiction). This local bureaucracy was only partly under government control, which did not matter as long as it was asked to do only what it wanted, but became crucial if the central government found itself forced into policies unwelcome to the locally influential. There is some evidence of political views affecting the choice of Justices of the Peace in the 1620s and 1630s. Even a few clerical J.P.s appeared. But this did not affect the broad pattern of an independent magistracy, enjoying local prestige. Office-holding could induce (with some help from the Privy Council) a governmental attitude: the sheriffs, chosen from the local gentry, achieved at first a good yield from Ship Money. But the non-payment eventually became substantial, and revealed clearly the fragile administrative basis of any attempt by the government to pursue what the localities regarded as innovatory policies. In short, the lack of a local bureaucracy became crucial when confidence had already been lost. It did not cause the government's weakness, though it certainly ensured that the collapse was rapid when it came.

More serious perhaps was the fact that this lack deprived the central government of much information, which was particularly important for an interventionist regime. The implementation of government plans, like the doing of justice, depended largely on local institutions and local men, who told the Privy Council what they felt it should hear. Much of the Council's business was instigated by private men with a grievance; it is inherently improbable that justice could be done both to them and their opponents, given the selective information available to the central government. Delegation of a dispute to local worthies might embroil the parties in the complexities of family feuds. The role of semi-official informers in enforcing many penal statutes and discovering concealed royal revenues is well known. They might abet as well as reveal such concealments, but the government had nobody else to use. The extreme Conciliar activity in the 1620s and 1630s created a stream of orders and inquiries about troops, ships, prizes, corn supplies, employment, prices, wages, public order, etc., but by and large not much could be done to ensure local compliance. Occasionally this might be to the government's advantage: for example, the poor enforcement of the Council's restrictions on building in London probably helped, rather than hindered, the maintenance of public order. Such bonuses were rare. England had an interventionist government which was ignorant and of limited effectiveness.

The central government itself was too small for some purposes, but too large for others. It was also insufficiently under control. For an important, and perhaps growing, part of the political nation, the central government was the focus of personal aspirations. In the first place it offered a career with varying opportunities for social and financial advance. But these opportunities were not great enough to satisfy the demand or to create a powerful bureaucratic elite which might have outweighed the influence of other aspirant groups. The 'ins' in English politics did not overtop the 'outs'. On the other hand, royal control over 'the King's servants' was not firm enough to eliminate private gain at the public expense. The Crown was in the worst position: it suffered much of the odium of a bureaucratic state without the reality of its power.

There were three main modes of entry into the king's service: purchase (the buying of a place); patrimony (the obtaining of a post already held within an applicant's family); and patronage (the favour of someone more influential). Often more than one of these methods were appropriate to a specific appointment. The king's direct control of appointments was extensive at the top: the great officers of state were his appointees and with few exceptions held office during his pleasure. The quality of the advice on policy which he received was therefore his own responsibility. But lower down his rights were delegated to, shared with, or usurped by politicians, courtiers or senior officers who saw the exercise of patronage as vital to their political standing and financial advantage. Many rights of patronage were established, but often they were vague. Whether established or precise, rights to exercise patronage were bitterly defended and were the cause of much disruptive political rivalry. Uncertainty and divided power weakened control of staffing. The system clearly did not encourage merit, which anyway was difficult to assess except in legal posts. (It should perhaps be said that merit was not necessarily ignored: other things being equal there was no reason for a patron to appoint an incompetent.) But control was further weakened by the tendency for middling and lower offices to be held for life, which remained very common despite some minor attempts at reform under Charles I, and for reversions to be granted which might not be effective for many years. The growing practice of exercising offices by deputy made matters worse.

These points illustrate the tendency to see an office as a freehold; as a form of investment which must be made to yield results. Official salaries and diets were low. Much more important were fees for services done and the range of perquisites to which office provided access and which varied widely depending on the place held. There was much room for accusations of extortion. Not everything was uncertain. The pressures of bureaucracy tended to establish many fixed payments: the fee for routine jobs performed hundreds of times a year could not be haggled over each time. But inflation made the situation more unstable, by diminishing the value of official salaries and making it more necessary for office-holders to try to increase the discretionary element in their fees. Ideally, fees should have been adjusted to cope with rising costs, but perhaps only Bacon and Wentworth appreciated the need to make such adjustment. The nearest the government came to recognising the need for this was when, in the 1620s and 1630s its Commissioners inquiring into Exacted Fees, whose purpose ostensibly was to eliminate increased fees and prevent further rises, accepted as base dates the fees claimed in various years in Elizabeth's reign, thus tacitly legitimising rises achieved by then. But this was already a generation out of date, and the Commissions' double functions of placating public opinion and raising royal revenue by fining extortionate officials made them totally unsuited to face the general problem of adjustment.

The government was faced with a problem of balancing demands without having effective control of the situation. The need to satisfy the demands of would-be bureaucrats for jobs and of actual bureaucrats for fees had to be measured against the dissatisfaction of fee-payers. Efficiency could be improved and political tension eased by ensuring that fewer hands did the same amount of work or by reducing the proportion of central government income that went into officials' pockets. But even if it was agreed that such reforms were worth the wails of anguished office-holders, implementation was another matter. Any 'reforming' minister was himself the product of the system: both Cranfield and Laud owed much to Buckingham. At the highest level the King himself had much responsibility for backing such a minister against vested interests which were often closest to the royal person. Buckingham gave brief tactical support to Cranfield's economy measures, but he rapidly dropped both this and Cranfield himself. The favourite was part of the network of clientage and patronage which depended on him for access to perquisites. Dangerous political isolation might attend the poacher-favourite who turned gamekeeper.

The consequence was drift, punctuated by reforming agitations. The bureaucracy grew somewhat in size, especially at lower levels where clerks, solicitors and 'secretaries' could easily proliferate. This was partly due to greater government responsibilities, but probably owed more to the pressure of demand. Equally, it is clear that the demand was unsatisfied. Limits were imposed by the difficulties of indefinitely expanding business and fees, and there were many signs that officials did not find their places profitable enough. Further proliferation of jobs tended to reduce each existing officer's share of the cake. This encouraged the bitter inter- and intra-departmental struggles for business which were so marked a feature of the Elizabethan and early Stuart bureaucracy. Such struggles were clearly an element in the great disputes between the ecclesiastical and common law courts in James I's reign: they were the be-all and end-all of many officials' lives.

But grants of office are only a specific instance of the role of patronage in government. The government was the source of grants of titles, honours, perquisites, privileges, pensions, franchises and real property. The exercise of this patronage was a single, if complex, problem of political and social management. The satisfying of a faction or connection involved a range of concessions from titles and honours to perquisites and posts. The value of each concession was reduced by inflation or by being shared with too many competitors. Every grant, whether of a title, monopoly, part of Crown revenue or office, was likely to offend someone. It might be the Earl of Arundel whose ancient lineage was insulted by the ennoblement of the sheepmaster Spencer; it might be the consumer, a rival group of merchants or a disappointed competitor. In general the government had to try to achieve a balance between satisfying an apparently insatiable demand and limiting the burden its grants imposed on others.

James I allowed access to royal favour to become dangerously concentrated on Buckingham, depriving those not in Buckingham's favour of opportunities of advance and dangerously equating opposition to Buckingham with opposition to the Crown. (Since Prince Charles remained infatuated with Buckingham there was not even a reversionary interest to appeal to.) Financially James granted away too much royal revenue for too small a return, either in services done or political support consolidated. But the exercise of, and demand for, patronage were facts of political life: the king could no more afford to risk denuding himself of political allies than any lesser politician could. The problem was not simply one of reducing favours but of finding the right level and pattern of patronage. It may be that the problem was insoluble: that the government was not big enough or rich enough to create a dominant class of dependents who would outweigh 'Country' opposition; nor was it small and powerless enough for the demands on it not to be generated. Certainly the problem was not solved. The assassination of Buckingham removed the worst abuses: there was never again such a concentration of influence. But the 1630s saw the Crown appearing to link itself more and more closely with a favoured circle of court aristocrats and leading City financiers. Links with the 'Country' were weakened both in England and, under Wentworth's driving, in Ireland. No longer was it possible, as it had been at the height of Buckingham's power, for the 'Puritan interest' to hope the government might genuinely support the ends they had in mind, even to the extent of a war with Spain. It is ironical, and symptomatic of the complexities of political management, that the 'popular' policy of 1624 involved the sacrifice of the 'reforming' minister, Cranfield.

The role of informers further illustrates the government's difficulties. Up to a point the King's interests coincided with the private gain or 'corruption' represented by the activities of informers. Improved revenue might well be obtained by using informers and allowing them to take their cut. It is certainly the case that the highest revenue from wardships in the late 1630s was directly connected with more intensive use of informers.[10] We do not know enough about the workings of government in the 1630s to say whether this was a generalised phenomenon, but it is interesting that Wentworth was able in Ireland closely to tie the improvement in the King's income with his own personal gains. The methods characterising 'Thorough' (in the person of the Lord Deputy) and 'Lady Mora' (in the person of Cottington, Master of the Wards) may not have been such poles apart as they have been represented. An improvement in the Crown's position was not simply a matter of reducing 'corruption'; it was a question of ensuring that the shared advantages of the Crown and private interests (whether represented by the Lord Deputy of Ireland, the discoverers of concealed wardships, recusants or forest rights, the grantees of monopolies, or whoever) were not bought at the expense of too great a rise in political feeling. This delicate balance was more difficult to achieve because the level varied with the situation. It had to be reduced when a parliament was in prospect or in session, but even after the dismissal of a difficult parliament – 1611, 1621 or 1629 – it seems to have been psychologically necessary to reduce 'corruption'. Certainly the level of private advantage (with government connivance at public expense) seems to have been highest in the later 1610s and 1630s when there had been long periods without Parliament (though the wars of the later 1620s as usual increased both the government's needs and the opportunities for private profit). The process had its own internal dynamic, since the employment of informers tended to reduce the co-operation of the localities further, thus encouraging more reliance on informers. By the end of the 1630s the government had slid far down this particular slope. It might have found a new equilibrium: it might, had it managed to avoid the Scottish adventure, have established a new basis for political life, with an extended bureaucracy, reducing the 'country', deprived of a parliamentary forum, to impotent grumbling. Such things were possible, if very unlikely. If they had been achieved, it would have been by drift rather than policy. There is no sign that the faction-ridden advisers of Charles I conceived that a new permanent political structure was possible. It was over-confidence, born of a few years' political quiet and some success with Ship Money, which led to the Scottish policy. Equally naïve was the belief that when it failed, it would be possible to pick up the old rituals of parliamentary life – bargaining over supply and grievances – as if the 1630s had never been. Lack of information, lack of analysis of political feeling, a hand-to-mouth policy of expedients, and an unreformed and cumbrous governmental machine, were as characteristic of the last years of the English *ancien régime* as they were to be of the French.

Usually the government attempted to postpone a solution to its problems, and what constituted policy was reaction to specific circumstances according to certain presuppositions. 'Attempts at administrative reform' were taken up at moments of political or financial tension, were pursued without any real appreciation of their consequences, were almost always ineffective, and were soon dropped (or more typically, quietly forgotten) when the immediate situation had passed. Many of the government's economic and social policies and even the so-called new departures of 'Thorough' may best be seen as a traditional reaction to a particular situation. The traditionalism of its response may well have encouraged the government in its belief that it had not lost widespread political support, just as the passivity of the country encouraged it to believe it was in control of events.

The delusion that it had freedom of manoeuvre, and the rapidity with which it committed suicide, may well also owe something to its apparent financial successes. Modern historians and contemporaries have paid much attention to the problem of balancing the Crown's budget. After a generation in which the effects of Burghley's fiscal caution, Elizabeth's war expenditure, James's largesse, and continuing inflation had seen the Crown staggering from one crisis and one fractious Parliament to the next, the increased income and the peaceful foreign policy of the 1630s might make it appear that this phase had been successfully passed. But balanced budgets were not typical of State finances in the *ancien régime*, nor on the whole did the stability of governments depend on them. Most governments were in debt, and higher revenues – as in the 1650s and 1690s – tended to generate more ambitious and expensive policies. It is perhaps true that because of

its dependence on local goodwill the English monarchy could not afford
an imbalance as large as that which was possible in some bureau-
cratically more developed continental regimes; but in the short term
the key problem was the same: that of credit-worthiness. Could the
government borrow enough to service its debt and to meet current
demands? Professor Ashton has traced the decline in the Crown's
credit-worthiness, culminating in a situation in which many of its
leading creditors in the City, who had inevitably become heavily
committed financially to the stability of the regime, actually welcomed
the Parliament, which was to destroy that regime, as the only means
to secure themselves.

In terms of its structure and resources, the government's freedom of
action was more limited and it was weaker than might appear from the
quiescence of the 1630s. In a sense we have been discussing further
examples of that ambiguity in its position which could easily induce
political miscalculation. We must now see how these miscalculations
were made in economic, social and religious policy; how apparently
traditional policies, which seemingly often had the support of the
politically influential, came to be regarded as innovatory and corrupt.

IV

What were the issues at stake in early seventeenth century economic
and social policy? If the economy is seen as a battleground in which
the Prometheus of Capital is struggling to free itself from moribund
restrictions,[11] then the reason for the government's unpopularity is
clear. Such abstract images appealed to Marx's Idealism and they now
delight some liberal economists at the other end of the political spec-
trum: if the goal to be achieved is that nineteenth-century ideal of
freely moving capital meeting freely moving labour, then any Stuart
restriction on the mobility of capital or labour, or any taxation of
commerce, may be seen as harmful. But whether the free movement of
capital and labour was economically beneficial (assuming this is
definable) depended on circumstances: it could be argued, for example,
that in the vital English cloth industry capital and labour were too
volatile.[12] Restrictions were not necessarily harmful in themselves, and
were certainly not unpopular with the business community, which
naturally preferred protection to competition provided its interests
were being protected. Investment in office and in loans to the government might be a waste of capital resources from the point of view of
economic growth, but that was the reverse side of the coin of dependence

by the business community on the government. Government intervention was expected and sought by commercial and industrial interests under monarchical and republican regimes alike. Attacks on some monopolies and the temporary liberalisation of entry into the cloth trade, which followed the commercial crises of 1586–7 and the early 1620s, should not be seen as attacks on the principle of regulating the economy. They were attacks on particular forms of regulation which seemed to have been found wanting, and which appeared to allow undue sectional gain at public expense. (See Chapter 7 below.)

The difficulties were not over the fact of intervention, but over its particular nature, and the specific problems of reconciling divers private and government interests. As in any economy, the interests of industries and trades were partly conflicting, partly complementary. So too were the interests of the different groups involved: employers and employees, producers, distributors and consumers. Within these groups the same complex relations existed. Again, the government's interest overlapped but did not coincide with any of them, and it was itself subject to group and individual pressures. Given these complications, it is not surprising that Professor C. Wilson has been able to write, 'flagrant inconsistency . . . was perhaps the leading characteristic of Stuart attempts at social and economic planning.[13]

The English government, like all governments, was concerned with its own security, and it shared its concern about public order with the politically influential. It was suspicious of unplanned economic expansion, the disruptive consequences of which had been shown in the too rapid growth of the cloth trade in the 1550s. Its view of social and economic welfare was inseparable from its view of its own security and function, and it was suspicious of radical changes in economic practice. Redistribution of wealth was anathema; its aim, so like Oliver Cromwell's, was a natural sufficiency at all levels of society, and the minimisation of that degree of poverty which made men destitute and desperate. This is properly called an ideal rather than an aim since there was little notion of how to achieve it. The government supported those institutions in town and country which regulated wages, production, labour mobility and consumption. It could envisage and welcome modest expansion in some fields, especially in areas of production which reduced imports or 'set the poor on work'. The relative youth of the population, the brevity of working life, preference for leisure rather than higher earnings, the difficulties of capital investment, the low level of technology and productivity, the seasonal nature of work in agriculture

and part of industry, the inelasticity of demand and the high proportion
of spending on necessities produced a situation in which, in D. C.
Coleman's view, 'labour (was) easily the most important factor of
production' and there was 'a persistent tendency towards chronic under-
employment'.[14] It is improper to imply that the government favoured
only luxury industries or armaments.[15] More judicious are Charles
Wilson's words: 'In the interests of trade and industry the export of
raw material, – wool and its ancillaries, fuller's earth, pipe clay, wool
fells – was strictly prohibited, so as to keep prices down for the native
manufacturer. The inflow of skilled artisans was encouraged, bounties
were granted to producers . . .'[16] But in commercial and industrial
policy the government apparently allowed both its fiscal needs and the
political need to satisfy its clients to dominate its practice, especially in
the 1630s. The ambiguity is pinpointed by Wilson: 'Ordinances,
proclamations and statutes formed the dynamic of a new economic policy.
Such regulations frequently served private ends; collectively their
object was to raise the economy to a new level of productivity and
profitability.' As in the case of patronage discussed above, the government appeared to be supporting private interests against the public
good. Such an ambiguity was always likely to arise in an economic
policy which was based on regulation, since regulations tended to imply
discriminating in favour of one group of producers, distributors, or
even (in the case for example of sumptuary legislation) of consumers,
at the expense of another. But by 1640 it had reached a new height, so
that the government's allies in the commercial and industrial worlds –
frequently the ruling oligarchies in London and other towns, the grantees
in the 1630s of corporate monopolies over a wide range of productive
and distributive processes, the monopolistic overseas trading companies,
and the Crown's creditors in the London money market – were too
disillusioned with their treatment, or too isolated in the face of competitive groups to defend the regime effectively. We should add the
relative weakness of mercantile interests in the House of Commons,
and the doubts which traditionalists felt about wealth acquired in
commerce or finance, to appreciate how the Crown's reputation
suffered from its association with these enemies of the common weal.

But the Crown might legitimately complain that it faced an unprecedented situation and that it tried to adapt its traditional responses
to cope with it. The two preceding generations had seen a notable, if
painful and hesitant, restructuring of English industry and commerce.
The growth of extractive and consumption industries; the beginnings

of the diversification of English exports away from their staple broad-cloth and their concentration on northern European markets; the growth of coastal shipping; the opening of extra-European trade routes and colonisation; the development of London as a centre of both 'mass and inconspicuous' consumption and of developing credit facilities. All these intensified the difficulties of managing an economy which was at once becoming more diversified and more unified. In particular, it was an economy of notable booms and slumps, the mechanics of which were only beginning to be understood, but which nevertheless led to rising expectations and demands for action. The situation in the cloth industry was especially serious when, as in 1586, 1622 and 1630, bad harvests meant that dearth coincided with unemployment. In Burghley's view, clothworkers were 'of worse condition to be quietly governed than the husbandmen',[17] and the government's immediate reaction in a depression was to try to keep production going and employment up even if it was uneconomic. J.P.s were to keep wages up and to ensure that the various processes of production and distribution were maintained.

But it was all of little use, except to weaken the government's reputation further. The gap persisted between the aspirations of government and political society to control economic change, and the reality of continued depression in the 1620s and 1630s – not only in the older branches of the cloth trade. The void between regulation and its effectiveness was not new, but it is less easily borne in a depression than in prosperity. 'Objectives might be agreed, but execution remained elusive.'[18] The reasons were partly intellectual: 'The government's main aim . . . was to keep the wheels of industry turning by encouraging or enforcing the circulation of capital, [but] . . . to throw open the trade, on the pretext of expanding demand, might only aggravate the slump. There were obvious economic limitations to a policy which contradicted the expectations of private capital.'[19] Even with a more developed appreciation of the reasons for the crisis, the government could have had little effect on it internationally, and not much more at home. Its power to stimulate demand was slight. The government was also hampered by the local devolution of its administration. 'Local acts and options in domestic social and economic policies proved realisable, when more general measures were not';[20] this was so because the former tended to represent the local consensus of the politically influential, while the latter might be conciliar or parliamentary acts conceived in the 'national interest' and cutting across local ones. The very frequency with which the Privy Council intervened in the minutiae of economic regulation are signs both that it accepted its responsibilities and that enforcement was beyond its capacities.

Depression was one reason why the gap between the intentions of the government and the reality of its power became more brutally obvious. Another was the general early seventeenth-century failure to maintain statutory control over economic developments. Political troubles prevented many regulatory bills from reaching the statute book, although, as we have seen, this was a period in which the economy was diversifying in its location, its products and even to some extent in its technology. How far the triumph of the mercantile over the handicraft element in the older industries was responsible for the decline of regulation in practice is in dispute,[21] but it is clear that the vulnerability of the cloth trade to changes of overseas demand led to most emphasis being placed on foreign trade in the 1620s debate. But whether the reason for the decline of statutory regulation was political, or a more fundamental economic change, the Privy Council itself took over regulatory functions from Parliament to an increasing extent. Mr. Hinton strongly defends this change:

> The greater part of government was simply a matter of prohibiting certain actions and permitting others. Patents were capable of this ... Some things could be done better outside parliament ... Government by patent enabled regulation to be more exact: at one time it was good policy to import a small fixed amount of Spanish tobacco and a larger fixed amount of American tobacco, guaranteeing minimum prices for the latter; an act of Parliament would have been useless, the only possible method was a tobacco monopoly. Until the government could afford a civil service, privileges were the only way of getting things done; indeed the distinction between privilege and office in this period is a fine one ... Government was normally initiated by a private person with a petition. It is not to be thought of as something imposed from the top, but as something granted in response to a demand, and accordingly we must not suppose people were hostile to it. There was plenty of scope for deceit and corruption, and much talk – some rather loose – about monopolies, but it is fair to say that the system itself (the idea of private men implementing public policy) was regarded on all hands as normal and proper.[22]

We agree that economic management of this sort was more naturally a function of the executive than the legislative branch of government and that economic management was expected of the regime. But the actual exercise of these powers required a delicacy which successive politicians rarely showed, if private interest was not to appear the motive force. The absence of Parliament in the 1630s made it much more difficult to take note of those outport, producers' and manufacturers' lobbies which had been apparent in Jacobean parliaments. The reversal of the policies of the 1620s, especially the restoration of the Merchant Adventurers' monopoly in 1634, owes much to the opportunities for influence open to a tightly organised London merchant community in competition with the diffused 'country' interests.[23]

But there was at least a respectable case for reversing the unsuccessful liberalisation of the 1620s. There was much less of one for the influence which projectors and courtiers acquired in the later 1630s over grants of monopoly and licences, which appeared to be simply a means of diverting money away from the consumer into the pockets of court parasites – to the extent of over £1 million a year, according to the Grand Remonstrance. These grants represented no new theory of economic organisation, and they might very well be justified individually on contemporary principles; but they appeared – and in politics appearance is all – to overstep that use of royal power legitimate in the interests of the common weal. In particular complaints, about monopolists, projectors, patentees, etc., always reached a peak after periods of especial royal financial difficulty, when the government raised money by granting away its economic powers. 'A greasy business it is' wrote Laud of the soap monopoly, 'but *lucrum ex re qualibet!*'[24]

In one sense grants of monopoly are merely an example of the government's ambiguous attitude to the economy: its interest in revenue did not necessarily coincide with its desire to encourage or depress certain economic activities. It may be well argued that there was some leeway to be made up after Burghley's political quietism. The increased impositions of Robert Cecil seem to have been absorbed without much further protest, after the dissolution of Parliament, in the commercial prosperity of the early 1610s; and the taxpayers' strike over the non-parliamentary levy of tunnage and poundage did not last even in the chillier commercial climate of the 1630s. But the legality of impositions and of tunnage and poundage was at least questionable; and, although it may be true that in absolute terms the government's revenue demands were not a heavy burden on English overseas trade (and internal trade was remarkably free), it is the relative size of the increase which is politically significant in taxation.

As in other spheres of its activity, the government's intervention in the economy in the 1630s was marked not so much by new departures, as by the development of policies which revealed its over-confidence and the narrowing of its political support. It passed the indefinable line between public and private interest. There was no natural break between the Crown's admitted rights of regulation and contested grants of monopoly, but contemporaries drew one. The Crown's policy had some fiscal and political value. No doubt some potential aristocratic *frondeurs* were deterred from rebellion (though memory of earlier perquisites had not deterred Essex in 1601, and Holland was not deterred in 1641), but the circle of profiteers was too small, and that of sufferers too large, to justify what was done in political terms. By continental standards the largesse available to the English Crown was small; it was also misused.

The government's social policy, or more specifically its attitude towards the problem of poverty, was of course inseparable from its general attitudes towards the economy. It also revealed similar problems and ambiguities, and its political consequences were equally doubtful. The government had a traditional and accepted framework of policy within which to act, but it received contradictory advice about the implementation of that policy from divers interested parties; it had only limited information and limited administrative power; and its activities seemed unduly mixed with private graft. The government of Charles I tried to act as the Tudors had done. The latter's policy had been hammered out in parliament and owed much to the experience of local communities and authorities in coping with the sixteenth-century problem.[25] Historians' traditional belief that Elizabethan and early Stuart Englishmen were concerned simply about over-population has been questioned and, in view of the significance of labour in the economy and in military strength, such doubts seem justified. Labour was a crucial commodity, but it had to be properly used. The government and the politically influential shared fears that depopulation, unemployment and mobility of labour would lead to vagrancy and social unrest, and they had the same interest in a settled yeomanry and husbandman class as the backbone of the English infantry. Whatever the level of depopulating enclosures in the early seventeenth century, the problem of poverty had not been reduced: it was marked by growing emigration (winked at by the government), the spread of London, unemployment exacerbated by recurrent cloth crises, a pattern of land-holding which may have been moving against small owners and tenants in favour of large estates with associated engrossing of holdings, and the possible narrowing of agricultural profit margins as the long inflation slowly subsided. In addition to the restrictions on mobility imposed by sixteenth-century legislation on apprenticeship, the organisation of poor relief and the punishment of vagrancy was on a parochial basis: the emphasis was on returning 'masterless men' to the more or less welcoming bosom of their home parishes. This was complementary to the frequent proclamations enjoining gentlemen to leave the delights of London and return home so that the 'meaner sort of people (may be) guided, directed and relieved'. The gentry were given forty days to arrange their affairs; vagabonds had to move more smartly. In dearth, as in 1630, the government busily issued streams of orders to ensure both regulation and relief of the poor, instructions to enforce apprenticeship, levy poor rates, redistribute and prevent the hoarding of what grain there was, and organise public works. It is doubtful how effective this activity was. The whole range of economic and social legislation was more effectively administered locally than centrally, but that might still depend on the local interests involved: levying poor rates, releasing surplus corn, or (as the 1631 Book of Orders permitted) rewarding informers, was not necessarily attractive to local governors. But on the whole we may suppose that in a crisis such policies commanded general support among the influential, who feared as much as the government the breakdown of social order.

It was not so certain that this attitude would be maintained when the emergency had passed. The indolence of the Justices of the Peace had filled the preamble to the Book of Orders, and it is not probable that Privy Council pressure on them to certify their proceedings led to any radical change in their attitudes. In Professor Jordan's words: 'An examination of these returns suggests that the Council was incredibly naïve in assuming that because a return had been filed the law was being enforced. The great mass of the returns are on their face evasive, vague, or misleading and could have given the Council little more solid information than they give us.'[26] The principles behind the labour legislation and poor relief might still be generally acceptable; what it required in cost and bureaucratic effort from the localities was less so.

The government still gave a high place to engrossing and enclosure as causes of depopulation. Mrs. Thirsk writes, 'Under James I and Charles I, however, the government lost much of its zeal for the cause. Indeed after 1607, when the last large-scale enclosure enquiry took place, it abandoned all opposition to the principle of enclosure, but continued to keep up the appearance of opposing it in practice. Commissions were issued from time to time for the discovery of offenders, but their crimes were pardoned on payment of a money fine. The punishment of enclosers degenerated into a money-raising device and little else.'[27] Professor Beresford's gloss is: 'A few oppressors of the poor and would-be depopulators were no doubt penalised or deterred but the victims seem to have been mostly land-owners who had enclosed by agreement and infringed the Acts of 1597 (unrepealed in 1624) by some small diminution of the area of tillage or the number of farm-houses.'[28] But unless would-be depopulators were aware they were not to be prosecuted, then any fines must be a deterrent – and the larger the fine for a small offence, then the bigger the deterrent. High profit to the Crown is perfectly consistent with an effective deterrent and a vexatious informing system; indeed, given the early seventeenth century administrative structure, they would seem mutually dependent. Fining was always a more realistic policy than reconversion to tillage or common, or rebuilding; this was recognised in most Tudor statutes, and in both the sixteenth and seventeenth centuries fining was a deterrent which increased the cost of what was a business operation.

Politically it hardly mattered what motive was behind the government's policy: fines for depopulation were of a piece with fines for continuing to reside in London against the proclamation, or with the mutilation of Prynne. All were affronts to gentlemen. They also revealed the gap between what the politically influential claimed they wanted, and their dissatisfaction when they seemed to be getting it.

Perhaps in no field was that gap as wide as in religion. The English Reformation exacerbated some problems and produced others; their slow working to a climax may be traced from 1540 to 1640. The Reformation itself was a product of anti-clericalism, both in the sense that the laity wished to pillage the Church and wrest control of office and political power from the clergy, and in the sense that the clergy's control of education and its pastoral work seemed to be failing to produce the orderly, disciplined society required by an increasingly peaceful property-owning laity. This does not necessarily mean labour discipline in the interests of nascent capitalist development. There were plenty of reasons why the politically influential should desire an orderly society in the later Middle Ages without any necessary change in the modes of production. Intense suspicion of clerical pretensions was matched by a realisation that a reformed, educated clergy had a central role in instilling – who else could do it? – Godly Discipline in the 'dark corners'. The secular aims apparent in the charitable bequests of the laity had their parallels in the social and economic policies the government was expected to pursue.[29] They may also be seen in the ambiguous place which society assigned to the clergy. The Church was expected to be pillaged, to lose its political influence and no longer be the chief recipient of charity; but it was also expected to be newly active. Greatly increased reliance was placed on the secular arm – the Godly Prince – to ensure both that the clergy were reformed in the required image and that they did what was needed 'in *this* world'. The 'Godly Magistrate' was expected to patronise the Church, and also (since this would reduce his demands on the laity) to participate in its despoliation, while at the same time ensuring that the clergy were educated, resident, non-pluralist and good preachers.

The situation was unstable. Whatever its intention, any ideology gives enhanced status to its practitioners and exponents – at least in their own eyes. Whatever weight it may have placed on lay participation, Reformation theology in all its branches (from Arminian through Calvinist to sectarian) could be interpreted as giving special status to the clerical order. Such claims were made by High Church Laudians in the 1630s, Presbyterian divines in the 1640s, and even (by implication) by the crowd-drawing radical preachers of the Interregnum. The established Church could not be prevented from trying to improve its immediate post-Reformation position, in which the social status of its clergy was low, its remaining wealth ripe for picking, and its political influence greatly reduced. The changes appear slowly through Elizabeth's reign. Her religious settlement stabilised through time and appeared less provisional. The upper clergy began to defend it actively, and to claim for themselves enhanced status and influence. The beginnings of the *jure divino* defence of episcopacy, and Whitgift's political influence and aggressive persecuting policy are well-known stages in this process. A clear division between the hierarchy and the laity began to appear over the treatment of the problem of the poverty of the lower clergy, itself exacerbated by clerical marriage and by such success as had been achieved in raising educational standards at parochial level. The bishops held that lay impropriation was the root of the trouble, the laity that redistribution of wealth within the Church was the solution.

These tendencies were inherent in the post-Reformation settlement. What is less clear is how far the secular government need have allied itself as closely and as disastrously as it did to particular episcopal pretensions. 'No bishop, no king' had its attractions, but it perhaps revealed an attitude of mind in James and Charles which would make the cliché a self-fulfilling prophecy. So much so that by the time of

Laud and Charles I, we may turn it on its head and say, 'If that bishop, then not that king'. Episcopacy played a bigger part in destroying the old monarchy than in preserving it. But in any case we need to ask what sort of bishop and what sort of monarchy, before the equation is accepted. Too often hierarchy in the State is held to depend on hierarchy in the Church, as if the principle of social subordination in early modern society were such a delicate plant that the most extreme manifestations of the hierarchical principle must always be maintained. The monarchy was assured, in Protestant thought, of full support provided it could be seen as accepting its responsibilities towards religion.

Ironically, moderate Puritans might have approved of much of what their arch-enemy Laud offered, were it not associated with other distasteful manifestations of clericalism. His social policy was traditional, and his desire to improve the standards of living, conduct and education of the clergy were well in line with orthodox Protestantism. But there had long been a deep suspicion of the independence of the lower clergy among certain elements of the episcopate, which revealed itself in an especial distrust of uncontrolled preaching. Preaching, as any form of education or news dissemination, was in itself politically neutral: it could either support or undermine the existing order. What mattered was its content. But by the 1630s the bishops seemed to have manoeuvred themselves into a distaste for the thing itself, except under the most carefully dictated conditions. They placed more and more emphasis on the elements of ritualism and ceremonialism which had been at a low ebb in the Elizabethan church. This was no doubt a natural reaction for any hierarchy, but it made more marked the revival of clericalism – in the sense of the clergy as an independent order of society – and cast serious doubts on the Laudians' claims that they too wanted a 'godly, preaching ministry'.

Politically there were two disastrous elements in Laud's policies. One was his apparently infallible tendency to do what raised the political temperature highest with the least effect on the distribution of power in ecclesiastical affairs. In politics Laud had the simplicity of the academic but none of the deviousness of the cleric. The show trials of the pamphleteers and preachers, Prynne, Bastwick and Burton, might have been calculated to offend the susceptibilities of lay gentlemen. When last did a cleric cut off a gentleman's ears ? Locally, the more forceful visitation policy and the pressure exerted by ecclesiastical courts could be seen as direct attacks on the gentleman's right to control what went on in his parish. But there could be no real revival of clerical independence while so much patronage and income of the Church was in lay hands. The early Stuarts may have stopped royal despoliation of the Church, but to undo lay impropriation would have been the work of generations, especially if common law procedures were to be followed. Laudianism in fact became bogged down in a series of disputes about ceremonialism (so beloved of English theological controversialists and so destructive of that peace of the Church at which Laud aimed) and a series of lawsuits about tithes and advowsons. The Church appeared to be concerned about its wealth and status at the expense of its reforming function. Dispute was maximised and effective change minimised.

It was the imposition of the Scottish Prayer Book which most clearly revealed the Laudian propensity to raise controversial issues without a proper assessment of the realities of power. The fact that the King's part was perhaps greater than the Archbishop's illustrates the second political error in the religious policy of the 1630s: the close association of the secular government with an extreme episcopal line. This had many facets which can only be summarised here: the influence of the Archbishop in Star Chamber and Privy Council; his aggressive role in secular questions, especially extra-parliamentary taxation and the punishment of offenders; the appointment of a bishop, Juxon, as Lord Treasurer; the role of Star Chamber in punishing libels against the ecclesiastical hierarchy; the use of ecclesiastical punishments for trivial and sometimes apparently secular offences. All this implied the interpenetration of monarchy and a particular brand of high episcopacy which was disastrous to the reputation of both. There were other parallels: in both Church and State the administration appeared slow, devious and costly, qualities which contrasted badly with the proclaimed high aims.

In short, religious affairs presented dilemmas similar to those we have outlined in other fields. The government was expected to implement unspecific and partly contradictory policies without the necessary well-established power base. Exasperation could lead to a dangerous combination of over-confidence and unconcern about the narrowing of its political support. If there was a clear distinction between Wentworth and Laud as exponents of 'Thorough', and the rest of the government in the 1630s, it was perhaps that the former were prepared to push to extremes their lack of concern for political allies and to break more readily the Court's surviving links with the country. The 'corruption' of Lady Mora still presented the possibility of political support through jobbery, which may help to explain why Cottington got off more lightly than Laud or Wentworth in the 1640s. But we must not exaggerate the difference: jobbery existed in Wentworth's Ireland and it certainly had not been reformed out of Laud's Church, while both in Ireland and in England it existed on too narrow a front to be an effective counter-weight to the opposition it aroused.

The importance of Irish and Scottish affairs may easily be exaggerated: it was in the south and east of England that the decisive battle for political support was lost by the government. But the Irish issues have been seen as a microcosm of the struggle in England,[30] given added force by the links between the Protestant 'new English' in Ireland and the opposition at home. Similarly the English Parliament believed they shared a cause with the Covenanters. It might very well seem, away from the nuances and complexities of London politics, that the royal power was strong enough in Scotland and Ireland to be asserted without reference to any specific interest group. This was not so, as the ultimate collapse of Laud's and Wentworth's policies shows. Although James I, by 1603, had achieved more independence than any recent Scottish king, this had been by astute balancing of interests, by taking advantage of jealousy raised by any over-powerful group of nobles, and by swallowing the insults of the Kirk. After 1603 he continued an extremely cautious policy, enticing the nobility with church lands and the fruits of English patronage, and moving very delicately in religion. The innovations of the 1630s were precisely those in liturgy and ritual which were most public, gave most offence, and created a vested interest only in controversy. In Ireland Wentworth's policy did not collapse so soon because both Catholic 'old English' and Protestant 'new English' had high hopes from the regime and envisaged Irish politics as a continuation of the old manoeuvring around the Deputy. It was only slowly that it became apparent that Wentworth aimed at, or at least seemed to be, pursuing an independent line, giving full support neither to the 'old English' with their pleas for security of possession and at least *de facto* toleration for Catholicism, nor to the 'new English' with their demands for further profitable investment in land and office and for a strongly Protestant church. 'In fact it was the deliberate policy of Wentworth in the sixteen-thirties to abstract the state still further from society in Ireland by creating a government wholly unresponsive to its local environment.'[31] Such an aim cannot be strictly realised (all politics mean compromise to some extent) but Wentworth came as near to it as makes no difference in view of the completeness of the collapse of the regime once he had been removed.

V

The crisis of 1640–1 did essentially concern the relationship of the State
to society, but we may point to a number of differences from Trevor-
Roper's model. The issue was not inflation of the size and cost of the
bureaucracy, but of the relation between its size and what was asked
of it. The English governmental structure was not large or powerful
enough to satisfy the demands made on it for economic, social and
religious management, or for jobs and perquisites; it was not insignificant enough for such demands to be unrealistic and thus be dropped.
In England the Renaissance State, like the Bourgeois Revolution, went
off at half-cock. Society (and the use of this vague term is meant to
indicate that no group or individual was to blame) did not appreciate
the gap between its aspirations and the political structure which it had
acquired. In face of this, the inadequacy of seeing the government
simply as the expression of class rule becomes apparent: faced with an
intolerable gap between ends and means the government increasingly
appeared as a distinct interest in society, and ignored the wishes of the
politically influential. The apparent unconcern at the consequences of
seeming to favour Catholics at home and abroad is paralleled by the
cultural isolation of Charles I's court, the aggressive fiscal legalism,
and the narrowing of the links with the financial and commercial élites.
Charles was more dignified than his father, but he was also more
unapproachable.

In view of all this it is not surprising that, once the Long Parliament
had eradicated the innovations in government, it should turn its attention to the problem of controlling ministers, which seemed to be the
decisive stage in bringing the 'State' once more to order. But it also
became clear that this was no panacea for political ills. Even when
Parliament directly appointed its own executive in the 1640s, the
structural problems remained. The government was still a centre of
aspirations: its bureaucracy and its interference continued to grow.
So too did the opposition. All political groupings in the 1640s and
1650s, from the royalists, through Presbyterians, Independents and
Levellers, to the Diggers, had some decentralising tendencies. But
only the politically insignificant Diggers seem to have conceived of
dismantling the central state, and they were remarkably unspecific
about how their commonwealth would be maintained. The government
raised its fiscal demands and military interference to heights which

made Charles's 'tyranny' seem derisory. Successive regimes collapsed much more rapidly than the old monarchy had done. But the seventeenth century, which saw the establishment of parliamentary 'liberties', ended with Leviathan much stronger, more able to raise troops and money, than it had been at the height of 'absolutism'.

2. County Government in Caroline England 1625-1640

L. M. HILL

THE powers of central government in seventeenth-century England were hollow without the active cooperation of the army of local authorities upon whom enforcement depended. Professor G. E. Aylmer has put this relationship as clearly as any scholar writing of the period:

> In the localities the will of the central government depended for its execution on the voluntary cooperation of a hierarchy of part-time unpaid officials: Lord and Deputy Lieutenants, Sheriffs, Justices of the Peace, High and Petty Constables, Overseers of the Poor, and Churchwardens. Without their co-operation the central government was helpless: witness the failure in 1639–40 to collect Ship Money or to raise an efficient army against the Scots.[1]

It is to these local officials that we must turn first in this discussion. Having provided *dramatis personae*, which space limits to the county officials alone, we shall then consider two instances of Caroline policy, conceived in Westminister but executed locally, which will serve to demonstrate the inter-relationship of the two tiers of government and the dependence of the superior tier upon the inferior to make government work in any effective sense. The two examples which we shall use are the Book of Orders of 1631 and the Ship Money levy of 1634-40. We shall conclude with a tentative assessment of what went wrong in local government in the decade before 1640 that contributed so materially to the ensuing rebellion.

Throughout our consideration we must keep clearly in mind that rebellion was not foreseen until the very end of the 1630's at the earliest. For this reason we cannot usefully indulge in grand generalisations about the causes of the Civil War when a detailed examination of the decade or so before the rebellion reveals how little men thought of the consequences of their actions.

Nonetheless tranquillity was the goal of churchwarden and Privy Councillor alike. Until they had left it behind, most men wished to preserve the peace in their corners of England. But peace was more a matter of negative restraint from violence than positive pursuit of harmony. Witness the words of Michael Dalton, the guide to so many of the local officials of the seventeenth century:

> Peace in effect (saith Master Fitzherbert) is the amity, confidence, and quiet that is between men: and he that breaketh this amity or quiet breaketh the Peace. Yet Peace (in our law) most commonly is taken for an abstinence from actual and injurious force, and offer of violence; and so it is rather a restraining of hands, than a uniting of minds. And for the maintenance of this Peace chiefly, were the Justices of Peace first made.[2]

Let us turn then to the Justice of the Peace to begin our study.

I

The Commission of the Peace was the Crown's most effective means of governing the counties. There had been occasions when the central government tried unsuccessfully to interpose itself directly into local affairs as in the case of the frustrated admiralty circuit of 1591.[3] But it was the Commission of the Peace, drawn largely from the shire, which could best represent national policy on the county level. The commission was the effective voice of the county and although it was not a political body as such it could take political decisions especially in resisting or at least impeding the will of the central government. Socially, the commission was the élite of the county and it represented the conscience of the élite, particularly since it administered the poor law and enforced labour statutes. Judicially, the commission was the most powerful tribunal under the assize. Very little in the yearly routine of the countrymen did not come under the scrutiny of the commission or of the individual Justice of the Peace.

J.P.s were named in the Commission of the Peace which passed under the Great Seal. The Lord Chancellor was responsible for nominating candidates to the Crown although he sought the advice of those assize judges, sitting justices, Privy Councillors and Lords Lieutenant who could identify suitable men of good standing in the county. The honour attendant upon being named to the commission was so great in the eyes of the county gentry as to make them keenly aware when one of their number was overlooked. It has been suggested that the commission was so important to the gentry that the Crown carefully weighed the advantages of removing a particular justice from the commission against the disadvantages which a restive gentry would bring to the fairly smooth functioning of county government. But we should not imagine that the commission was simply a committee of obstreperous gentry digging in its heels against all outside intrusion.

There were four major groups of commissioners, and we shall see from their composition the degree to which the county was kept under surveillance by the Westminster authorities.[4] In the first group we find eminent statesmen of national significance such as the Lord Chancellor (or Lord Keeper) or the Lord Treasurer. Their names headed the commissions, but they rarely played an active part in the Quarter Sessions. The second group, which included judges of assize, several serjeants at law and occasionally a Baron of the Exchequer, served a functional as well as an honorific role on the commission. These judicial figures assured central government of a means to bind the Quarter Sessions to the central courts and the half-yearly assize.

The remaining two groups were distinguished by being of the county rather than *ex officio* outsiders. In the one we find the Lord Lieutenant and other men of rank (i.e. the peerage) or of great distinction. But in some counties there were simply no peers at all. In Norfolk for instance from 1572 until 1605 there was neither a Duke of Norfolk nor an important resident peer. In 1605 and again in 1614 James I appointed as Lord Lieutenant respectively, Henry Howard, Earl of Northampton and Thomas Howard, Earl of Arundel. They constituted the peerage in the county and they were not often present. The last, largest and most important group of commissioners was drawn from the ranks of the leading county families. They gave to the commission its distinct gentry colouring and were the backbone of the bench. These Justices accounted for nine-tenths of the membership of the commissions at any one time. The most senior Justice in the commission came to be styled *custos rotulorum* which, despite the name, was not a clerical position but was the presidency of the bench. The *custos* was in many cases Lord Lieutenant, which further underscored the link between the commission and the great magnates.

The clerical business of the commission was performed by the Clerk of the Peace who had originally been a Crown appointee but who had from the sixteenth century been named by the *custos*. The Clerk was no sinecurist; his duties were extensive and as the records of the seventeenth century show he was responsible for an ever-widening range of executive and legal duties out of sessions in addition to the clerical duties that he performed on quarter-days. In Somerset we find that, in addition to the Clerk of the Peace, there was a joint-clerk, a deputy clerk, as many as four attorneys and at least five ordinary clerks whose duties were entirely secretarial. Furthermore, each J.P. had a clerk who either accompanied his master to the Sessions or represented him there in the Justice's absence. The sheer number of clerks gives us some indication of the volume of business which came before the Quarter Sessions and hints at the even greater volume handled out of Sessions by the individual J.P.

We have spoken of Quarter Sessions but without having properly explained it. The sessions were the judicial and administrative meetings of the Commission of the Peace four times each year in principal towns throughout the county. The meetings were limited by a fourteenth-century statute to a duration of three days although two day sessions were the norm. Although in theory the whole commission met at the Sessions in fact those justices who were at all active would attend two or at most three of the four sessional meetings a year. The Sessions could be convened by as few as two Justices, one of whom was of the quorum. While more than two Justices appeared at the Wiltshire Sessions there were some years when at least half of the commissioners appeared at no sessional meetings at all.

It has been said that the Quarter Sessions was the field day of the Justices and the *omnium-gatherum* of the shire. Certainly the quarter days were among the great events of the provincial year. Grand juries and juries of presentment, the sheriff, undersheriffs, bailiffs, constables and so on throughout the petty hierarchy of the county; all of these would be present to wait upon the Justices of the Peace. Quarter Sessions was the crucial organ of co-ordination of the full range of duties which were placed upon the Justices. Both legal and administrative affairs (there was an unclear line between them) were brought together in the Sessions. Although the commission was a judicial bench much of its criminal jurisdiction had been taken over by the assize. Thus we do not find in the early seventeenth century much concern with criminal matters of a felonious nature. But Professor Hurstfield has observed that the criminal jurisdiction which was exercised was marked by its rough quality: fines and whippings punished alleged breaches of the social and economic laws which were the mainstay of Elizabethan and early Stuart domestic policy. Punishment was meted out to vagrants, parents of bastard children, poachers, trespassers and rioters, while undertakings were demanded that there would be no further disturbance of the peace. But these criminal punishments generally enforced the extensive civil jurisdiction which the J.P.s exercised. They were responsible for providing poor-relief, some pensions, trade regulations, food supplies, regulation of ale-houses and the collection of local taxes. In addition the actions of inferior courts and inferior officers in the county were subject to appeal to the Quarter Sessions.

The J.P. could accomplish only a limited amount of work in Quarter Sessions because of the statutory time-restriction and because usually there was only a fraction of the commission in attendance. Much of the J.P.'s charge could be met only if he were present and active in the limited local area that he knew well and in which he was known. Thus much of the nominal authority of the Sessions was exercised by one or two Justices in the 'divisions' which were the administrative districts of the county. Within the division the Justice performed most of his work. This reliance upon divisional service was only partly the result of the Justices' inability to cope during Quarter Sessions; it was also the result of Tudor and Stuart legislation which had transformed the J.P. into the county's principal administrator. It is not difficult to appreciate why the Quarter Sessions tended to regard the time available to the Justices in their divisions as being of infinite duration. Thus a crucial error was made early on when it was assumed that the J.P.s, either alone or in small numbers, possessed a limitless capacity to administer and adjudicate. This misconception and the decision taken by Privy Council in 1631 to burden the Justice further with the Book of Orders were intimately related.

The Lord Lieutenant was the closest to a viceroy that the county knew. There had been lieutenancies at times of crisis during the sixteenth century but it was only after the Armada that the office came to be regarded as permanent. The Crown named a principal peer to the lieutenancy whenever possible and occasionally it would group several counties into one lieutenancy. The Lieutenant's primary duty was to provide for the military defence of the county and to serve as the police power of last resort should public order be seriously threatened.

Assisted by several deputy lieutenants, the Lieutenant caused the county to be divided into workable districts within which to raise and train the militia. Over each of these divisions there presided a muster commission of J.P.s and the occasional deputy lieutenant. It was the commission's duty to prepare and periodically to revise the muster roll. Once or sometimes twice a year there was a divisional muster of all able-bodied men and boys who were paraded in rag-tag array before the Lieutenant and his representative. The muster masters, generally pensioned NCOs, were in charge of the training of the men and the repair of the county's arms and munitions. The Lieutenant and the commissioners were authorised to levy a tax for raising, training, arming and transporting the militia. Part of these funds was well spent, but a part was largely waste because the militia was divided into two entirely different organisations of distinctly different quality. The first, the 'trained band', tended to be worth the money spent on it. Its members were relatively well-disciplined and, being largely responsible to the local gentry, they were assured of home service within the county except in the most dire emergency. This home service was intended to provide a well trained force to defend the county in the event of invasion. The second organisation, if such a term can be used, was the levy of untrained county men for extraordinary service, usually overseas. The levies were pressed in the same way that crews were pressed into naval service. The pressed levies were riotous and mutinous gangs who resented the dangers and the abhorrent conditions to which they were subjected. The marked contrast between their service and that of the trained bands contributed to their low morale and to the pathetic foolishness of the Crown's reliance upon them in 1640 after the Scots had crossed the border. Because of the work involved in preparing the muster rolls, levying taxes, accounting for and maintaining the equipment stores, the lieutenancy was heavily engaged in clerical and administrative duties while the training and levying was done by amateurish captains recruited from the gentry or by the muster masters.

During the reasonably pacific reign of James I the Lieutenants' duties became more and more a matter of routine. The trained bands assembled periodically, the levies were only occasionally called and the Lord Lieutenants with their deputies spent less and less time on their military duties. When Charles I ascended the throne with Buckingham pressing ambitious foreign adventures upon him, the military machinery was thrown into high gear for the first time in nearly twenty-five years. As Professor Barnes has said:

> ... the next sixteen years were a time of alarums and excursions, threats of invasion, real and supposed. The defence of the kingdom through the agency of the counties received new emphasis, at times equal in intensity to that when the Armada came, far surpassing the years of the Armada in prolongation for over a decade and a half. The full weight of this emphasis fell on the institution of lieutenancy, still young and immature, foredoomed to perpetual weakness. The

terrible climax came at the end of this period when the Scots'
invasion put the lieutenancy to the test.[5]

Leaving this brief description of the lieutenancy we should note
that the non-military potential of the office was never fully realised,
either by the county or by the Council. Ideally a leading magnate with
strong ties in both court and country would have been an invaluable
bridge between the two. In fact the Lord Lieutenant was rarely in his
jurisdiction because the very eminence that made him Lieutenant
caused him to be called to the centre on the Crown's service. Thus the
deputy lieutenants, who were often J.P.s as well, did the Lieutenant's
job and the bridge between court and country existed in name alone.

Although the sheriff had lost his actual pre-eminence in the county
in the thirteenth century, it was not until the sixteenth that the Crown
had replaced the sheriff's nominal primacy in the county with the J.P.
and the Lord Lieutenant. This declining office was onerous, and great
skill was employed by those members of the gentry who wished to
avoid being selected. Why then do we bother with any discussion of the
sheriff if he was so unimportant? It will become apparent below that
the sheriff, after years of decline, was suddenly in the 1630s turned into
a minister of substantial, although unsought-after, authority and power
as the collector of the Ship Money. If there were no other reason for
discussing the sheriff, his connexion with the Ship Money would be
cause enough. The shrievalty was in a state of advanced decline when,
along with the lieutenancy and the bench, it was jerked back into life
during the 'personal rule'. As with the other offices, the shrievalty
could hardly stand the shock.

The sheriff was elected each year by an ancient ceremony on the days
immediately following All Saints' Day. Members of Council and the
judges of the central courts met in the Star Chamber to prepare a list
of three nominees for every county. The first name was usually their
first choice but when the list was presented to the monarch he could
and often did 'prick' or choose one of the other candidates. 'Pricking'
involved puncturing the list with a needle. For the next year the sheriff
could not leave the county without the express consent of the Crown
and thus could not normally sit as an M.P., a point not overlooked by
the early Stuarts when they wished to quiet a difficult Member. During
the shrieval terms the incumbent served in a largely ministerial capacity,
in other words his official discretionary power was limited. He was
charged with serving the writs of the central courts, impanelling juries

either at Westminster or in the county and with executing the judgments of the common-law jurisdictions. The sheriff was also the official host to the assize judges when they visited the county. But the enforcement of local penalties fell to the sheriff as well. The welter of brutal punishments which served no useful deterrent purpose but which made up the bulk of the penalty clauses of the social and economic statutes were the sheriff's responsibility along with the constables. Whippings, brandings, confinements and hangings: these in addition to the more prosaic levying of fines were within the sheriff's charge. One might suppose that a police function would naturally adhere to such an office but this was rarely so. Those disturbances with which the constables and Justices could not deal were more effectively quashed by the trained bands than by the legal riot which was grandly known as the *posse comitatus*.

There was another area of shrieval responsibility, as ancient as any which the incumbent exercised; the collection of the Crown's traditional revenues. These arose from the Crown's estates and franchises as well as from the 'fruits' or profits of justice as administered in the courts. An elaborate structure had been erected to assure the honest collection and return of these accounts but the amount of revenue gathered was not only declining absolutely but also relatively in comparison with the burgeoning fiscal demands of the early Stuarts. It is therefore of some curious note that the Exchequer and Council devoted a disproportionate amount of time and energy to the sheriffs' accounts. Year after year commissions would sit and officials would confer about more effective means of controlling the sheriffs, an energetic pursuit after little gain. But these efforts were sufficient to make the shrieval dignity all the less attractive to the gentry. The sheriff was aided by an under-sheriff and several bailiffs, some of whom worked directly for the sheriff and some of whom were assigned to the various hundreds within the shire. The under-sheriff was meant to be an annual appointee along with the sheriff but he tended to become a rather permanent civil servant whose knowledge of the office made him, by the seventeenth century, effectively the sheriff in all but name. The under-sheriff and the bailiffs did the work and extracted what profit there was to be made; they removed much of the drudgery of the shrievalty from their master's shoulders but they were not able to assume the responsibility that he owed to the central government. As a result the sheriff found himself in an untenable position. He could not in one year, with little interest in becoming deeply involved, impose effective control on his subordinates. Equally, he could not avoid the office. The Crown expected honesty and efficiency from him and was not greatly interested in mitigating circumstances. Thus the sheriff was in a hopeless position and one which, because of the attendant charges and expenses, was unprofitable. In addition we shall see that the sheriff was to be further burdened with the collection of the Ship Money, and this proved to be the last straw.

The J.P., the Lord Lieutenant and the sheriff constituted the trinity which governed the county but they had to depend upon an army of even more local officials to cause the Crown's writ to run to the parish, the manor and the hundred. The hundred, which comprised no uniform territory but varied from region to region, was the responsibility of the high constable named by the commission of the peace. The high constable was the direct link between the J.P. and the people of the hundred. In addition there were three clearly unique responsibilities which belonged to the high constable.

The first concerned local police authority. It was the high constable's duty to maintain the watch, and cause beacons to be erected and maintained. The matter of beacons was of particular importance along the coast, where the threat of invasion was often real and was always imagined. The watch was useful in quite another way. While the maintenance of good order was always an official desideratum, the watch had an additional function to perform. The parishes within the hundred had no desire to welcome vagrants, wandering bands of soldiers, pregnant women whose children might become local charges, beggars and the like. While there were provisions for some relief for the poor, the prevailing technique was simply to keep them moving. Thus the watch exercised important social responsibilities in addition to providing good order.

The second of the high constable's duties concerned local works. Although there were surveyors and commissioners charged with the repair of bridges and roads, it was ultimately the responsibility of the high constable either to see that the work was done or that action was taken to punish those who refused to effect repairs.

By far the most important of the high constable's duties, and the third in this discussion, was the enforcement of the annual wage scale which was established by the commission of the peace. The high constable would summon the masters and servants of the hundred to 'statute sessions', there to examine conditions of employment and the wages paid. It was his duty to prepare presentments to the Quarter Sessions in which breach of statute and of employment contract were sent up to the commission for redress. At these same hundredal sessions presentments were also made for minor nuisances and for the repair of bridges and roads.

Within the manors there were petty constables who were the only elected officials in the county outside the towns. In the court leet of their manors, the petty constables were chosen by the steward or were elected by their fellow householders. In those manors in which the court leet no longer sat, the householders elected the petty constable from their own numbers or they established a rota. Although the office was supposed to be tenable for a year, the tendency was for the petty constable to serve for much longer terms. When we consider this position in which the petty constable found himself we can appreciate the advantages of long terms of service because trust and confidence and knowledge were crucial in performing his task. Although there is little mention of the petty constable in the statute books,

'nevertheless his undistinguished shoulders carried the base of the pyramid of local government . . . In his own sphere he was quite as truly as the justice of the peace in his, the man-of-all-work for the community and the central government [being] the union of policing and administration.'[6]

Briefly stated, the petty constable was the general purpose official in charge of all detection and presentment of crime in the manor, while he was also responsible for punishing the wide range of petty offences which cluttered daily life. In addition it was his responsibility to preserve order in his jurisdiction and to raise hue and cry to assist in apprehending felons. Crowning all these duties was the petty constable's task as the ultimate tax collector. If one can use the conduct and the attitudes of the J.P. as a gauge of gentry opinion, one can surely use the petty constables in a similar fashion to assess yeoman opinion. It is interesting to observe the extent to which the government had to depend upon these most minor officers to enforce major social legislation. A vagrant would not be apprehended if the petty constables were not willing to pursue him. But the petty constables were beset with problems. Many of them were illiterate, yet they were expected to know their place in the law and not to transgress the statutory limitations which surrounded them.

Furthermore they were liable to a fine if they failed to make an arrest. They had to maintain a bastard child if it could be proven that the father had escaped through their negligence. Evil doers did not respect them because they were ignorant, timorous and powerless; the Justices did not respect them because they were lazy, disobedient, and negligent. [7] The shortcomings and difficulties of the parochial officials were of a similar nature. It was with the problems of the minor local authorities in mind that Council attempted the reforms found in the Book of Orders.

The Poor Law of 1597 brought out of relative obscurity the smallest unit of local government, the parish. The ecclesiastical and civil responsibilities of the parish were largely undistinguishable although the clergyman had rather little to do with the non-spiritual affairs of the parish which he served. Ever since the Henrician Reformation there had been a continuous accretion of responsibility to the parishes: the maintenance of roads and bridges, the fabric of the church and church buildings (such as tithe barns), and finally the care of the poor.

The churchwardens who presided over the parish were elected annually. Originally all the parishioners had had a part in the election, but by the early seventeenth century it had become the concern of a smaller group of the householders of the parish. These electors had been known by several names but they came generally to be known as the vestry. In the light of the taxing power which the Poor Laws placed in the churchwardens' hands, it is not surprising that the substantial householders of the parish had secured control over their election.

The 1597 Act distinguished several categories of the poor. There were poor children, the elderly and the infirm, the unemployed, and the vagrants and sturdy beggars. Different treatment was to be meted out to each of the categories. The poor children, including the illegitimate, were to be apprenticed, but this was a costly affair because the parish had to raise the necessary money to provide clothing and to pay a lump sum to the putative masters. Of course if the fathers of bastard children who were born in the parish could be identified and apprehended, the J.P.s were authorised to issue an affiliation order which forced the father to pay maintenance until the child was twelve years old. The basis of such an order was information provided by the parochial authorities.

In the case of the aged and infirm, the parish was interested in looking after its own. Collections had been taken for this purpose before the 1597 Act gave the overseers of the poor within the parish the power to assess a poor rate. The money provided for outright relief, for the parochial expenses involved in the apprenticing of poor children and bastards and for the provision of stocks of material to be used in 'setting the poor on work'. The workhouse, which was intended for the unemployed in the parish, was a form of subsidised industry which was reasonably successful except when it ran up against entrenched competition. At the very least the workhouse could provide some of the staple requirements of the poor of the parish, at best it could make a profit which would be turned back into more relief ventures. Fortunately for the parish relief system, the good folk of the country found that the gifts of money to the parish for the benefit of the poor bridged the gap between what could reasonably be raised in rates and the total funds that were required.

The rogues, vagabonds and 'sturdy beggars' were the one class of poor for whom there was no sympathy. It was a part of the Poor Law that these types could be moved on from parish to parish until they arrived at the parish of their birth. Watch was maintained at the borders of counties as well as of parishes to keep wanderers out or to hurry them on before nightfall. The system had in it the seeds of a workable relief programme, but excessive reliance upon private bequests and excessive sloth caused the care of the poor to run down to a dangerously low level and occasioned the formulation of the Book of Orders in 1631.

II

Professor Barnes has provided us with an invaluable analysis of the Book of Orders through which the Privy Council sought to revitalise a largely moribund county magistracy. By examining the case which he makes for the Book of Orders, we can draw together the many strands of early seventeenth-century local government and view the problems of the 1630s as a whole rather than in fragments.

The accession of Charles I occasioned a change in the tempo of government. Although the new King was neither a reformer nor a slogging administrator, he was nevertheless committed to active policies which required efficiency and purpose of his subordinates. From Buckingham's foreign adventures, Laud's domestic house-cleaning marked a sharp reversal. Archbishop Laud was a very demon for detailed administration. He was hardly the tyrant which legend has portrayed but he was an unbending man who could not conceive of his role except in terms of a reformer of church and state beneath the King. On Laud's influence during the 'personal rule' Professor Barnes observes:

it is difficult to fix responsibility for any single project upon any single minister or indeed upon the King himself, but there can be little doubt that the spirit infused into the Council and Court by William Laud nurtured the ideas culminating in the Book of Orders.[8]

There was an abiding fear of social unrest in the seventeenth century just as there had been in the century before. While there were no large scale rebellions, social discontent simmered none the less. Poverty was hardly a novelty but there had been nigh-Aristotelian notions that the poor were a fixed and natural proportion of society, a proportion which Christian charity required men to relieve. This notion had been disturbed because the poor were seen to be more abundant. They placed greater demands on a community which did not have the capacity to cope. The causes of this increase in the numbers of poor were manifold. In a static agrarian society the number of poor was constant but with the introduction of industry the concentration of the poor in towns created entirely new problems. Furthermore the overall population was growing; as there were more people there were thus more poor. But with this growth there was not a corresponding increase in wealth to pay the necessarily increased taxes and poor rates. The years 1629 to 1641 were marked by economic instability although the two years 1629–31 were the worst. As a result of this depression a great proportion of agricultural labourers as well as artisans lived in biting poverty. It is interesting, although depressing, to note the complaints of London chandlers in 1634 that for the past five years their trade had been damaged by the reliance of the poor upon horsemeat, peas and oatmeal.

Because of their concern for the maintenance of good order the government had already made the initial overtures to revitalising local authorities. In 1627 and again in 1628 the bands of runaway soldiers on the roads had occasioned directives from the Council calling upon the local authorities to suppress them. Such a policy would have commended itself to the local governors who were faced with the pillage of footloose soldiers; but there were other directives which, while equally important, were less popular. For instance the restrictions on the movement of grain or the licences to export grain, either of which were important national policies, met with intense local hostility. In Kent there were numerous instances of near riot when groaning waggons lumbered down to the coast carrying grain for export as starving locals stood by and watched. Similarly in Somerset the passage of a grain waggon could lead to civil commotion. But as Professor Barnes has pointed out, if the magistrates were to bear down on the movement of grain the result might well be the starvation of an adjoining city or town. In 1630 there was a notable incident near Bath as grain was being transported from Somerset through Wiltshire to Bristol. The problem was one of hunger in both town and country, and the government, despite severity on the local level, had no choice but to show leniency to the offenders.

Apart from the control of the movement of grain, the government was equally concerned with controlling the way in which the existing stocks of grain were used. In order to conserve as much grain as possible the alehousekeepers and maltsters came under especial scrutiny. They consumed an inordinate amount of grain and thus had to be restricted. To effect this restriction a book of instructions was sent out to the shires containing an updated set of regulations and requiring monthly meetings of the justices the better to enforce the Council's will. This was, according to Barnes, the immediate predecessor of the Book of Orders which was issued four months later.

It was, after all, concern for the poor (or what the rebellious poor might do) that motivated the Council. The questions of grain stores was but one aspect of the necessary provision for the poor. By January 1631 the Council saw the necessity for devoting its own attention to the problem of the poor. It first designated itself a commission for the poor and then divided itself into subcommittees each of which corresponded to an assize circuit. Thus prepared, the Council by the end of January issued 314 Books of Orders, each with a conciliar letter mandating its use, to sheriffs, commissions of the peace, and borough authorities. In the greatest detail these books ordered a point-by-point enforcement of the existing law and made it quite clear that no excuses would be tolerated. The Book of Orders was disarmingly simple: a straightforward conflation of the existing law with a clear directive to enforce its every detail.

> Save for the requirement ... that houses of correction should henceforth be built adjoining the common gaol, there was nothing novel in the government's demand, nothing which had not appeared in one order or another during the preceding thirty years. What was novel about the Book of Orders was the inclusiveness of the program contained in it, the intensity with which the program was executed subsequently, and the duration of that intensity.[9]

Inclusiveness, intensiveness and duration: the desiderata which had hitherto been absent in any previous attempt at reform. While the poor loomed largest among the concerns of the Book of Orders, it was not only concerned with the pauper. It was equally interested in tightening up the responsibilities of local authorities at all levels. Such was its inclusive quality. Intensity was the product of the Council's concern that the laws of the land had simply not been enforced in the past, but that every effort should henceforth be applied to enforce these laws. But these two qualities alone, as Barnes has indicated, would not have been of particular note had it not been for the third quality: duration. For a decade the Privy Council did not let up on the pressure and for a decade it did not hesitate to remind the justices and the sheriffs of their duties in minute detail. This was so despite the fact that the Council ceased to maintain direct pressure after 1635 because by then the execution of the Book of Orders could be left to the judges of assize and did not require conciliar interference. It simply was not worth the attendant difficulties for a local official to neglect his duties which were contained in the Book.* This accounts in large part for the continuation of the Ship Money collection with relative ease as late as 1638–39 even though the Ship Money was not a part of the Book of Orders.

One cannot extrapolate the experience of Somerset to the rest of England, but Barnes's argument can usefully be contrasted with other parts of the realm. This is particularly so in the matter of the petty sessions and their relationship to the Book of Orders. As already mentioned the J.P. conducted the greatest part of his business when the Quarter Sessions were not meeting. This divisional work was the only way in which he could manage a reasonably constant application of his judicial and administrative talents to local affairs. Barnes has told us of the injunction to the J.P. contained in the book of instructions which preceded the Book of Orders and was subsequently amalgamated with it. The injunction required the justices to meet monthly out of Sessions and to report the results of these meetings to the sheriff. The sheriff would then transmit the reports to Council. Barnes regards this monthly meeting as the beginning of petty sessions. While this was doubtless so in Somerset and elsewhere, there were many 'petty sessions' throughout the country which preceded 1630 and had little if anything to do with the Book of Orders. In Essex two or more J.P.s had met periodically to license alehouses and had called their meetings petty sessions. In Northamptonshire there had been for years a 'three weeks' sessions'

---

* For a contrasting view of the effectiveness of the Book or Orders, see ch. 1 above. Our estimate of its effectiveness must depend partly on the date we are considering, since its effectiveness declined with the passage of time. (Ed.)

which was held to be of ancient origin. Indeed, the Northamptonshire petty sessions were in one instance alleged to be the model upon which the Book of Orders was based. With reference to the Book of Orders and the establishment of petty sessions, M. G. Davies has commented: 'the temporary success of the Privy Council's directive [i.e. the Book of Orders] may have been due as much to the fact that what it enjoined was already an accepted institution in at least certain districts as the force of conciliar government at this period.'[10]

But whether or not petty sessions were universally the result of the Book of Orders, at least in Somerset they were clearly the product of the Council's drawing in the reins on local authority. Indeed, Barnes has given the highest marks to the establishment of these sessions. He believes that no institutional development between the establishment of the Quarter Sessions and the creation of the county councils was as important as the emergence of the petty sessions. They are, he said 'a truer representative of an ancient and traditional ideal of government than any other institution, central or local, that England now possesses – the judgment and punishment of the evildoer by his neighbors'.[11]

As the Poor Law was central to the Book of Orders, it is not surprising to find that the resulting petty sessions were concerned first of all with the rapid implementation of the multitude of provisions for the poor which had previously either been neglected or ignored. Parochial poor rates were increased, materials were put by for the workhouse, and apprenticing was more rigidly controlled. When an able-bodied pauper was ordered to enter employment by petty sessions, he obeyed or was packed off to a house of correction. 'Probably for the first time since the reign of Elizabeth, these troublesome citizens felt the full weight of the law.' In addition alehouses were closed and the proper use of stores of grain was at least momentarily realised. All of this activity was accompanied by reports to the Privy Council which were forwarded by the sheriff. A by-product of all this concern for the poor was the increased awareness of the Justices of the Peace in the petty sessions of their other responsibilities. Bridges and roads were better maintained because the Justices were taking seriously that requirement in the Book of Orders that they should devote special attention to the supervision of their subordinate officers.

But the Justices' zeal was not limitless. The passion for efficiency and obedience which the Justices had initially displayed had waned by the end of 1631. The reason that Barnes ascribes to this dwindling ardour was local resistance to some of the provisions of the Book of Orders. In keeping with the Statute of Artificers, the Book required the Justices to force apprenticeship upon pauper children and upon those who might become a burden on the parish. So long as the paupers were the only persons burdened by this requirement the householders of the district had no reason to object. But when the 1629–31 depression had turned the tables, the position of the community by the end of the first year had changed rapidly. The Justices were still requiring children of the poor and the near-poor to be apprenticed, but the prospective masters of these apprentices did not wish to bear the cost of a new employee at that time. When the Justices began to apply pressure the masters pressed back and the Justices cooled. The Council responded to this waning zeal in a matter that made clear its position without diminishing its authority. The Judges of assize were to assume the responsibility for the supervision of the Book of Orders. It was to become an unexceptional part of county life which would not require extraordinary conciliar direction. By 1635 the Privy Council had backed out of direct administration, leaving the task to the Judges in their respective circuits. At the same time the predominant concern of those who executed the Book of Orders shifted from poor-law enforcement to the more general business of punishing vagrancy and other misdemeanors; but the withdrawal of conciliar supervision did not materially alter the quality of enforcement. The Judges had been well briefed for their supervisory duties and the Justices were not allowed to slip into casual disregard of theirs.

When we consider the overall effect of the Book of Orders we cannot but be impressed by the initial success that it enjoyed, and by its continuing, although reduced, effect throughout the 1630s. The poor were better treated and better cared for than ever before. Grain stocks were better administered and waste was curtailed. The quality of local government was markedly improved and little doubt lingered as to the Council's ability to cause the king's writ to run into local parts with considerable authority. The lax magistrate who could not be bothered with hearing causes out of Sessions was no longer tolerated. But it was unfortunate that the implementation of the Book of Orders was one of the few domestic successes in Caroline policy.

The 'personal rule', of which the Book of Orders was an outstanding part, had positive achievements to its credit despite its subsequent reputation. Professor Aylmer has summed up the period with great precision:

BK. of orders - success

It is perfectly true that in the years of economic distress (1629–31) due to bad harvest conditions coinciding with harvest failures at home, the King and his Council had made a real effort to see that the laws concerning poor relief were properly enforced. They also imposed a prohibition on the export of corn while there was a scarcity at home, bullied employers into keeping their workpeople even when there was no work to do because of the slump, and used the full vigour of the law against some profiteers. Perhaps their orders to J.P.s and other local officials to levy poor 'rates', to find work for the willing able-bodied poor, to flog the idle and to relieve the helpless were more detailed and emphatic than those issued in previous crises . . . In general it would be called a return to an Elizabethan policy of 'paternal' state control, and it contrasts favourably with the ineffectualness of James' government in the economic crises of the early 1620s.[12]

While a left-handed compliment, this is a fair summary of the effect of the Book of Orders.

III

If we can ascribe success to the Book of Orders, we must ascribe failure to the six years of Ship Money collection which ended in 1640. But success or failure require a word of qualification. Both policies were immediately successful if we look only to statistical evidence of the fulfilment of their respective briefs. The Book of Orders surely provided a higher level of efficiency in local government and alleviated the worst conditions of the poor. So too the Ship Money, over a six year period (even taking account of virtual non-collection in its last year), yielded an average £107,000 per year. This was the highest peace-time direct tax receipt ever recorded.[13] Taken in these terms we would have to regard both policies as successful. But the Book of Orders did not contribute to dividing the country and its short and long-term goals were realised. The Ship Money, on the other hand, while realising its short-term goals in unqualified financial terms, failed utterly in the long run and was a major divisive element in the build-up to civil war.

The levy of ships was an ancient practice. There was no doubt in anyone's mind of the Crown's duty to provide for the security of the kingdom and little doubt that it was the Crown's right to use any means available to defend the kingdom and thus meet its obligations. But the Ship Money was understood to be an occasional extraordinary levy and

not a supplementary tax. By 1634, when Ship Money was again introduced there was every reason to believe that the going would be
reasonably smooth. The execution of the Book of Orders had progressed
to such a point that the Privy Council was about to leave its routine
administration to the judges of assize. The nation was apparently quiet
and without Parliament what dissidence there was did not have a central
forum; thus it seemed to the Council that there was no disaffection at all.
Even Laud and his policies had not become sufficiently notorious to
give a focal point to anger and disquiet. On the continent the wars
were not going well for England's interests, while the English fishing
boats required protection from foreign vessels. These causes gave
credence to a request for the Ship Money but it was assumed that the
writs would only run to coastal regions and that they were temporary,
which meant one time only. Professor Barnes has suggested that English
notions of maritime sovereignty, which were at odds with those of her
continental neighbours, lent an element'of chauvinism to the reception
of the first writ. But the second writ gave the lie to the transitory nature
of the writ; 'the permanence of the ship money was an effective antidote to the seductiveness of jingoism.'[14]

The Ship Money writs were administratively unique and possessed
a putative efficiency. They assigned a lump-sum charge upon the county
and made the sheriff solely responsible for meeting this obligation
although he was given a detailed, indeed a contradictory, set of instructions telling him how to raise the money. It should be kept in mind
that Council was aware of the dangers of a regressive tax which would
simply create more social tension than already lay dormant in the land.
The Council ordered a self-rating scheme which could have been a
useful means to prevent or at least postpone ultimate rejection of the
measure. But this contradictory element in the instructions gave to the
sheriff the final authority to accept or reject local rating. As we shall see
this was one of the greatest intrinsic weaknesses of the entire scheme.

When the writ reached the sheriff he first turned to the boroughs and
incorporated towns within his jurisdiction. Their mayors and the sheriff
met to determine the proportion of the charge which the corporations
would pay and to set the rate at which their share would be levied.
The remainder of the charge was to be collected from each of the hundreds and tithings in the county. The original Ship Money writ gave a
day certain for the collection of the money and it was the high constable
who collected from the parishes and remitted to the sheriff who in
turn remitted to the Treasurer of the Navy. But regardless of the in-

volvement of local rating men, high constables and mayors, it was the sheriff alone who was personally responsible for the entire charge even if it had to come from his own pocket. The sheriff's accounting procedures in Exchequer allowed him to fudge his books and to find ways of wriggling out of his obligations especially by passing on to his successor the unfulfilled charges of his own term of office. But this procedure could not be used with the Ship Money writs. Each sheriff was responsible for his own debt and could not pass it on. In 1640, Barnes reports, there were in Somerset four ex-Sheriffs who were trying to collect Ship Money which was due from their respective years.

If there was a fair degree of co-operation in the first year of Ship Money, the honeymoon had ended with the second writ. The change of attitude first manifested itself in rating complaints throughout the kingdom, although Somerset enjoyed the doubtful distinction of having troubled the Council with complaints more often than any other county during the six years of the Ship Money writs. Rating complaints had an interesting characteristic: they were largely avoidable. We mentioned above the contradictory instructions to the sheriffs which allowed them to step in after the parish had determined its rates and to alter the assessment as they saw fit. Whatever their reasons for altering their rates may have been, the sheriff would have been much safer and in a far stronger position if he had not had the opportunity to intervene. As a neutral administrator collecting a self-determined tax from those who had determined it, the sheriff might well have been successful. But as a para-magisterial official who could alter the rate the sheriff faced opposition at every turn because no one could regard him as being without bias.

Although there was a modicum of co-operation in the first year in Somerset, the county hierarchy in Wiltshire divided against itself by 1635. The J.P.s there were implacably hostile to the writs, and told the sheriff that they did not have the authority to obey the Ship Money writs. The Sheriff had thus to deal with the constables without any support from the commission. He found that without their co-operation organisation on a county-wide basis was difficult, and even when the high constables collected the money the bench would not co-operate in forcing them to turn it over to the sheriff. It was axiomatic that when the senior officials of the county stood together there was little hope of more junior officials' thwarting their will. In similar circumstances the will of the central government could only penetrate the solid phalanx of the county's entrenched establishment with some difficulty. But when the establishment was divided against itself different circumstances obtained. In the first place the junior officials had less to fear as a consequence of disobedience if the senior officials were quarrelling amongst themselves. Furthermore, the sheriff who was ranged against leading members of the commission could muster precious little authority when there were those as mighty or mightier leading the opposition to the collection of the Ship Money. When in Somerset, Sir Robert Phelips, a J.P. and deputy lieutenant, stood out against the Ship Money in the very first year and was subsequently joined by his brother-Justices Sir Henry Berkeley, Sir Charles Berkeley and Sir Francis Dodington in the second and third years there was little chance of the sheriff's being able to counterbalance their authority. Had there been a thorough re-rating by Quarter Sessions, when the complaints were first ventilated, the opposition at an early stage would have found that their strongest card had been trumped. The legality of Ship Money during the first three years was not as yet publicly questioned by many Englishmen and inequality of rating was the best opposition that could be raised. By 1637, when the Council had ordered just such a re-rating, the task appeared so awesome in anticipation that nothing was done. Also the Justices were by that late date in no mood to assist the government in developing more effective means of collecting a hated tax. In addition, the Justices had only to look to the Council for confirmation of their own suspicion that the rating difficulties were the sheriff's fault anyway. The Council usually supported hundredal complaints of shrieval rating errors and thereby further undercut the very officer upon whom the success of the Ship Money collection depended.

Objections to rating gave way in 1637 to individual refusals to pay the tax, and by 1638 myriad individual refusals to pay were focused on the case of John Hampden, who was had up before the Exchequer Chamber to force payment of the tax which he alleged was illegal. The decision for the King was by a narrow 7–5 division which was as good as a defeat in the eyes of thousands of Englishmen. The King and his advisers however persisted in a myopic legalism which caused them to count the decision a clear victory. At this time the personal refusals to pay shaded into official refusal to enforce collection, and it was here that the Ship Money was to founder. When the undersheriffs and constables refused to act on the sheriff's behalf to enforce the Ship Money writs, the system had all but failed.

In December 1637 the Sheriff of Lincolnshire, Sir Anthony Irby, complained mightily to the Privy Council that his predecessor, Sir Walter Norton, had sent for the undersheriff and had told him that 'he hoped [Irby] had not engaged him to assist . . . in the ship business, and advised him that if he were clear of it, he should not meddle with it, for he knew [Irby] should procure . . . many enemies by it.' Irby then bluntly told the Council:

It will be impossible for me to answer his Majesty's expectation without the assistance of the county ministers and my own officers, especially the under-sheriff. How far the discouragement of so near an officer may cause neglect in the more inferior, I leave to your consideration. What others [Norton] has or intends to dissuade I rather fear than know.[15]

From the pulpit, preachers inveighed against Ship Money; to judge from the reaction of the High Commission their homilies appeared successful. Richard Powell, vicar of Pottishall, Northamptonshire had articles laid against him alleging drunkeness, irreverence and immorality. In addition it was alleged 'that he preached against ship-money and that thereupon all his parishioners refused to pay the same, and many of them having been consequently distrained upon; the defendant in his next sermon inveighed against tyrannical princes that laid cruel and unjust taxes upon their subjects.'[16]

Even if we assume a desire to co-operate on the part of the local officials, there were situations which made co-operation a virtual impossibility. In September 1638 the Sheriff of Northamptonshire, Sir John Hanbury, tried to explain why he was unable to keep pace with his responsibilities. There was plague in the county, as there had been for some time. The county was still providing £148 per week to relieve the sick. His personnel were ill, as were many officers in the hundreds. Corn was scarce and prices were high. Many people in the county had withheld payment while awaiting the decision of Hampden's case, and the whole county was still recovering from a purveyance tax levied the year before by the previous sheriff. Hanbury had managed to collect £2500 and had distrained the goods of nearly 200 men. Even those men whom he had arrested were proving an unusual burden because he could not send them to the gaol in Northampton. The city was still infested and no one would risk going there with the prisoners.[17] Within a month of Hanbury's letter we find that two of his collectors of the Ship Money had been chased across the county by the constables and had finally been arrested on a charge of horse theft arising out of distraining a mare of the Earl of Peterborough. Even though the charges were eventually dismissed, men of such humble station were surely frightened by the arrest and overawed by the station of their opponent. Their will to serve the Crown and the sheriff must have been strained beyond endurance. But even without such overt harassment most junior officials, such as the constables, had been cautious in the early days of the collection of the Ship Money and by the time their distaste for the job surpassed their caution there was little that the Council could do to beat them back into obedience. The pressure of the constable's neighbours and the magnates in his region were more awesome in the long run than the pressures of either bench, sheriff or council.

With the first war with Scotland in 1639 the seeming composure of central government changed to incipient panic. The rising in Scotland against the Prayer Book was known quickly throughout England and soon the Scots had crossed the border. By this time the antipathy to the Ship Money had reached such intensity that Englishmen were identifying their cause with that of the Scots. Collection under these circumstances became nearly impossible. In 1639–40, the last year of the Ship Money, the Sheriff of Somerset was unable to collect more than 4 per cent of the charge on the county. His 96 per cent arrearage was not unique amongst his fellow sheriffs. The Privy Council reacted with arrests, dismissals and peremptory orders to sheriffs to pay out of their own pockets by July 1640 all outstanding balances. And in utter desperation it called upon the escheators in the counties to perform a service which Professor Barnes has compared to 'political commissars who would report the sheriffs' activities to the Council in return for which they would receive such reward "as their services respectively deserve".' This was the first time in more than a century that the escheators had been employed in the counties except in their traditional roles. Barnes has observed, regarding the use of the escheators: 'Probably never before had the central government so patently employed the services of a minor, fee-taking local official to spy on a local governor. Yet never before had the Council been so desperate and so distrustful.'[18]

Crown and Council found that the Ship Money had utterly failed and by the end of 1640 the Long Parliament had made the Ship Money illegal. A committee was set up to consider cases of 'rigorous levying of Ship Money,' and more memories proved to be longer than might have been expected. A Norwich lawyer in 1640 petitioned Parliament against the zealous rating and collecting of John Anguish, that city's mayor in 1635.[19] Sheriffs, and mayors too, having had to contend for six years with conciliar pressure to levy the tax rigorously were now liable to Parliament for having obeyed their instructions. But neither Crown nor Council seemed fully to appreciate what had happened. They believed that, without reservation, the sheriff was the sole cause of the failure of the Ship Money. What they failed to appreciate was the depth of opposition. Professor Margaret Judson has written that, during the controversy that led up to the civil war, 'the belief [that] the subject possessed property which was truly his own and could not be taken from him without his consent played a major part in shaping men's beliefs and in determining their policies and actions'.[20] When the Crown encroached too much upon this proprietary individualism the result was that even moderates were driven into the ranks forming behind the more radical leadership of parliamentary opposition. The Petition of Right of 1628 was an early and respectful manifestation of the same alliance which would dismantle the powers and agencies of prerogative government in 1640 and 1641. The government seemed unable to distinguish simple rating grievances from principled refusals to pay the tax under any conditions. Furthermore the government was convinced that stern law and clear reason could overcome the opposition when in fact the opposition ran to the deeper level of philosophical and political antipathy to the Ship Money in particular and, more generally, to the politics of the 'personal rule'.

IV

If we recall Professor Aylmer's observations about the reliance of the central government upon the co-operation of local officials for the execution of its will we can perhaps appreciate the magnitude of the collapse in 1640 of central authority as it had been known. Under the new dispensation of the Long Parliament, central government took on a new, parliamentarian leadership which belongs more to the Civil War and the interregnum than it does to the origins of the conflict. But there remains a useful comparison with Professor Aylmer's observation on which to leave this discussion of local authorities and central government before the Civil War. Robert Ashton, writing of the Crown's fiscal policies under the early Stuarts, ventured the hypothesis that the ends of government economic policy were too ambitious in relation to the administrative means at the government's disposal. He went on to suggest that the credit demands of a relatively highly organised state upon a relatively underdeveloped business community simply could not, in the end, be met.[21] Perhaps this dichotomy could be applied beyond the realm of finance. Both the Book of Orders and the Ship Money may be seen as the over-ambitious projects of a relatively sophisticated central government which could not succeed if it had to depend upon the relatively underdeveloped agencies of local government that eventually collapsed under the burden of responsibilities for which it was not equipped to deal. While such speculation takes no account of important political and constitutional divisions, nor of religious, social and economic factors, it does perhaps suggest a functional administrative flaw which has received rather less attention than it deserves. Taken in conjunction with other more conventional causal factors this functional question may aid us in developing a more balanced understanding of the origins of the Civil War.

3. Parliament and the King's Finances

CONRAD RUSSELL

1

'THE power of Parliament, and especially of the Commons has always depended in the last resort on control of taxation'.[1] Professor Roskell's judgement is not invalidated by the fact that Parliaments had always been concerned with many other issues, of which the most explosive were a recurring desire to influence the King's choice of ministers, and an almost invariable desire to attack the clergy. Many members agreed with the opinion of Sir Robert Phelips in 1628 that 'I never think that Parliament truly happy, that intends nothing but money'.[2] Yet however much members' sense of their dignity might make them want to feel that their advice was wanted as well as their cash, money remained the chief bargaining weapon with which they could induce the King to listen to their advice.

The power of Parliament therefore came to be closely connected with that most expensive of royal hobbies – war. War called for some measure of extraordinary taxation, and extraordinary taxation, in practice even more than in theory, demanded the consent of the political community, since they had the task of collecting it. Seventeenth-century Parliamentarians who quoted Magna Carta were perhaps nearer the mark than they have sometimes been recognised to be. The crisis which produced Magna Carta was an unpopular and unsuccessful foreign war, and no less than two thirds of Magna Carta's clauses prohibited various methods by which the king had been raising money. Many more crises occurred before the principle was firmly established that the King needed the consent of the political community for extraordinary taxation, and even more before it was clear that Parliament was the proper body to express that consent. In this context, Sir Edward Coke's grateful use of the precedents of the reign of Edward III was entirely appropriate, since the emegence of Parliament as a frequently recurring occasion owed much to Edward III's attempt to conquer France. It is not a coincidence that the century from which seventeenth-century Parliamentarians drew most of their precedents was the century of the Hundred Years' War. During the Hundred Years' War Parliaments acquired a number of further powers, of which some of the most important were the right to audit accounts, to appropriate the money they granted to specific purposes, and to pay it to special treasurers appointed by themselves.

By the beginning of the seventeenth century these powers had lapsed. When seventeenth-century members quoted them as precedents, 'what actuated them was a consciousness of continuing or recurrent constitutional and political realities or situations'.[3] These recurrent political realities were foreign wars for which the Crown could not afford to pay: the Armada war of 1588 to 1604, the war against Spain and France simultaneously in the later 1620s, and the Scottish war of 1639–40. The last two of these wars produced another 'recurrent political reality': crass mismanagement of the war, leading to the same sense of national disgrace which had been so powerful a weapon against Edward II. The third, the Scottish war of 1639–40, was also the most unpopular foreign war the Crown had planned since the thirteenth century.

We have often missed the similarity between later medieval and seventeenth-century Parliaments not merely because we have underrated the power which the Hundred Years' War gave to medieval Parliaments, but because we have overrated both the powers and the ambitions of early seventeenth-century Parliaments. Neither medieval nor early Stuart Parliaments were able to impose significant restrictions on the Crown unless the Commons were backed by powerful forces among the Lords. There is, as Dr. Ball has reminded us, no notion of Parliamentary sovereignty in early Stuart Parliaments.[4] Their most far-reaching aims, like those of their medieval predecessors, were to force the King to accept Councillors in whom they had confidence. When the King searched the study of Sir Dudley Digges, one of the managers of the impeachment of Buckingham in 1626, he found, not a paper urging the King to rely on the advice of his Parliament, but a paper urging him to rely on the advice of his nobility.[5] It is commonly appreciated that when Sir Peter de la Mare appeared as leader, and first known Speaker, of the Commons in 1376, he owed much of his importance to his position as steward of the Earl of March. It is not so commonly appreciated that John Pym, in 1640, was almost equally dependent on his backers among the peerage: without them, indeed, it is doubtful whether he could have succeeded in obtaining a regular seat.

Any plans formed by Parliamentary leaders for a serious take-over of power had to depend on groups of peers, operating within something resembling the existing constitution. Parliamentary government is possible only if Parliament can be kept in regular session, and it can be kept in regular session only if most of its members can afford town houses. The proportion of members who could afford town houses rose sharply after about 1590, which may be one reason why Parliament grew more vigorous. However, in the early Stuart period, long sessions such as that of 1628 were still severely disrupted towards the end by the tendency of members to go home, and even in 1641, the atmosphere of acute political crisis did not prevent a massive return of members to their country houses as harvest time approached. Long stays in London were expensive. In 1625, one member estimated that, they were collectively spending £7,000 a week, and in 1626, Eliot estimated the cost to the members of a session over four months long as equivalent to a subsidy.[6] For many established Commons men their 'country' was their county and however much they might like occasional visits to London, they expected to return shortly to the real centre of their power.

If this picture of Parliament's development is correct, it remains to explain why Parliament should have lost its medieval importance, and why it should have begun the process of recovering it in the early Stuart period. One reason is the exceptional increase in the Crown's landed estates during the fifteenth century, in which its acquiring of the Duchies of Lancaster (1399) and York (1459) were the most important elements. It was these, together with an exceptionally high standard of land administration, which enabled Edward IV to make his rash promise to the Commons in 1467 that from then on he intended to 'live of his own'.

Another reason is that there was an alternative method of expressing discontent. Any regime will provoke discontent, and most discontents tend to find expression. But from about 1450 to 1603, Parliament was not the best method of expressing discontent, since a rival candidate for the throne might reverse the King's policies more thoroughly than any Parliament could ever hope to do. From the middle of the fifteenth century down to the accession of James I, it was always a promising policy to offer support to a pretender, or even to a possible legitimate successor. It is perhaps not a coincidence that effective Parliamentary opposition to the Crown increased soon after the accession of James I, who had two sons, put an end to the long series of crises about the suc-

cession. In the later seventeenth century, when the succession again became disputed, much of the opposition shifted back again from constitutionalism to conspiracy after an intriguing mixture of the two
during the Exclusion crisis. Among all these reasons however, probably
the most important is the end of the Hundred Years' War, and its
replacement by the concentration of Edward IV and Henry VII on
making France pay for peace.

It is remarkable, in the light of the great Tudor inflation, that Parliament's constitutional power did not substantially increase during the
Tudor period. Between 1544 and 1550, about £3.5 *million* was spent
on wars in France and Scotland,[7] and this on a royal income which is
unlikely to have been much over £150,000 a year. Undoubtedly the
reason why this expenditure did not give Parliament a stranglehold on
the King is the dissolution of the monasteries. The Reformation Parliament is commonly quoted as having increased Parliament's importance.
It certainly increased the members' sense of their own importance, but
however flattering it might be to the Reformation Parliament to find
itself so deeply involved in doings of such momentous significance, it
was involved no more deeply than the King and Cromwell chose, and
could force no policy on them which they did not wish to follow. That
Parliament's most powerful rearguard action, against the Statute of
Uses, ended in defeat. At the same time, by giving the Crown an
enormous endowment of landed wealth, in whose distribution Members of Parliament shared, they sold much of their political power in
return for an increase in the rewards of royal service, which itself did
much to increase the King's power to secure co-operation from his
leading subjects.

Forced loans and the euphemistically named 'benevolences' continued
to be levied during the Tudor period, and help to explain the comparative
rarity of Parliamentary sessions during it. The principle that extraordinary taxation could not be levied without Parliament was, however,
kept alive in spite of breaches in times of recognised emergency such
as the Spanish Armada of 1588.

Yet life grants of tunnage and poundage, monastic lands and forced
loans were not enough to make Tudor monarchs altogether independent
of Parliament. One reason for this was the structure of local government: the very people who would have to be relied on to collect unparliamentary taxes were the same ones who would be asked to consent
to parliamentary ones, and their co-operation was much the more
easily achieved if the King had consulted them.

In the event all that the monastic lands did was to postpone for about sixty years a collapse of the royal financial system which had become inevitable. The reason for this collapse was the great inflation of the sixteenth century, which began about 1510. If prices in 1510 are taken as 100, they had risen by 1588 to 346, and by 1597 to a peak of 685. After 1597, the rise was less dramatic, but the figure remained over 500 for most of the early seventeenth century. These figures are necessarily only tentative. The Crown's ordinary expenses were thus likely to rise about fivefold during the century, even without any additional extravagance. It is possible that the Crown may have been more hard hit than these figures suggest. Like the modern cost of living index, they are based on a notional 'average budget', in this case that of a building labourer. The Crown's budget differed in many ways from that of a building labourer, and it may have been affected by the price rise in different ways.

It would appear that in the sixteenth as in most other centuries, the cost of warfare inflated faster than other costs. This may have been partly due to developments in military technology, but this can only be matter for conjecture. What is clear is that some of the most rapid increases were in the price of cheap foods, and these increases had a devastating effect on the cost of feeding armies. In 1640, a postponement of Charles I's Scottish campaign forced him to dispose of 1,500 tuns of bad beer, and of 1,200 firkins of butter, which being nearly two years old were 'unfit for the king's service'. Fortunately, Charles got the butter contractors to pay back most of his purchase price in return for being allowed an export licence for the butter, but he was not always so successful.[8] The kings of France and Spain, whose power to raise taxes was for practical purposes largely unfettered by political controls, were able to adjust to expenses of this type, but the English monarchs were not. As Mr. Cooper has recently remarked, 'the cost of trying to match effectively the scale of continental warfare in Charles I's time had profoundly affected English governments by 1559, however much their subjects hankered after memories of past glories.'[9]

Many of the English Crown's expenses may have been exceptionally susceptible to inflation, but this would not have mattered if their revenues had also kept pace with the rise in prices. Part of the cause of the financial crisis was that the Crown's revenue was exceptionally ill-suited to adjust to inflation. This is particularly true of its land revenue, which at the beginning of the inflation was its most important single source of revenue. Land revenue was made up of a large number of miscellaneous bits and pieces, necessarily administered locally. The local man often had local loyalties, and these, together with natural inertia, tended to prevent Crown rents from rising with inflation. Moreover if the Crown were to keep friends it had to reward people, and so the stock of crown lands steadily diminished.

Many of the Crown's other revenues depended on land valuations of estates in private hands, and these also failed to rise with inflation, chiefly because the local commissioners responsible for valuation were also suffering the effects of inflation, and were the friends and relations of those whose estates they were valuing. Assessments for Parliamentary subsidies suffered even more severely than most other sources of taxation. Even Bedford, in the middle of his plans to reform the Crown's finances, was prepared to protest in 1628 that his assessment to pay £300 towards the subsidy was too high, even though he may have been worth £15,000 a year. Dishonest assessment ran much further down the social scale. In 1628, one of Pym's Somerset tenants was assessed as worth £1.4s though he had recently paid Pym an entry fine of £460 for his lease.[10] The yield of a Parliamentary subsidy, which had been about £130,000 in the early sixteenth century, had fallen by 1628 to £55,000. Queen Elizabeth, who was not as good at handling long-term administrative problems as she was at dealing with short-term diplomatic crises, did almost nothing to counteract this tendency of her income to fall behind inflation. At the end of her reign, royal annual income was in the region of £330,000, having rather more than doubled since 1510, while prices had increased over fivefold.

Queen Elizabeth's method of meeting inflation was not to increase her income, but to exercise a rigorous control over her expenditure. As Sir Francis Seymour said in Parliament in 1625, 'she governed by a grave and wise council, and never rewarded any man but for desert, and that so sparingly, that it was out of her abundance, not taking from the subjects to give to others'.[11] This speech is a case of distance lending enchantment to the view. Many of Queen Elizabeth's contemporaries were less certain of the deserts of Leicester and Essex, and some of her economies were undignified, to say the least. When she directed her troops to crawl round under the walls of Edinburgh castle (under fire from the enemy), in order to collect cannon-balls for economy re-use, she is likely to have provoked comments somewhat less flattering than those of Sir Francis Seymour. The same is likely to have happened when she and Burghley decided the household could not afford breakfast.

Queen Elizabeth's niggardliness probably served to worsen the already severe strain on her administrative system. Official salaries had always been small, and inflation had rendered them insignificant. Attempts to increase fees, piecework payments from clients, were repeatedly resisted. The only part of an official's income which could be made inflation-proof was gifts, and gifts therefore tended to cross the very thin dividing line which separated them from bribery. Throughout James's reign complaints about fees, corruption and administrative malpractices were the Commons' most consistent theme of complaint. It is of course impossible to say whether there was an increase in official corruption in the late Elizabathan and early Jacobean period, since no one kept accounts of his bribes. It is, however, possible to say that complaints of bribery and corruption grew more frequent and more vehement.[12]

Another cause of vehement complaint was monopolies, which were in effect a form of indirect taxation for the benefit of the officials. When for example Sir Robert Harley was granted a monopoly of the fines for abuses in making gold and silver thread, he was being rewarded, through the opportunity to charge higher prices, both for the inadequacy of his salary as Master of the Mint, and for being the brother-in-law of Secretary Conway. Some of the case for monopolies arose from the inadequacy of government machinery to supervise commerce. When, for example, Charles I set up the monopoly office of 'searcher and gauger of red herrings', he was delegating a piece of work (the prevention of the sale of bad fish) which no department of his own administration was suitable to undertake. On the other hand, few traders in red herrings are likely to have seen why they should pay 2s. a time to a private individual for sticking his seal on their barrels. Other forms of reward granted by the Crown could be even more curious. In 1632, Charles I granted a fine of £1,000 imposed for incest to the Dean and Chapter of York for repairing the church, installing a new organ, adorning the altar and paying a library keeper – an ironic side-light on the 'beauty of holiness'.[13] However, if the crown had no money, it had to offer rewards like these. The result was a rapidly increasing tension between country gentlemen in the Commons and royal administrators – a tension in no way lessened by the fact that some of them were or hoped to become royal administrators themselves.

The war with Spain in 1588 therefore fell on a financial and administrative system which was already creaking at the seams. In the next four years, the war cost over £1 million, and the cost soared even further after 1601, when a rebellion and a Spanish landing created a need for a large land force in Ireland. The chances of Parliamentary co-operation in meeting this cost were as good as they were ever likely to be: Parliament had some complaints against the Queen's government, especially in religion, but they supported the war, they trusted in the honesty and efficiency of the leading ministers and commanders, and above all, since the English were winning, they were not tempted to find scapegoats for defeat. The Puritan Chancellor of the Exchequer, Sir Walter Mildmay, succeeded in 1589 in getting a vote of two subsidies instead of the normal one, though he created untold embarrassment for his successors by promising that such a sum would never be asked for again. It was soon apparent that this promise could not be kept: in 1593, the government got a vote of three subsidies and six fifteenths (a fifteenth was an old-fashioned tax worth about £30,000). In 1597 they got three subsidies and six fifteenths, and in 1601 four subsidies and eight fifteenths. By the standard of previous precedents, these grants were fantastic. Yet, partly because the yield of subsidies fell as the number increased, they came nowhere near the meeting the cost of the war. The Queen raised £339,000 by sales of crown lands, thus severely diminishing her successor's income, and left behind her a debt of at least £400,000 as well.

Since the highest figure James I's debt ever reached was £900,000, in 1618, nearly half his debt was left behind by Queen Elizabeth, as the price of her victory over Spain. It looked uncomfortably clear that, failing some really drastic alterations in the financial and administrative system, England could not afford to have a foreign policy. As Mr. Cooper has remarked, 'one of the most important symptoms of political crisis under the Stuarts was their inability to pursue an effective foreign policy'.[14] This was the fact which restored the potential power of the House of Commons. Their use and abuse of this power forms the subject of the remainder of this chapter.

II

At this stage, when it was vitally important to convince the political community in Parliament that the King had not enough money, the throne was inherited by one of the most extravagant kings ever to occupy it. Queen Elizabeth's annual expenditure had not risen above £300,000 except in wartime, and was often well below that figure. James's rose almost immediately to over £400,000 and, by 1614, was up to £522,000. Much of this money moreover went on extremely conspicuous consumption at court, or on fees and pensions to courtiers, an item which rose immediately by £50,000. The cost of the household doubled, from about £40,000 to about £80,000. It should be remembered, however, that like Henry IV of Lancaster, who got into equal trouble with his Commons for making 'outrageous grants', James was the first representative of a new dynasty not yet securely established, and could not escape the need to buy support. In some fields, such as the sharply rising expenditure on ambassadors, James's increasing expenditure met a crying need: under Elizabeth, appointment as ambassador had been so poorly paid as to be almost a form of punishment, and a king who wanted to be adequately served had to increase the rewards available. For much of James's expenditure, there was a very sensible administrative and political case, but for much else there was not. His extravagance was sufficiently obvious to make it easy for members of the Commons who had themselves been hard pressed by the exceptionally rapid inflation of the 1590s to reply to requests for extra money by suggesting that the King be asked to reduce his expenditure.

At the same time, members of the Commons reacted with some hostility to the first serious attempts since Mary's reign to increase the royal income to keep it up with inflation. Most of these were inspired by Robert Cecil, Earl of Salisbury, and they lost momentum with his death in 1612. His attempt as Master of the Wards to raise the normal selling price for wardships, brought in an extra £2,500 a year, and helped to create a demand for the abolition of wardship. He made herculean attempts to improve the Crown land revenue, which ultimately foundered on the cost of the supervision necessary to make them effective, and on the inertia of Exchequer procedure.

The only important part of the Crown's income which could readily be made inflation-proof was the customs revenue, and this is one reason why so many of the constitutional crises of the early Stuart period centred on the customs. The first thing done with the customs was the institution of the Great Farm, in 1604. The customs were farmed (i.e. leased) to a syndicate of businessmen who paid a fixed rent, and kept any profit above that figure. This avoided the difficulties which had been caused by the collaboration of almost unpaid customs officers in smuggling rings, but it also contributed to the growth of a world of somewhat shady characters on the frontiers of business and politics who did much to help the King, in return for fat profits, shady commissions, export licences and titles. This of course caused great jealousy among country gentlemen in the Commons, especially when mere merchants were given titles, and in 1628 Sir Robert Phelips appeared to argue that the profits which would go to the customs farmers were a sufficient reason against letting the king have tunnage and poundage.[15]

By far the most important case concerning customs however was Bate's case in 1606, a constitutional test case which deserves all its fame. The original case was not very far-reaching, since it concerned only one stage in a long-standing trade war against Venice. But the logic of the judgement, as Cecil quickly appreciated, allowed the King to impose any customs duties he chose, provided only that he was willing to assert that the purpose of the duties was the regulation of trade, and not the raising of revenue. Since such an assertion could not be challenged in the courts (the King being the only authority on his own motives), this meant that Parliament stood to lose all its control over customs duties, which had been the cornerstone of its political power ever since 1340. When Cecil quickly put on a new set of customs duties, known as the impositions, it looked as if Parliament was on the way to extinction. The original impositions were worth about £70,000, and by the 1630s, when they had been joined by the New Impositions and the New New Impositions, they were worth £218,000 a year. It is not surprising that many Parliamentarians took the line that the King's abandonment of his claim to impositions would have to be a necessary condition for them to help him out of his difficulties. Why, indeed, should they help him if he intended to raise money without them anyway? It is a mark, both of the seriousness of the situation and of the financial incompetence of James and Charles, that the Impositions did not in fact enable them to dispense with Parliament entirely.

Another entirely legal device for keeping pace with inflation was involved in the controversy by the fact that a new Book of Rates was issued at the same time as the impositions began. A Book of Rates, like a modern rating valuation, laid down the supposed rateable value of the item which was to be taxed, and the customs duties were then levied in the form of a proportion of this official value. In a period of inflation it was thus necessary, if the real value of customs duties was to be kept up, that new books of rates should be issued frequently. The Commons however began to claim that they were the sole authority for imposing a new book of rates, and in 1628 gave an extremely rough handling to an official who had been working on a draft for one.

These were among many distrusts which contributed to the failure of the most statesmanlike financial proposal of the reign, Salisbury's Great Contract of 1610. By this proposal the King was to surrender purveyance and wardship, two of his more unpopular ways of raising money (worth about £70,000), in return for an annual grant of £200,000. Many M.P.s were not convinced that the King really needed all this money, and one remarked that 'the Commons find the Exchequer to be like the ocean, whereunto, though all rivers pay tribute, yet it is never satisfied'.[16] Others thought it would give the King so much money that he could dispense with Parliament entirely, and for whatever reasons, the proposal failed.

After this, there was no other course left to the Crown but to attack departmental expenditure, which was done by Cranfield between 1618 and his fall in 1624. He uncovered some remarkable administrative frauds, and achieved a saving of £87,000 a year together with an annual increase in revenue of £37,000. These gains came near to putting the king's revenue and expenditure in balance but, like Salisbury's attempts to improve Crown land revenue, they could not be kept up without a degree of supervision which was impossible to achieve for long. It was difficult to go round the household every morning to make sure that no one threw away a used candle-end before it was finished. A few years after Cranfield's fall, many of the frauds he had detected were in full swing again.

All these various efforts meant that James left a financial situation little worse than he inherited, but they did no more than keep the situation stationary: they did nothing to improve it. Above all, they only enabled the Crown to keep going in peace-time with no margin to spare. They did nothing to make it possible for the Crown to fight a war, with or without Parliamentary support. This was the more serious because the Thirty Years' War, which broke out in 1618, aroused a complex of emotions like those aroused by the Spanish Civil War or the Vietnam war in this century. Like the other two, it was one in which no essential national interest demanded English participation, but the fact that the King's son-in-law was one of the main participants did much to arouse public emotion. It was not in fact what Rudyerd and other M.P.s thought it was, a grand international conflict between the forces of Protestantism and Catholicism, since the 'Protestant' side was largely inspired by the French, under Cardinal Richelieu. But for a generation brought up during the Armada war, the myth mattered as much as the reality.

Whenever the English tried to do anything abroad, the whole constitutional and financial situation would come to a head. This moment came in 1624. In that year, the Duke of Buckingham, James's homosexual favourite and *de facto* King of England, was in the process of carrying out the difficult manoeuvre of changing from being James's favourite to being that of his son. At this time, when he was most vulnerable, Buckingham decided to enter into an alliance with Parliament. One of the conditions of this alliance was that England should go to war with Spain.

This war was undoubtedly popular with the Commons, many of whom had overseas investments, and most of whom wanted to revive the supposed lost glories of Queen Elizabeth's reign. But if the war were to be a success, the Commons would have to rouse themselves to vote sums of money they had been quite unwilling to consider in 1588.

The Duke of Buckingham was not, perhaps, the best man to induce them to do this. He was never the sort of inflexible opponent of Parliament that Charles later became, since it is doubtful whether he had any principles which he regarded as worth inconvenience. However he was not conspicuous for his competence, and was extremely conspicuous for his extravagance. Apart from untold gifts from the King, he derived a large income from the fact that almost no office could be obtained without paying him. He was vulnerable to any critic who might choose to ask why, if the crown was so poor, it could afford to pay him so much. In addition to its suspicions of Buckingham, the Parliament suspected (rightly) that James did not have his heart in preparations for war, and were 'as wary and suspicious as though dealing with enemies'.[17]

It was an unpromising beginning to what was necessarily to be a make-or-break experiment in royal collaboration with Parliament. Spain was a much superior enemy, and if war was to be carried on without disaster, Parliament would have to vote sums far bigger than any Parliament had ever voted before, in addition to paying off royal debts which amounted to £666,666. In this event, meetings of Parliament were likely to become so regular that at least one shrewd observer expected a rapid rise in the level of Westminster rents. On the other hand, if Parliament failed to vote the sums needed, the King would still have to raise the money, or else face a serious risk of invasion. Thus, if Parliament did not vote enough, or if the price it asked for its money was too high, it was an almost inevitable consequence that the King would make a serious attempt to impose new taxes without Parliament, and thus that Parliament's usefulness would be at an end. Rudyerd put the issue before the Commons succinctly: 'I am afraid if this Parliament fail, it will be the last of Parliaments; if it go well it will be the beginning of many.'[18] As spokesman for the Earl of Pembroke, who was

Parliament's best friend on the Council, Rudyerd should have compelled belief, but for five years, the issue hung in the balance, while he
continued to repeat similar warnings. In 1629, when the King gave up
the attempt to come to terms with Parliament, Rudyerd's warnings were
justified by the event.

Why did this attempt to come to terms with Parliament fail? This
question is central to any attempt to explain the origins of the Civil War.
It did not fail because Parliament refused to vote supply: the Parliament
of 1624 voted three subsidies and two fifteenths, the Parliament of 1625
two subsidies, the Parliament of 1628 five subsidies, and in 1626 a vote
of four subsidies was lost by a premature dissolution. As members
repeatedly pointed out, these sums were bigger than had ever been
voted before. Moreover, they were voted at very short intervals, and
during a period of acute economic depression. The reason given for
abandoning fifteenths was that they pressed too heavily on the poor,
and this excuse may have been genuine. Many members protested
that they could not vote large sums of money without obtaining redress
of grievances, for fear of the reactions of their constituents, and it is
possible, especially among those whose real ambitions were for power
in their countries, that these protests may have been sincere.[19]

Another reason is that a number of members simply could not understand the magnitude of the sums which were needed. For a successful
war, something over a million in a year was needed. When the King
asked the 1624 Parliament for six subsidies and twelve fifteenths, he was
asking for rather less than he needed, but when the Commons heard
the sum, they were 'amazed', and not one shout of 'God save the King'
was heard as he went away. Sir Edward Coke, who should have known
better, said that the sum came to near a million, and 'all England hath
not so much'. He was not the only member whose estimates were
wildly short of the mark. In 1626, Sir Walter Earle, a fairly typical
member of moderate importance, estimated that '£200,000 would
make the king of Spain swim in his own channel'. Sir Dudley Digges,
who was one of the members most concerned to be helpful on financial
questions, also thought £200,000 a year could carry on a satisfactory
naval war.[20] In 1624, only two members could be found to support a
request for the sum for which the King was asking. One was Sir Edward
Wardour, the Exchequer official who would actually receive the money,
and the other was John Pym, who thus already showed an awareness
of financial realities which sharply distinguished him from most of his
Parliamentary colleagues.[21] Finally, Sir Robert Phelips, who was one of

the Commons' leaders chosen by Buckingham to help him to manage the House, seems to have reached a compromise with some of the Privy Council on a figure of three subsidies and three fifteenths, which was duly granted.

This sum, though extraordinarily generous from the Commons' point of view, was woefully inadequate from the government's. Even for this sum, a double price had to be paid. Part of the price was the impeachment and disgrace of Lord Treasurer Cranfield partly because, as James I sagely observed, all good treasurers were unpopular. The other part of the price was proposed by Rudyerd, whose patron Pembroke was Buckingham's worst enemy on the Council. The Commons at his instigation revived two medieval precedents by appropriating their subsidies to the war, so that they could not be used to relieve the King's debts, and by paying them to treasurers of their own nomination, thus preventing Buckingham from getting his hands on them.[22] So blatant a distrust of Buckingham's competence, though entirely justified, was not a promising beginning to the great new alliance between him and Parliament.

How justified the distrust was emerged as the war proceeded. James was reluctant to enter a war, and no significant campaigning started until the autumn of 1625, after Charles succeeded to the throne. Then an expedition to Cádiz landed the troops under the midday sun, with the wine and without the food. The results can be imagined. During 1625 and 1626, moreover, it became apparent that Buckingham was trying to pick a quarrel with France as well as Spain, and during these two years the Commons' alliance with Buckingham turned into a bitter hostility, culminating in his impeachment in 1626. By 1627 England was at war with France as well as Spain. These were the two greatest powers in Europe, and in almost permanent hostility to each other. The absurdity of the situation was as great as if Britain should today find itself at war with Russia and the United States simultaneously. Fortunately, France and Spain were distracted by a new Italian war. Otherwise either could have conducted a successful invasion, as many Englishmen were well aware. An expedition against the French in 1627 was even more disastrous than the one against the Spaniards in 1625. Meanwhile Moorish and other pirates were regularly taking captives from the English coastal towns and selling them into slavery. The government's complete failure to deal with the pirates perhaps did more to disgrace it in the eyes of its subjects than almost anything else.

It is not surprising that in these circumstances, faced with war taxation and a large forced loan, and the billeting of riotous soldiers added to military disgraces, many members began to feel it was as important to change the king's ministers as to reform the government's finances. As Rudyerd said in 1628, 'is it a small matter that we have provoked two mighty enemies and not hurt them, made them friends to themselves to agree to destroy us ?'[23] On the subject of money, the Commons' leaders appeared to split into two groups. Political groupings in the 1620's were fluid and were liable to form in different patterns on different issues. It should not be supposed that these two groups on money matters necessarily corresponded to groups on any other issue.

On the one side were Seymour, Phelips, Coke, Earle and Eliot,[24] and it is their analysis of the financial situation which was widely accepted in the Commons, and is still widely accepted among examination candidates. According to these members, the King had quite enough money, if it were competently administered. Sir Robert Phelips contrasted the Stuarts' failures with the success of 'that glorious Queen, who with less supplies defended herself, consumed Spain, assisted the Low Countries, relieved France, preserved Ireland'. He forgot that the debts left behind by the 'glorious Queen' in the course of these successes accounted for many of their current difficulties. He added, with a typical backbencher's piety, 'they dishonour the King, that think money can give him reputation'.[25] Eliot and Earle, who as west-countrymen were particularly concerned about pirates, repeatedly and wrongly insisted that want of money was not the reason for the government's failure to suppress them. They repeatedly pointed out that the Crown had been granted more money than ever before, and complained that the reason for the Crown's poverty was that, in Seymour's words, 'these great sums have come to particular men's purses'. This view produced Seymour's only constructive proposal, that they should follow medieval precedents, and pass an Act of Resumption of grants of Crown lands. Eliot in 1626 claimed that over the past two to three years, he had found public record of £76,522 issued by the King to Buckingham.[26] For this group the analysis was simple: stop corruption, restore efficient administration, and the King would have enough. Coke in particular was the only strict adherent of the supposedly classical financial theory that 'the King must live of his own', and persistently argued that the King should only ask Parliament for money on extraordinary occasions, and that his ordinary revenue could meet his ordinary expenses.

It was this group of members who were responsible for the most misguided decision of the period, the decision in 1625, when Charles came to the throne, to vote him tunnage and poundage for one year only, instead of for life. Earle, who moved the limitation after a hint from Coke, argued that tunnage and poundage was designed to guard the sea, and that until the King guarded the sea against the pirates, he should not have tunnage and poundage. Phelips, who seconded the motion, had a special and long-standing concern with the issue of impositions, and hoped to get it established once and for all that customs duties could not be levied without the consent of Parliament. Professor Roskell is right that the Commons were well within their legal rights in making this limitation. Nevertheless, the limitation did not make political sense. Charles was, after all, engaged in a war, which, as he reminded Parliament, he and his father had entered on their advice, and on their somewhat vague promises of support. Moreover he had to live, even in peace-time. Tunnage and poundage was his biggest single item of revenue, and without it, as he told the Commons in 1628, 'I neither may nor can subsist'.[27] Charles was therefore forced to levy tunnage and poundage without Parliamentary authority, thereby creating another major ground of dispute and making the idea of living without Parliament seem very much more attainable.

The other group in the Commons was a very small and isolated one, consisting of Sir Nathaniel Rich (who was easily its most important member). Sir Benjamin Rudyerd, Sir Dudley Digges, and John Pym. They agreed with the Seymour-Phelips analysis of what was wrong, so far as it went: they agreed that Buckingham was crassly incompetent and that much money was wasted. When, in 1626, the Commons lost patience and attempted to impeach Buckingham, the Rich group did their best to make the impeachment a success. But they did recognise that if Parliament was to survive, they could not afford to make it financially necessary for the King to levy unparliamentary taxes. They appreciated that, in addition to occasional subsidies, some measure of permanent reform was needed. After the 1626 Parliament, when Pembroke and the Commons were forced to accept that Buckingham was a fixture, these members bowed to the inevitable with a better grace than Coke or Seymour, and resumed their natural strategy, which was to seek to buy some measure of power in return for money. One of the things these four members had in common, apart from their attitude to the King's finances, was that all of them were closely connected with leading peers.

Of the four, it was Rudyerd whose ideas were least far-reaching. He usually confined himself to arguing in favour of the grant of a large number of subsidies; but he also argued, in 1626 and 1628, that something should be done to reform the assessment of subsidies. He said that though everyone's rents had risen since Queen Elizabeth's time, everyone's subsidy assessments had fallen except those of the nobility and clergy.[28] Digges in 1628 strongly supported Rich's attempt to renew the grant of tunnage and poundage, and also attempt to persuade the Commons to draw up a new book of rates – a proposal which might have done much to improve the king's permanent revenue.[29] Pym, who was the most junior and the most taciturn member of this group, was generally helpful over subsidies, but otherwise confined himself to supporting Rich's 1626 proposals for a committee to consider improvements in the king's revenue, and his 1628 proposal to settle tunnage and poundage[30].

Rich, the Earl of Warwick's man of affairs, might well have emerged as the leader of the Parliamentarians if he had not died in 1636. In addition to his other propsals, Rich had been trying since 1622 to supply the King with an acceptable settlement for the problem of impositions. His first proposal was for the King to take, instead of impositions, a monopoly of the import of tobacco and pepper, together with the right to sell licences to retail tobacco. The licences to retail tobacco were introduced in the 1630s by Charles I, who probably thereby increased the suspicion of the Parliamentary leaders that the King might pick their brains without employing their services.[31] Similarly, when Pym's patron Bedford, after the dissolution of Parliament in 1629, drew up a scheme to settle the customs by Act of Parliament, and to increase them by £52,000 a year, Charles I adopted much of the scheme, without calling a Parliament to implement it.[32] By 1626, Rich had given up his tobacco and pepper scheme, which, though useful, would not have raised enough money, and was trying to induce the Commons to take up a promise of James I, that if Parliament confirmed his existing imposition, he would in return renounce his right to create any further impositions without the consent of Parliament.[33]

The proposals of this group, though not so far-reaching as they later became, were certainly helpful and constructive, and they showed some readiness to consider the responsibilities which might go with office. This cannot be said of members like Seymour and Phelips, who had all the distrust of the executive of the congenital backbencher. In the House, it was Seymour and Phelips who spoke for the bulk of the members. So far from wanting Parliamentary sovereignty, most of them did not want the least degree of responsibility that might fetter their freedom to criticise and complain, or force them to understand the values of the government, as well as those of their county neighbours. They were happy to legislate on small issues, like the importing of Irish cattle or the exporting of Welsh butter, or to complain on large ones, but they were quite unwilling to accept any of the responsibilities of power. In 1628, Phelips's support for a motion to compel holders of baronetcies and Irish and Scottish peerages to pay extra subsidy showed all the distrust of court circles that was to be typical of the eighteenth-century country member: 'I beseech you lay a mark upon those that domineer over us: they murther all English gentry and get places to free themselves from us which our predecessors never knew'.[34] If Parliament were ever to make the settlement of the King's finances which was the necessary price of its continuance it would need to acquire attitudes very different from these.

III

Since this chapter is concerned with Parliament, it is fortunately unnecessary to tell the financial history of the 1630s in detail. Charles succeeded in raising his income from about £600,000 to a figure in the region of about £1 million. The most important element in this was increases in the customs, caused partly by better bargains with the customs farmers, and partly by a steadily increasing use of impositions. In addition he was getting nearly £200,000 a year from Ship Money, which, since it was in theory an emergency levy only, could not be accounted as ordinary income, but happened to be levied every year. His other methods of fund-raising, such as knighthood fines and forest fines, are too well known to need description here.

Why this large increase in income did not enable Charles to dispense with Parliament for ever is a question which is still largely unanswered. Increases in expenditure, especially in the household, are part of the answer, but these increases have not yet been investigated in detail. They cannot be ascribed to inflation, which, except for the freak years of 1631 and 1638, was slowing down considerably after 1620. The cost of interest on the debt he inherited from the war years caused some difficulty. But the significant cause is that he had still not made himself able to fight a war without the consent of the political community.

When, in 1639–40, Charles blundered into war against his Scottish subjects, it emerged that the reasons for this inability to fight wars without consent were by no means only financial. Charles's structure of local government still depended very heavily on exactly the same county gentry whom he could not trust to help him in Parliament. The gentry themselves often suspected Charles of intending to replace them by the increasing use of clergy as Justices of the Peace, but though Charles may have had such an intention, it had not by 1640 gone far enough to be effectively implemented. Moreover the Deputy Lieutenants, who controlled the militia, were all laymen – many of them already overwhelmed by the work of collecting Ship Money.

In the last years of Charles's regime, when these people were being asked to make unprecedented efforts to raise taxes and an army, they were faced by an extraordinary public hostility. Part of this was due to a slump, which made the collection of taxes in 1640 peculiarly difficult, and part of it by a widespread public sympathy with the Scots' cause. One of the Secretaries of State reported that even the army the King sent against the Scots 'receive it as orthodox that the rebels have been redeemers of their religion and liberty'. In these circumstances, it became possible to produce something approaching a taxpayers' strike, in which some of those who should have been collecting the taxes took part. Others, particularly after the under-sheriff of Hereford was murdered while collecting Ship Money, may have refrained for fear. The gentry and the peerage, who did not like this degree of insubordination among the lower orders, appear usually to have done their best to co-operate with the King. Even Warwick and Bedford, who were still Lords Lieutenant of their home counties, appear to have done their best to help the King to raise an army. It was easy to hang or imprison one man, or even ten men, for mutiny or tax refusal, but it was impossible without a disciplined standing army to hang or imprison whole villages and counties. The point was, as the Deputy Lieutenants of Shropshire reported, that they had 'a persuasive, but no compulsive power'.[35] The King did not have the physical power to force the major part of his subjects to perform actions they did not want to perform.

Even in these unpromising circumstances, the sum by which Charles was short might still have been raised. Something between half a million and a million was still needed. Charles's first attempt to raise it, from the Short Parliament in April and May 1640, failed, but it failed by a narrower margin than many people, including Charles, supposed. It is true that almost the only member to give explicit support to supply was Rudyerd, still arguing that it was the way to purchase future Parliaments. Yet there was a real split in the Short Parliament, which Charles might well have managed to exploit. Even the most irresponsible of country members were patriotic, and, Puritan or not, they did not like Scots, especially when they invaded England. The future royalists, Seymour and Hopton, did not refuse to grant even the enormous sum of twelve subsidies for which the king asked, provided that he would first abolish Ship Money and redress their grievances. On the other hand, Pym and his new lieutenant Oliver St. John were not now prepared to grant supply under any circumstances.[36] Though they had more awareness of administrative realities than Seymour, they were also far more dangerous opponents, since, unlike the country members, they had a real desire for power and for major changes of policy. In 1640, unlike 1628, they would not make any settlement with Charles without cast-iron guarantees. Since the Scottish army was the only means of extorting such guarantees, they could not afford to dispense with it. From their point of view, any measures which enabled the King to defeat the Scots would be disastrous, since they would only allow the King to go back to the regime of the 1630s. After three weeks, the Parliament was suddenly dissolved, apparently in order to forestall an attempt by Pym to get Parliament to declare its support for the Scots against the King.[37]

There remained the possibility of borrowing. Most kings could borrow a year's income without too much difficulty, and Charles's failure to borrow the money he needed in 1640 is one of the more important, and more mysterious, points in the story. Most of those who refused to lend pleaded poverty. This may have been a genuine reason, in the light of the slump and of a crisis of business confidence which had provoked a rapid flow of capital from the country. However poverty was the conventional polite excuse on such occasions, and many of those who failed to lend may have been too much out of sympathy with the regime to have any desire to help it out of its difficulties. Others may have expected Charles to lose, or simply remembered that he had a bad record as a creditor.

Since borrowing failed, Charles had to try Parliament again. The Long Parliament which met in November 1640 had a far more purposeful leadership than any previous seventeenth-century Parliament. Many of the leaders were associates from the 1620s, and many of them, with the conspicuous exception of Bedford, had been closely associated during the 1630s in the company for colonising the island of Providence, in the West Indies. The key members of this group were almost all peers, and Pym, acquired much of his sudden new-found reputation from being known to be the peers' chief spokesman in the Commons. This group approached the meeting of Parliament with a very clearly defined programme. This programme was not to obtain 'Parliamentary government', but to get themselves into office, and to use triennial Parliaments as a means of keeping themselves there. Their aims were not so much for changes in the constitution, as for changes in policy. The sort of aristocratic *coup d'état* which the peers planned had many precedents, which they cited correctly. In so far as their aims were 'constitutional', they were concerned with the position of the peerage, as well as that of Parliament, and Bedford's commonplace books make it clear that he believed neither in the sovereignty of the King nor in that of Parliament, but in the sovereignty of the Privy Council. As early as 1628 Bedford had been prepared to cite Simon de Montfort in favour of the proposition that 'if the King will refuse to do justice, the baronage ought'.[38] This policy, including the use of Parliament as the baronage's chosen instrument against the King, was in the authentic tradition of medieval English constitutionalism. Unlike medieval barons, they had no army and therefore they were forced to rely on an agreement with the Scots whereby the Scots were to keep their army in England until the *coup d'état* was completed.[39]

Much of the programme of this group is very well known. The measures designed to prevent the King from ruling again without Parliament and those designed to sweep away the Laudian regime in the church, are too familiar to be recounted here. What is less well known is that they had a constructive programme for settling the King's finances, which was to have been implemented by Bedford as Treasurer, and Pym as Chancellor of the Exchequer. This programme had been carefully thought out, and in forming it, they had access to information from a large number of senior departmental administrators in the Exchequer and elsewhere. The revenue balances, on which Bedford was to start work, were being prepared by Sir Robert Pye, who was Hampden's relation by marriage, and by Sir Edward Wardour, who had been a trustee of Pym's estate and was a close friend of Bedford. In the Wards, they could rely on Rudyerd, the Surveyor, who was a trustee of Pym's and Bedford's estates, and in the Duchy of Lancaster on Pym's friend Sir Gilbert Gerrard. Of the two treasurers of the Navy, the younger Vane was Pym's friend, and Sir William Russell was Bedford's close friend and cousin. On crown land revenue, Pym was himself an expert, and they were also receiving advice from Sir Christopher Vernon, one of the Exchequer's experts on concealed crown lands. In the customs administration, Sir John Harrison the customs farmer offered his services to his 'great and noble friend' the Earl of Bedford.[40] The fact that these men were prepared to support a compromise settlement did not make them potential rebels, and not all of them became Parliamentarians. Much of this financial programme was put into effect by Pym in 1643 as a means of enabling Parliament to win the war, but it was all ready to be implemented in 1641 as part of a settlement with Charles I. First, Parliament was to vote enough money to pay the king's existing debts, so that any new financial system would have a good chance of success.[41] The next proposal was to deal with the falling yield of the subsidy, by the method ultimately successfully implemented for Pym's Weekly Assessment in 1643. Instead of voting subsidies, which were a proportion of taxpayers' supposed income, and therefore could be reduced by dishonest valuation, Parliament was to vote a fixed sum.[42] Parliament was to fix how much each county should pay, and then the county commissioners were to proportion the sum among the taxpayers as they thought fit. It would then become impossible for dishonest commissioners to reduce the total yield of the subsidy. At the same time, the leaders proposed to abolish certificates, a device by which people could evade taxation in one place by certifying that they had paid it in another, so that 'gentlemen scapt in London for a song, and so got a discharge for the countries' (i.e. counties). In future, people were to be taxed in every place where they held land.

Both these proposals aroused a good deal of opposition in the Commons, even when introduced for the emergency purpose of paying the Scottish army. Pym's first attempt to switch over to the lump sum method of parliamentary taxes was thrown out, and the proposal to abolish certificates was strongly opposed by many of the richer members, 'and thus, as Sir B[enjamin] R[udyerd] saith, the country fenced against the Parliament, or rather the Parliament against the King'. One member said the new proposal was the fashion of the conqueror, or the Turk.[43] Even more indignation was caused by the attempt to get peers, who had previously taxed themselves at most dishonest rates, taxed by the same methods as everyone else. A proposal by Pym that the King should be given tunnage and poundage or a recompense for the abolition of Ship Money was obstructed by Sir Walter Earle, who moved that the committee should confine itself to Ship Money.[44]

Some of Bedford's other proposals were much better designed to gain Parliamentary support. There was likely to be little objection to the confiscation of the lands of 'delinquents'. Equally, the Commons were likely to take kindly to proposals to increase the income raised from

fines on Catholic recusants. A much more important proposal was for
the confiscation of the lands of Deans and Chapters. This had probably
first been suggested in the 1620s, but the detailed scheme for it which
survives among Bedford's papers probably dates from 1640. The lands
of the Deans and Chapters were to be leased out at low rents and high
entry fines, thus combining the paying off of the King's immediate debts
with a series of attractive bargains for potential tenants. Throughout
the document, the author is as concerned to prove that the bargains
were attractive to the tenants as that the yield to the King would be good.
The idea seems to be that Bedford and Charles could use these bargains
to buy the support of the Parliamentary classes, as Cromwell and Henry
VIII had bought their support with monastic land. The specific
proposal was for the King to gain an annual income of £120,000, and a
capital sum of £420,000 in entry fines.

At least one well-placed observer believed that the Parliamentary
leaders intended to revive the Great Contract of 1610, and another undated memorandum among Bedford's papers, in the same hand as that
for the Deans and Chapters, sets out proposals for the abolition of wardship. Here again, the author's concern is as much to prove that the
bargain is attractive to holders of lands formerly liable to wardship as
that it is advantageous to the King. The annual revenue to be raised in
rents on lands formerly liable to wardship was only £48,666, which was
well under the £75,000 a year the King was making from the Court of
Wards. On the other hand, the King was to gain an immediate capital
sum of £239,333 in entry fines. Again, a bribe to the landed classes to
accept the settlement is to be combined with an immediate windfall to
pay off the King's debts.[45]

This scheme was never seriously raised in Parliament, and it almost
certainly died with Bedford in May 1641. At Bedford's death, the task
of negotiating with the King was taken over by Viscount Saye and Sele.
Much of the opposition to Bedford's proposals from within the Parliamentary leadership had come from Nathaniel Fiennes and Sir Walter
Earle, Saye's son and son-in-law resectively. When, within a few weeks
of Bedford's death, Saye accepted the highly profitable office of Master
of the Wards, he almost certainly abandoned the scheme to abolish
wardship.

As always, however, the crucial question was the settlement of
customs, and particularly of tunnage and poundage. On this issue,
negotiations did continue after Bedford's death, and the failure to bring
them to a conclusion is something of a mystery. From May 1641 until

the Civil War, the House of Commons repeatedly voted tunnage and poundage for a few weeks at a time, but no settlement was ever reached, to Charles's great indignation. One stumbling block was the question of guarantees. The Parliamentary leaders were well aware that, in voting tunnage and poundage to the King for life, they ran the risk of making him sufficiently solvent to manage without Parliament. They had, it is true, passed an Act saying that Parliament was to meet every three years, but after the Petition of Right of 1628, it is doubtful whether many of them believed that a mere Act would bind Charles against his will. It is true that the Act contained clauses for calling a Parliament without the King's consent, but it was doubtful whether the clauses would be implemented.

Bedford, Pym and St. John had worked out a plan which was more nearly foolproof. They intended to vote Charles tunnage and poundage for three years at a time, so that his right to his customs would expire whenever a new Parliament was due. They also planned to take over the farming of the customs themselves, so that if Charles failed to call a Parliament, they would be able to refuse to pay him his customs. Moreover, as a memorandum submitted to one of the Parliamentary leaders pointed out, control of the customs conferred control of intelligence, and would therefore give early warning of any plan to bring in foreign troops. Another advantage of the scheme was that if Charles intended at some future date to ditch Parliament and his Parliamentarian ministers, he would need to raise large loans, and it had become increasingly clear over the past twenty years that only the customs farmers had the resources to make loans on the required scale. Control of the customs farm would have given the Parliamentary leaders almost as effective a stranglehold on Charles as they later attempted to obtain by control of the militia. This scheme was sufficiently advanced of Pym's step-brother Francis Rous to write to him petitioning for the Collectorship of customs at Dartmouth.[46] Control of posts as small as this would have given the Parliamentary leaders an almost Walpolean volume of patronage, and so provided them with another weapon to persuade the House of Commons to accept an adequate financial settlement.

Why did this scheme fall through? Parliament did finally draw up its new Book of Rates, which proved good enough to survive the Restoration. However, tunnage and poundage was never settled, and the Excise, the biggest of Pym's financial proposals, a sales tax which ultimately brought in £300,000 a year, was never put before the

Commons until 1643. We have only Clarendon's authority that it was ready for introduction in 1641. It may be that the scheme fell through because Charles was not prepared to accept the restrictions involved. That Charles should be unwilling to accept a complete surrender of power is natural enough, and this may be a sufficient reason for the scheme's failure.

It may not, however, be the only reason. Clarendon claimed that one reason for the Parliamentary leaders' failure to reach a settlement with the King was their inability to persuade Parliament to vote a sufficient financial settlement. It may be that Charles's would-be ministers in 1641 foundered, like all his previous ministers, on the rock-like obstinacy of country members' refusal to accept the real cost of government. If Clarendon is right, he was himself one of the guilty members. In December 1641, the then Edward Hyde opposed a proposal by Pym, St. John and Pye for a general settlement of the King's finances, arguing, with an absurdity worthy of Coke or Earle, that the sums spent in the past two years were enough to conquer Germany.[47] But the opposition to this financial settlement went nearer the centre of the Parliamentary leadership than Hyde. Between May 25 and June 1, 1641, Bedford's men Pym and St. John, the chief enthusiasts for a financial settlement, had to fight two major battles against Holles and Strode, both of them later among the Five Members. Lacking the support of their old patron Bedford, Pym and St. John lost both battles. The first was an echo of an old contention of 1629; Pym and St. John wanted to vote the king tunnage and poundage, which necessarily involved them in coming to an agreement with the customs farmers, while Holles and Strode wanted instead to condemn the customs farmers as delinquents for collecting customs illegally: a move which would probably prevent any settlement with them. Pym suceeded in deferring this issue for a week, and finally lost. The other issue was whether the interim vote of tunnage and poundage for a few weeks, which was to be made pending a settlement, was to be made to the king or to commissioners for his use. Once again, Holles and Strode persuaded the House to vote the money to commissioners for the King's use.[48]

According to Clarendon, Charles wanted Pym and St. John to do him service before they were taken into office. After they had suffered these two defeats in the House, he may well have doubted whether they had the power to do him adequate service. The dominant spirit in the House of Commons was not the responsible opposition of Pym and St. John, willing to accept the cost involved in the changes of policy they

demanded. The dominant attitude was still the irresponsible distrust of
the executive characteristic of Phelips and Seymour: the rooted distrust
of government for its own sake which was to form the 'country' opposition of the eighteenth century. The House of Commons, as Cromwell
was to discover, was not yet ready to accept the responsibilities of power,
and this fact does much to explain its failure to reach a settlement with
the King before the Civil War. It may have been the unwillingness of
backbenchers to trust the executive with a financial settlement that
pushed the Parliamentary leaders into their final desperate position,
that they would not vote Charles tunnage and poundage for life until
he allowed Parliament to elect the great officers.[49] Many members probably wanted to be as free to obstruct Pym and St. John as ministers as
they had been to obstruct Laud and Strafford.

It was thus inevitable that Charles's financial and administrative
system should break up, and almost inevitable that the Commons would
not be willing to help him out of trouble. The breakdown of Charles's
financial machinery in the face of war did much to allow the other
passions Charles had provoked to grow into Civil War. But though
financial difficulties provided the opportunity for the Civil War, it
would be an exaggeration to say they made it: men do not usually kill
each other for the sake of a few shillings, but, as Dr. Christopher Hill has
said, 'about serious issues of principle which roused large numbers of
men to heroic activity and sacrifice'.[50] Among these issues of principle,
the religious issues described by Dr. Tyacke and Dr. Clifton raised up
more soldiers than the financial issues here described. These financial
issues made a constitutional crisis inevitable, but without the passion
provided by religious troubles, it would not have been inevitable that
the constitutional crisis should end in war.

Section Two

4. Puritanism, Arminianism and Counter-Revolution

NICHOLAS TYACKE

I

HISTORIANS of the English Civil War all agree that Puritanism had a role to play in its origins. Beyond this however agreement ceases. For some, particularly the Marxists, Puritanism was the ideology of the newly emergent middle classes or *bourgeosie*, as they are sometimes called. Puritan ideas, it is argued, complemented and encouraged the capitalist activities of 'progressive' gentry, merchants and artisans alike. On the assumption, again made by those most under the influence of Marxism, that the English Civil War was a 'bourgeois revolution' the Puritans are naturally to be found fighting against King Charles and his old-world followers. An alternative and widely held interpretation sees Puritanism as a religious fifth column within the Church of England, and one whose numbers dramatically increased during the first decades of the seventeenth century; by the early 1640s, with the collapse of the central government and its repressive system of church courts, the Puritans were thus able to take over at least in the religious sphere. These two schools of thought, the Marxist and the fifth-columnist, are best represented by the writings respectively of Dr. Christopher Hill and Professor William Haller.

In the following essay however a different view will be put forward, to the effect that religion became an issue in the Civil War crisis due primarily to the rise to power of Arminianism in the 1620s. The essence of Arminianism was a belief in God's universal grace and the freewill of all men to obtain salvation. Therefore Arminians rejected the teaching of Calvinism that the world was divided into elect and reprobate whom God had arbitrarily predestinated, the one to Heaven and the other to Hell. It is difficult for us to grasp how great a revolution this involved for a society as steeped in Calvinist theology as was England before the Civil War. But whether or not we agree with the arguments of Christopher Hill, it is clear that the Puritan ideas to which he ascribes so much importance for the development of modern, capitalist society are in the main predestinarian ones. Similarly with Haller's thesis concerning the growth of Puritanism, the message preached with such success from Puritan pulpits was rooted in the Calvinist theology of grace.[1]

At the beginning of the seventeenth century, a majority of the clergy from the Archbishop of Canterbury downwards were Calvinists in doctrine, and the same was probably true of the more educated laity. So Puritanism in this Calvinist sense was not then seen as a political threat. Only when predestinarian teaching came to be outlawed by the leaders of the established church, as was the case under Archbishop William Laud, would its exponents find themselves in opposition to the government. Any doubts that the Church of England was doctrinally Calvinist, before Laud took control, can be resolved by reading the extant doctoral theses in divinity maintained at Oxford University from the 1580s to the 1620s. There, year after year predestinarian teaching was formally endorsed, and its opposite denied. The following are a representative selection of such theses, translated from the original Latin and listed in chronological order: 'No one who is elect can perish' (1582); 'God of his own volition will repudiate some people' (1596); 'According to the eternal predestination of God some are ordained to life and others to death' (1597); 'Man's spiritual will is not itself capable of achieving true good' (1602); 'The saints cannot fall from grace' (1608); 'Is grace sufficient for salvation granted to all men? No.' (1612); 'Does man's will only play a passive role in his initial conversion? Yes' (1618); 'Is faith and the righteousness of faith the exclusive property of the elect? Yes' (1619); and 'Has original sin utterly extinguished free will in Adam and his posterity? Yes' (1622). The licensed publications of the English press tell the same Calvinist story, albeit in a more popular vein, as do many religious preambles to wills where the testator confidently affirms belief in his divine election. A good example of this type of Calvinist will is that made by Lord Treasurer Dorset, who died in 1608; George Abbot, future Archbishop of Canterbury, was so impressed by Dorset's claim to be an elect saint that he quoted the will verbatim when preaching his funeral sermon in Westminster Abbey. Calvinism at the time was clearly establishment orthodoxy, and contemporaries would have found any suggestion that Calvinists were Puritans completely incomprehensible.[2]

Puritanism around the year 1600, and for more than two decades subsequently, was thought of in terms either of a refusal to conform with the religious rites and ceremonies of the English Church, or as a presbyterian rejection of church government by bishops. At that date conformists and nonconformists, episcopalians and presbyterians all had in common Calvinist predestinarian ideas. Here however we come to the crux of the matter, for Calvinism also helped to reconcile the differences between them. Thus the late Elizabethan Archbishop of Canterbury, John Whitgift, who was a Calvinist in doctrine, regarded Puritan nonconformity in a different light from that of the Arminian Archbishop Laud. This did not stop Whitgift as Archbishop from attacking nonconformists, especially with Queen Elizabeth hard on his heels, but it did impose important limits on the extent of his persecution. Before the advent of Laud, nonconformists and even presbyterians were never regarded as being totally beyond the pale; they were seen instead as aberrant brethren deserving of some indulgence. Symbolic of the pre-Laudian state of affairs is that in the 1560s Whitgift had been a nonconformist and Thomas Cartwright, the later presbyterian, a candidate for an Irish archbishopric and, despite a long history of public controversy between them, they ended up on good terms in the 1590s. Calvinist doctrine provided a common and ameliorating bond that was only to be destroyed by the rise of Arminianism. As a result of this destruction, during the 1620s, Puritanism came to be redefined in terms which included the very Calvinism that previously had linked nonconformists to the leaders of the established church, and the nonconformist element in the former Calvinist partership was driven into an unprecedented radicalism. The Arminians and their patron King Charles were undoubtedly the religious revolutionaries in the first instance. Opposed to them were the Calvinists, initially conservative and counter-revolutionary, of whom the typical lay representative was John Pym. These are the developments which we must now consider in detail. First however something more needs saying about the definition of a Puritan.[3]

One possibility would be to define Puritanism in terms of Calvinist predestinarian teachings, and certainly many modern writers agree in labelling this body of ideas as in some sense Puritan. We have already noted that such labelling involves the paradox of making Archbishop Whitgift and most of his fellow bishops into Puritans. Doctrinal Calvinism does not however explain why Elizabethan Protestants became nonconformists, presbyterians, and sometimes separatists. Here what seems to have been critical was a difference in attitude to the authority of the Bible as a religious model, although the distinction is by no means clear cut. Indeed the point needs making that it is extremely artificial to start drawing hard and fast lines between Puritans and 'Anglicans' in the Elizabethan and Jacobean periods. There are far too many cases which defy categorisation. For example in a sermon collection published in 1585, Archbishop Sandys of York asserted that 'in the scriptures . . . is contained all that is good, and all that which God requireth or accepteth of', and that this was no empty claim is clear from his will, dated two years later, where he wrote 'concerning rites and ceremonies by political constitutions authorised amongst us, . . . in the church reformed, and in all this time of the gospel (wherein the seed of the scripture hath so long been sown), they may better be disused by little and little'. Despite these declared views Archbishop Sandys himself conformed, and was prepared on occasion to prosecute in the church courts those who did not. At the other extreme however the separatist leader Henry Barrow, writing in 1591, justified his separation from the Church of England on the grounds that 'every part of the Scripture is alike true, inspired of God, given to our direction and instruction in all things'.[4]

But if Calvinism did not cause Puritan nonconformity there was as we have said a willingness among predestinarians to tolerate such aberrations, or at least not to regard them in a very serious light. This can be illustrated by a visitation sermon preached in 1605 about 'the lawful use of things indifferent'. The author was a doctrinal Calvinist, Sebastian Benefield, who later as Lady Margaret professor of divinity at Oxford became well known for his attacks on Arminian heresy. In his sermon of 1605 he took as his model St. Paul, who became 'all things to all men' that he might 'by all means save some', and placed ceremonial conformity firmly in the context of the elect's calling to salvation by the sowing of 'the immortal seed of the word of God'. Preaching he described as the human means 'whereby the foreknown of God from all eternity, and the predestinated to life of God's pure favour, are effectually called from the state of servitude to liberty'. This task of preaching took priority over any conscientious scruples about wearing surplices and the like, and it was the duty of a minister to conform rather than be silenced. On the other hand, although Benefield did not explicitly make the point, those in authority logically should exercise great restraint in applying ultimate sanctions against nonconformists lest their evangelising services be lost. Another doctrinal Calvinist whose writings exhibit an even more marked ambiguity than do Benefield's as regards nonconformity, was Samuel Gardiner. His theology can readily be deduced from a series of surviving sermons which he preached in 1611 on the subject of God's eternal predestination. Earlier, in 1605, he had published a work in dialogue form concerning 'the rites and ceremonies of the Church of

England,' in the course of which the conformist admits to his opponent that 'if the laws had not been in these cases already made, I should never, for my own part, wish to have them made.' But for the present ceremonies were to be tolerated until 'it shall seem good by higher powers, they may as superfluous or little profitable, grow out of use.' The views of Benefield and Gardiner are highly relevant for understanding official attitudes to Puritan nonconformity before the time of Laud, because both men became chaplains to George Abbot, archbishop of Canterbury from 1611 to 1633. Abbot, a committed predestinarian, was chided by King James in 1613 for advancing 'one of the puritans' arguments', when he maintained that 'Scripture doth directly or by consequence contain in it sufficient matter to decide all controversies, especially in things appertaining to the church.' This links Abbot with Archbishop Sandys, who, as we have seen, believed that the rites and ceremonies of the Church of England needed further reformation.[5]

In the light of such evidence it should already be apparent that the first decades of the seventeenth century in England did not witness any straightforward contest between an 'Anglican' hierarchy on the one hand and the serried ranks of Puritanism on the other. This becomes even clearer if we take the case of William Perkins, whom Christopher Hill has described as 'the dominant influence in Puritan thought for the forty years after his death' in 1602. His funeral sermon was preached by James Montagu, shortly to become dean of the chapel royal and subsequently bishop of Winchester, and the chief critic of Perkins's works was answered in print by Bishop Robert Abbot of Salisbury, whose intellectual position was identical to that of his brother the archbishop. While this blurring of religious differences seems characteristic of the period, a further complicating factor was the religious standpoint of the monarch, as supreme head of the English Church. James I was much more sympathetic to Calvinist doctrine than his predecessor Elizabeth, and to that extent those Puritan nonconformists were correct who hoped for better things on the queen's death in 1603. The proof of the king's Calvinist affinities was conveniently published as a pamphlet in 1626, by Francis Rous, who was the step-brother of John Pym and an outspoken parliamentary critic of Arminianism. Two examples of this royal Calvinism must suffice. In 1604 James was officially quoted as saying that 'predestination and election dependeth not upon any qualities, actions or works of man, which be mutable, but upon God his eternal and immutable decree and purpose.' Similarly in 1619 he wrote that 'God draws by his effectual grace, out of that attainted and corrupt mass [mankind], whom he pleaseth for the work of his mercy, leaving the rest to their own ways which all lead to perdition.' Yet having demonstrated James's Calvinism, and therefore the existence of a common and potentially reconciling bond with Puritan nonconformists, one is faced with the problem of his celebrated outbursts against Puritans – as for instance when he described them in March 1604 as a 'sect unable to be suffered in any well-governed commonwealth', and the deprivations for nonconformity which occurred during his first years on the throne. The explanation, however, would seem to lie in *raison d'état*, as that was interpreted by the King. His exposure in Scotland at an early age to Calvinist theology had left him favourably disposed towards its teachings, yet his experience there of religious rebellion had also made him politically suspicious of anything remotely akin to presbyterianism. Whereas for Elizabeth political considerations had complemented her religious antipathies, with James there was thus something of a conflict. The preface to the 1603 edition of his book *Basilicon Doron*, where James withdrew some earlier unflattering comments about Puritans, has often been seen as propaganda aimed at smoothing the path of his succession to the English throne. But the same sentiments recur, notably in some royal remarks paraphrased by Robert Cecil during a Star Chamber speech in 1605. 'For the puritans . . . [the King] would go half way to meet them, and he loved and reverenced many of them, and if they would leave their [nonconformist] opinions, there were some of them he would prefer to the best bishoprics that were void.' King James himself put the dichotomy more succinctly in July of the previous year. 'To discreet men I say, they shall obtain their desires by grace, but to all I profess, they shall extort nothing by violence.'[6]

These distinctions would be rather academic had James's fear of Puritan nonconformity continued to dominate him as much as it did during the earliest years of his English reign. Increasingly however, a countervailing political factor emerged in the shape of an intensified fear of Catholicism. This was particularly the case between 1608 and 1615, a period in which the King himself wrote as many as three works on the subject of the oath of allegiance. The latter was a modified form of the supremacy oath, enacted by statute during the aftermath of Gunpowder Plot in an attempt to isolate politically disloyal Catholics. Any chance of success which the scheme might have had was effectively wrecked by strong papal opposition and an ensuing pamphlet war. Almost inevitably Puritanism benefited from this redirection of government energies. Religious differences among the various royal champions who entered the lists were subsumed in a cloud of zeal against the common papist enemy. Catholic charges that Puritans differed on doctrinal grounds from the established church were publicly denied even by emergent Arminians like Bishop Andrewes, and there was a widespread campaign to ban the use of the term Puritan completely. Suggestive also is the fact that from 1611 until 1618 no work directed specifically against Puritanism, either in its nonconformist or presbyterian guises, is recorded in the Stationers' Registers as being licensed for the press.[7]

In part symptomatic of the altered climate was George Abbot's own promotion to Canterbury in 1611. The Jesuit Father Coffin wrote of the new primate as 'a brutal and fierce man, and a sworn enemy of the very name of Catholic'. Certainly his elevation occurred during a two-year period which witnessed a third of all the Catholic martyrdoms under James. The supposition that these events were linked is further strengthened by the terms in which the appointment of Toby Matthew to the archbishopric of York had been canvassed back in 1606. Already at that date there was alarm in government circles over conditions in the north, as an area 'overpestered with popery and not with puritanism'. Cecil was urged to promote the appointment of 'a painful and preaching successor' to Archbishop Hutton and one 'industrious against papists'. Policy however was often inextricably interwoven with patronage; just as Cecil was Matthew's patron, so Abbot had been recommended as archbishop by the current royal favourite Dunbar. Abbot, as Dunbar's chaplain, had been instrumental in helping reconcile the Scottish Church to episcopacy, and his Puritan proclivities almost certainly contributed to the success of that enterprise. Compared with his Protestant predecessors at Canterbury, Abbot in his general outlook seems most to have resembled Edmund Grindal. The latter has recently been described by Professor Collinson as 'one of the very few Elizabethan bishops who enjoyed the full approval of the protestant governing class and the equal confidence of all but a small embittered minority of the godly preaching ministers.'[8]

By contrast, the archiepiscopal predecessor whom Abbot least resembled was the man he immediately succeeded. This was Richard Bancroft, whose policies more than those of any other churchman prior to the Arminian Laud drove Puritan nonconformists to extremes. Bancroft's loathing of Puritanism amounted almost to paranoia, and his espionage methods threatened to make real the Puritan conspiracy which originated largely as a figment of his own imagination. He was also among the first Protestant churchmen in England to disassociate himself from the predestinarian teachings of Calvinism, and therefore lacked the restraining influence of a theology shared with his nonconformist opponents. Fortunately, from the point of view of political stability, Bancroft's extremism was kept in check by King James. Indeed the appointment of Bancroft to Canterbury in 1604 was a Jacobean anomaly; his Elizabethan record of severity against Puritans apparently recommended him as the man of the hour, when nonconformist clergy, backed by gentry support, seemed to pose a serious political threat. As Archbishop, Bancroft had from the start been a rather isolated figure. Those who succeeded him in the bishopric of London, a post which administratively ranked second only to Canterbury, were all Calvinists during his lifetime. One of them, Richard Vaughan, who was Bishop of London from 1604 to 1607, became well known for his tolerance of Puritan deviation from the strict letter of the law. Moreover in 1608 Bancroft was forced to acquiesce in the publication of an official Calvinist commentary on The Thirty-Nine Articles – the Church of England's confession of faith. After his death in 1610 Calvinist dominance became even more marked, and the combined religious and political atmosphere generally favoured a *modus vivendi* with Puritan nonconformity. In addition to government attacks on Catholicism, which distracted attention from disagreements among Protestants, the chief posts in the church were filled by men whose views at many important points merged with those of their nonconformist brethren. Both Archbishop Abbot and John King, Bishop of London from 1611 to 1621, had been lecturers in the 1590s, and the former expressed the hope during a parliamentary debate in 1610 that he would die in the pulpit. They were also sabbatarians, Abbot successfully intervening in 1618 to preserve the Puritan Sunday from the threat of the royal Declaration of Sports. A third very powerful Jacobean cleric was Bishop James Montagu of Winchester, editor of King James's collected works and a Privy Councillor. He had been the first master of Sidney Sussex College in Cambridge where he had not enforced conformity, and we have noted his connexion with the 'Puritan' theologian William Perkins. His brother, Sir Edward Montagu, had been a prominent spokesman on behalf of nonconformist Puritans during the parliament of 1604. All three bishops were Calvinists, Montagu assuming a watching brief for doctrinal orthodoxy at Cambridge and Abbot placing his brother Robert and his chaplain

Benefield, respectively in the Regius and Lady Margaret chairs of divinity at Oxford. At the same time, with royal fears of Catholicism still in the ascendant, these churchmen had the support of the new favourite Buckingham. Archbishop Abbot was on sufficiently familiar terms in 1616 to call him 'my George', being dubbed 'father' in return, and Montagu, who died in 1618, described Buckingham in his will as 'the most faithful friend that ever I had'. In Montagu's view the period since the accession of King James in 1603 had on the whole been one of 'harmony' with the Puritans.[9]

This impression of comparative calm receives some statistical confirmation from a recent study of Puritan lecturers in London by Dr. Seaver. Between 1604 and 1606 out of twenty identifiable Puritan lecturers only six came before the church courts, and of these six only one was permanently suspended from preaching. From 1607 to 1609 the pattern was 'much the same'. During the second decade of the seventeenth century prosecutions for nonconformity were even fewer and Seaver conjectures that 'at a time when controversy was at a minimum, when no great issues divided public opinion . . . some puritanically inclined ministers might have found little cause for militancy and small reason not to conform'. A situation similar to that in London existed in the northern province, under Archbishop Toby Matthew, where citations for nonconformity were rare despite the existence of many potential offenders. According to Dr. Marchant's account of Puritanism in the diocese of York, a 'general policy of toleration' prevailed there until the late 1620s. Matthew was a Calvinist and employed at least one moderate nonconformist, John Favour, as his chaplain, as well as being an indefatigable preacher himself. With archbishops like Matthew and Abbot in command, Puritanism presented no real problem.[10]

There was however an element of uncertainty in the situation, since much could depend on the vagaries of international politics and the shifting sands of court favour. Just as the oath of allegiance controversy, and its associated anti-Catholic attitudes, had worked to the benefit of Puritan nonconformity, so with plans for marrying Prince Charles to a Catholic Spanish infanta the process seemed about to go into reverse. By 1618 there was talk of tolerating Catholicism, as a condition of the Spanish marriage. The concomitant of this would be a slump in demand for polemic against the popish Antichrist, and tighter government control over the diversity of Protestant practice. That this threat did not materialise was mainly due to a political crisis in the Low Countries, which was deemed to affect England's foreign policy interests. In the

United Provinces, Oldenbarnveldt and Prince Maurice were engaged in a struggle for power, and had enlisted on their respective sides the rival Dutch church parties of Arminian and Calvinist. King James, for reasons which included theology, supported Maurice and the Calvinists, and in late 1618 sent a delegation, under Bishop Carleton of Llandaff, to participate in an international synod at Dort. This gathering proceeded to condemn the Arminian theology of grace, and affirm its Calvinist converse, and was an event which has never received the emphasis it deserves from students of English religious history. For the Calvinist doctrines at issue in the United Provinces were fundamental to English Puritanism before the Civil War, in a way that ceremonies and discipline were not. Calvinist predestinarian teaching was, as we have indicated, a crucial common assumption, shared by a majority of the hierarchy and virtually all its nonconformist opponents, during the Elizabethan and Jacobean periods. Indeed it is not too much to say that for many people in the early seventeenth century the basic issue as between Protestantism and Catholicism was that of divine determinism versus human freewill. Calvinist affinities between the bishops and their critics lent substance to claims that rites and ceremonies were matters of indifference. Accordingly the assertion of predestinarian Calvinism made by the Synod of Dort, with English delegates participating and its published proceedings dedicated to King James, served to emphasise afresh the theology binding conformist and nonconformist together, and the limits which that common bond imposed on persecution.

Hindsight is often the curse of the historian, and none more so in attempting to reconstruct the religious history of the pre-Civil War era. The battle lines of 1640–2 were not drawn by the early 1620s in this any more than other spheres. The parliaments of 1621 and 1624 were remarkable for a dearth of religious grievances. 'Godly reformation' was limited to allegations of corrupt practices by certain ecclesiastical officials, and requests that the recusancy laws be more strictly enforced. Among the clergy an appeal from Bermuda in 1617 by the presbyterian Lewis Hughes, to avoid persecution by emigration, fell on deaf ears. Moreover in 1621 Hughes's own form of catechism concerning 'public exercises of religion', as well as a tract on strict sabbath observance, were licensed for publication by one of Archbishop Abbot's chaplains. When therefore the Spanish marriage negotiations finally collapsed in 1624 it was natural for the favourite Buckingham to cultivate closer relations with John Preston, at that date 'leader of the Puritan party', again to quote Christopher Hill. Two years before, Buckingham had secured for Preston the mastership of Emmanuel College, Cambridge, and now held out promises of further preferment. Preston was a Calvinist conformist and the Cambridge protégé of John Davenant, who had been a delegate to the Synod of Dort and was now bishop of Salisbury. Far from being an untypical eccentric, Davenant was in the mainstream of Calvinist episcopalianism, and that Preston also found favour was of a piece with Jacobean religious developments. Indeed Preston might well have ended up adorning the episcopal bench. This was the context in which John Pym, during the parliament of 1621, rejected 'that odious and factious name of Puritans' which a fellow member had tried to fasten on the promoters of a bill for the better observance of Sunday. Pym thought that the speech was especially reprehensible in that it tended to 'divide us amongst our selves . . . or at least would make the world believe we were divided'. As it turned out however Preston died in the ecclesiastical wilderness in 1628, and a doctrinal revolution took place within the established church which shattered the Jacobean dispensation. The two events were intimately connected, for during the 1620s the Calvinist heritage was overthrown and with it the prerequisite of English Protestant unity. The result was a polarisation of extremes unknown since the Reformation, and one which rendered earlier compromises unworkable. It is this triumph of Arminianism, and its divisive consequences, which we must now consider.[11]

II

England in the early seventeenth century was doctrinally a part of Calvinist Europe, and it is within this ambience that the teachings of the Dutch theologian Arminius at Leyden have to be seen. During the first decade of the century, Arminius elaborated a critique of doctrinal Calvinism so systematic as to give his name to an international movement, namely Arminianism. He was concerned to refute the teachings on divine grace associated with the followers of Calvin, but he spoke as a member of the fully reformed and presbyterian Dutch Church, whereas his doctrinal equivalents in England were part of a different ecclesiastical tradition. There the most notable survivor of the English Reformation, apart from episcopacy, was the Prayer Book which, as its critics were pleased to point out, was an adapted version of the old Catholic mass book. Consequently Arminianism in England emerged with an additional, sacramental dimension to that in the United Provinces. Arminius was read with approval by anti-Calvinists in England but adapted to the local situation. English Arminians came to balance their rejection of the arbitrary grace of predestination with a new found source of grace freely available in the sacraments, which Calvinists had belittled. Hence the preoccupation under Archbishop Laud with altars and private confession before receiving communion, as well as a belief in the absolute necessity of baptism.

By the 1620s the Church of England had been Calvinist in doctrine for approximately sixty years. There had however always been a minority of dissidents, who led a more-or-less clandestine existence; in so far as these had a collective designation in the Elizabethan period they were known as 'Lutherans', after the second-generation followers of Luther who had rejected Calvinist predestinarian teaching. Not until Bancroft did the English 'Lutherans' find a champion holding high office and, as we have noted, not even he was strong enough to swim against the Calvinist tide. But after Bancroft's death in 1610 other lesser figures emerged to lead what it now becomes proper to call the Arminian party within the Church of England. The most powerful member of this early Arminian leadership was Bishop Richard Neile, although it also included Bishops Andrewes, Buckeridge and Overall; Laud was still a relatively obscure figure, dependent on Neile's patronage. They were not allowed to air their Arminian views in print, but managed to register them in a variety of covert ways. For example, in 1617, Neile, on his translation to the bishopric of Durham, had the communion table transformed into an altar at the east end of the cathedral and supported Laud in a like action the same year at Gloucester, where the latter was dean. A few years later Overall and Andrewes can be found advocating the novel practice of private confession before receiving the communion. As Laud was to say, during the 1630s, 'the altar is the greatest place of God's residence upon earth, greater than the pulpit; for there 'tis *Hoc est corpus meum*, This is my body; but in the other it is at most but *Hoc est verbum meum*, This is my word.' Such a view involved the replacement of preaching as the normal vehicle of saving grace, and one restricted in its application to the elect saints, by sacraments which conferred grace indiscriminately; baptism of all infants, without qualification, began the process of salvation, and this was to be followed by the regular receiving of communion as a result of which all partakers, provided they confessed past sins, were renewed in grace. This flank attack on predestinarian Calvinism has misled historians into thinking that the Dutch and English Arminian movements were unconnected. In fact both Arminian parties considered themselves to be engaged in a mutual duel with Calvinism; as early as 1605 the views of Arminius were being cited with approval by anti-Calvinists in Cambridge, and the Dutch Arminians can be found from 1613 until the eve of the Synod of Dort appealing for help to Arminian bishops like Andrewes and Overall. But the latter were powerless to intervene in the United Provinces, engaged as they were in their own English struggle for survival.

If the situation was ever to alter in favour of the English Arminians, their best hope lay in trying to capture the mind of the King or at least that of the royal favourite. This was the course on which they embarked, during the aftermath of the Synod of Dort. Neile was the chief intermediary between the Arminians and King James, while Laud came to play an equivalent role in Buckingham's entourage. Apart from direct theological argument in favour of Arminianism, one powerful lever was to suggest that Calvinist conformists were Puritans at heart and as such politically subversive, or again that predestinarian Calvinism lent itself to so much popular misunderstanding that its widespread propagation inevitably led to religious conflict. By 1624 arguments of this kind seem to have affected adversely James's attitude towards Calvinism. Fear of approaching death may also have helped sap his confidence in deterministic teaching, for should doubt as to whether one was an elect saint ever become unbearable, there was always the Arminian possibility of denying that the predestinarian scheme was true. As regards Buckingham, opportunism was the most effective argument for his listening sympathetically to the Arminians. In 1624 he was identified with war against Spain, and was temporarily the hero of the parliamentary and ultra-Protestant camp. Buckingham was well aware however that the situation could rapidly change and a need arise for new allies. His willingness to support the Arminian Laud, while at the same time patronising the 'Puritan' Preston, was part of a double insurance policy for the future.

It was in this more hopeful atmosphere that the Arminian party decided on a test case. This took the form of publishing a book in 1624, by the Arminian Richard Montagu, which while ostensibly answering Roman Catholic criticisms of the Church of England also rejected predestinarian Calvinism, on the ground that this was no part of the teaching enshrined in the Thirty-Nine Articles. The interpretation of these articles was and still is debatable, but not only were Bishop Neile and his chaplains able to get Montagu's book, the New Gag, past the censor; they also managed to prevent its subsequent suppression. In terms of previous Arminian experience in England this was a dramatic breakthrough. Outraged Calvinist clergy appealed to Parliament; John Pym took up their cause in the House of Commons, and Archbishop Abbot made representations to King James. The only result was a royal request that Richard Montagu clarify his views by writing a second book. Yet it soon became clear that the final arbiter of England's theological fate would be the heir to the throne, Prince Charles. Prior to his accession some observers considered Charles to be inclined towards Puritanism, but those closer to him, among them the Arminian Mathew Wren, claimed the reverse was true and that on this score his reign would contrast with James's. Wren's prediction was to prove abundantly true, for King Charles became the architect of an Arminian revolution which had at most been dimly foreshadowed in the last year of his father's reign. As the House of Commons was to complain in 1629: 'some prelates, near the King, having gotten the chief administration of ecclesiastical affairs under his Majesty, have discountenanced and hindered the preferment of those that are orthodox [i.e. Calvinist], and favoured such as are contrary.'[12]

The suddenness of James's death in March 1625 seems to have taken most people by surprise. Buckingham survived as royal favourite, but it was now Charles who increasingly made the religious pace. The new King had never apparently been a Calvinist; certainly a decisive bias in favour of Arminianism became clear during the first few months of his reign. Calvinist bishops were excluded from the royal counsels, and in July 1625 the Arminian Richard Montagu was placed under Charles's personal protection. In February of the following year Buckingham, clearly acting with the approval of Charles, chaired a debate at York House on the subject of Montagu's writings, in the course of which he made plain his Arminian sympathies. The Arminian Bishop Buckeridge was pitted against the Calvinist Bishop Morton, and during their exchanges the question arose as to how predestinarian doctrine could be reconciled with Prayer Book teaching on the sacraments of baptism and communion. 'What,' exclaimed Morton, 'will you have the grace of God tied to sacraments?' Buckeridge's seconder, Dean White of Carlisle, replied that all baptised infants were 'made the sons of God by adoption', and Buckingham told Morton that he 'disparaged his own ministry, and did . . . debase the sacrament'. White further argued that the Synod of Dort, by limiting Christ's redemption to the elect, had overthrown the sacrament of communion; he asked how on such predestinarian assumptions could ministers 'say to all communicants whatsoever, "The Body of our Lord which was given for thee", as we are bound to say? Let the opinion of the Dortists be admitted, and the tenth person in the Church shall not have been redeemed.' This clash of interpretation underlines the sacramental emphasis of the English Arminian rejection of Calvinism, whereby the Prayer Book was thrown into the scales against the Calvinist interpretation of the Thirty-Nine Articles which had been so prevalent in Elizabethan and Jacobean times.[13]

The York House conference was however far from being a mere wrangle among theologians. It had been called at the request of Viscount Saye and the Earl of Warwick, who were two of the government's most prominent critics and subsequently leaders of the Parliamentary party in the Civil War. Moreover Bishop Morton's seconder at the conference was the 'Puritan' John Preston, and their ability to collaborate in this fashion exemplified the sixty-year-old shared Calvinist assumptions which were now at risk. Immediately after the conference, the Arminian John Cosin was reporting that the King 'swears his perpetual patronage of our cause', and the rebuff that Calvinism received at York House was the signal for the House of Commons to begin impeachment proceedings against Buckingham for alleged gross mismanagement of the government. The fiction was maintained by the opposition that Buckingham's policies were distinct from those of the Crown, but this became increasingly unconvincing especially as regards religion. In June 1626 Buckingham was foisted on Cambridge University as chancellor, and all predestinarian teaching was forthwith forbidden. This was backed up by a royal proclamation which effectively outlawed Calvinism on a national basis. The London and Cambridge printing presses rapidly succumbed. At Oxford University however under the chancellorship of the Calvinist third Earl of Pembroke predestinarian views were preached and printed for another two years. But even Oxford yielded when in late 1628 Charles reissued the Thirty-Nine Articles with a prefatory declaration which insisted on their 'literal and grammatical' sense and commanded 'that all further curious search be laid aside, and these disputes shut up in God's promises, as they be generally set forth to us in holy scriptures'. As Prideaux the Oxford Regius Professor of divinity put it, 'we are concluded under an anathema to stand to the Synod of Dort against the Arminians'.[14]

Reaction in Parliament to this Arminianisation of the Church of England became increasingly strident, and the situation was made worse by the readiness of the Arminians to brand their Calvinist opponents as Puritans. We know from Laud's diary that in 1626 he had been promised the succession to Canterbury, and from this date he comes into prominence as the chief religious spokesman of the government. His sermon at the opening of Charles's second parliament in February 1626 was remarkable for its aggressive tone. He conjured up the vision of a presbyterian conspiracy, aiming at the overthrow of church and state. 'They, whoever they be, that would overthrow *sedes ecclesia*, the seats of ecclesiastical government, will not spare (if ever they get power) to have a pluck at the throne of David. And there is not a man that is for parity, all fellows in the Church, but he is not for monarchy in the State'. The reply of Pym and numerous other Calvinist members of the House of Commons was that on the contrary they were the true orthodox loyalists and that the new Arminian religion was both hetero-dox and the means of introducing Roman Catholicism into England. Some went further and claimed that the denouement would be the murder of the king at the hands of Jesuit-inspired plotters. They took particular exception to Richard Montagu's use of the term Puritan – a use shared by Laud who in 1624 had written on the subject of 'doctrinal Puritanism'. A Commons committee reported in 1625 that Montagu 'saith there are Puritans in heart' and that 'bishops may be Puritans'; since Montagu also defined predestinarian Calvinists as Puritans, the committee were quite correct to conclude that 'by his opinion we may be all Puritans'. More generally the Commons appealed to recent his-tory in justification of their Calvinist exposition of English religion.[15]

Arminianism was of course only one among a number of reasons for the breakdown of relations between Charles and his parliaments in the late 1620s, but some idea of its relative importance is conveyed by the last parliament before the Personal Rule, that of 1628-9. The first session was largely taken up with the Petition of Right, in an attempt to prevent any future resort by the crown to forced loans, but the second session saw Arminianism as an issue taking precedence over other questions; charges of heterodoxy were levelled at Neile and Laud, who had both been made Privy Councillors in early 1627, and it was claimed the path of ecclesiastical preferment was blocked to all but men of their persuasion. The debate on Arminianism was opened on 26 January 1629 by Francis Rous. The issue he said was 'right of religion . . . and this right, in the name of this nation, I this day claim, and desire that there may be a deep and serious consideration of the violation of it'. The violations, he thought, reduced to two, consisting of both a growth of Catholicism and Arminianism, the latter being 'an error that maketh the grace of God lackey it after the will of man, that maketh the sheep to keep the shepherd, that maketh mortal seed of an immortal God'. Moreover he claimed that the two phenomena were biologically connected, 'for an Arminian is the spawn of a Papist', and it was now high time for the Commons to covenant together in defence of true religion. Arminianism and the more mundane subject of tunnage and poundage were the main items of the session until it was forcibly terminated on 2 March. Rous and all the other contributors to the debate on religion, with one Arminian exception, spoke as Calvinist episcopalians. The rise of Arminianism was seen as a function of clerical pretentiousness, but was not yet considered to discredit the episcopal order as such. Indeed Sir John Eliot, speaking of Richard Montagu who had been consecrated a bishop in August 1628, said 'I reverence the order, I honour not the man'. But this reverence was subject to the continued existence of other bishops 'that openly show their hearts to the Truth'.[16]

John Pym was not given to the rhetoric of Eliot and Rous, but he more than any other M.P. inspired the Commons' case against Arminianism. From 1624 to 1629 he can be found chairing committees, delivering reports, and preparing impeachment charges on the Arminian question. Like many of his fellow M.P.s, Pym had imbibed Calvinism both in the home and at university. For them cynical calculations of the kind made by Buckingham were not a primary motive, nor in most cases did their religious stance disguise materialistic hopes of stripping the church of its remaining wealth. Nevertheless speeches on the floor of the House of Commons were not made *in vacuo*, and it is therefore particularly interesting to penetrate where possible behind the public image. While this cannot on present material be done for Pym, considerable evidence has survived for Oliver St. John who was to inherit the leadership of the Long Parliament on Pym's death in 1643. St. John, who was about fourteen years younger than Pym, had been a pupil of Preston at Cambridge, and there still exists a religious commonplace book which he kept during the 1620s and early 1630s. This allows for a reconstruction of his beliefs before the Civil War experience intervened, and an illuminating portrait emerges. He appears quite prepared to accept the order of episcopacy and has no objection to ceremonial conformity, in both cases quoting with approval the views of Bishop Davenant. Especially noticeable however is his dominating concern with predestinarian theology, Calvinist views being listed at length and their opposites labelled as 'heterodox'. Although he seems to agree with

William Prynne's hostile views on the subject of bowing at the name of Jesus, so did Archbishop Abbot. The only other signs of Puritanism are some doubts about whether clergymen might hold civil office, and strong disapproval of men growing their hair long or any similar marks of what St. John calls 'effeminacy'.[17]

All the indications are that Pym's brand of Puritanism was much the same as that of St. John. This is supported by a mass of material relating to the fourth earl of Bedford, who was both St. John's employer and Pym's close associate. The evidence, again consisting of commonplace books, has only recently become available to historians and investigation is not yet complete. Like St. John, Bedford appears to be a firm Calvinist and much exercised about the predestinarian controversy. At the same time he does not think of himself as a Puritan, whom at one point he dismisses as a person who 'will eat his red herring on Christmas day, and his roast beef on Good Friday'. He sees Arminianism leading logically to Catholicism, writing of the former as 'the little thief put into the window of the church to unlock the door', and cites Bishop Williams against the altar-wise position of the communion table. Unfortunately such entries cannot be dated as accurately as those from St. John, and the *terminus ad quem* is Bedford's death from smallpox in 1641. Thus it is not clear from how long before the Long Parliament dates his dislike of lordly bishops. He writes, or quotes from some anonymous authority, that 'lordship [was] forbidden to the apostles, Matth. 20.25, therefore dars't thou assume it?' But he also notes that when the Hussites thrust out bishops there was left 'neither bishop nor earl'. His general social conservatism and concern to preserve the aristocratic order are revealed in a number of passages, as for instance when considering the rise of favourites or quoting Viscount Saye on the ambitions of plebeians. Bedford perhaps carried the greatest weight among the leaders of the opposition to Charles I. His religious views seem to have been fairly typical of the opposition leadership as a whole, although Saye, his son Nathaniel Fiennes, and Lord Brooke all held more radical beliefs. Their families, who tended to intermarry, sometimes had formidable Calvinist matriarchs in the background like Elizabeth Clinton, countess of Lincoln. It was she who campaigned against the upper class practice of putting children out to wet nurses on the ground, among others, that the infant might be 'one of God's very elect . . . to whom to be a nursing mother, is a queen's honour'. Her son, the fourth earl of Lincoln, was also a pupil of the 'Puritan' Preston at Cambridge, and married a daughter of Viscount Saye. He distinguished himself by raising troops to fight for the recovery of the Palatinate, and in 1626 refused to contribute to the forced loan. Not very surprisingly he ended by siding against the King in the Civil War. Another Calvinist bluestocking, this time from the upper gentry, was Lady Mary Vere, wife of the hero of the siege of Mannheim and instrumental in securing the archbishopric of Armagh for James Ussher in 1624. Ussher was a close friend of some of the leading Puritan nonconformists, and his scheme for limited episcopacy put forward in the first months of the Long Parliament looked briefly like proving an acceptable compromise. With the subsequent destruction of the hierarchy he was appointed, at the instigation of St. John, lecturer at Lincoln's Inn. Indeed the 'godly bishop' long remained a legitimate Puritan aspiration.[18]

Among the clergy in the late 1620s, as with the laity, the hallmark of opposition to the Arminian policy of the government was still Calvinist episcopalianism. Puritan nonconformity although subsumed within this Calvinist episcopalianism was not the question at issue. As for presbyterianism, it was a negligible element in the situation, being confined to a handful of survivors from Elizabethan days. Nevertheless, it has been argued by Christopher Hill that English Puritanism in the first decades of the seventeenth century was taking on a new and looser institutional form, along the lines of congregationalism *within* episcopacy. In so far as this was the case, it still implies a compatibility of religious approach prior to the Arminian 1630s. The continued failure however of Calvinist episcopalianism to withstand the pressures of Arminianism was bound in the longer term to result in its being discredited as a viable church system. Charles's decision in 1629 to rule without parliament brought that time nearer, for it meant there was now no court of Calvinist appeal left. In 1630 died the third earl of Pembroke, who had been the most influential Calvinist among the king's privy councillors. He was moreover succeeded as chancellor of Oxford by Laud, who since 1628 had been controlling the London printing press as Bishop of London. The York primacy had been filled with a succession of Arminians since the Calvinist Matthew's death in 1628, and from 1632 was occupied by Neile. At Canterbury the Calvinist Abbot, in disgrace ever since refusing to license a sermon in support of forced loans in 1627, lingered on until 1633 when he was succeeded by Laud. By this process the court increasingly isolated itself from Calvinist opinion in the country. Arminian doctrines were now freely published while Calvinism languished in silence. An instance of the lengths to which propaganda went is supplied by the 1633 edition of the standard Latin–English Dictionary, compiled by Francis Holyoke. Published at Oxford and dedicated to Laud, this new edition contained for the first time the word *Praedestinatiani*, who were defined as 'a kind of heretics that held fatal predestination of every particular matter person or action, and that all things came to passe, and fell out necessarily; especially touching the salvation and damnation of particular men'. While Calvinists would regard this as misrepresenting their views, the definition was clearly aimed at them. This is confirmed by its citation in a book of 1635 by the Arminian Edmund Reeve, called *The Communion Catechisme Expounded*. Dedicating the work to Bishop Wright of Coventry and Lichfield, he claimed Bishops Overall and Buckeridge as his mentors. The exposition, which grew from the needs of his congregation at Hayes in Middlesex, contains an explicit refutation of predestinarian Calvinism and is a typical product of the decade.

Theory went hand in hand with practice. In November 1633, three months after Laud became Archbishop of Canterbury, King Charles by act of Privy Council established the precedent that all parochial churches should follow the by then general cathedral practice of placing communion tables altar-wise at the east end of chancels. We have already had cause to comment on the sacramental undermining by English Arminians of the Calvinist theology of grace, and on the basis of this Privy Council ruling Arminianism during the 1630s was made manifest throughout every parish in England, the sacrament of the altar becoming henceforth a propitiation for the sins of all partakers. These were the years too which saw an unprecedented onslaught on the lecturing movement, the *cause célèbre* being the dissolution of the Feoffees for Impropriations in 1633. The Feoffees were a trust, administered by a group of clergy, lawyers and merchants, and set up in an attempt to improve the level of clerical incomes. Laud, supported by Charles, claimed that a plot was involved to destroy episcopal jurisdiction. This sinister interpretation was not however shared by bishops like Morton, who in 1630 can be found recommending an impoverished curate to the charity of the Feoffees. Morton was, as we have seen, a Calvinist, and did not agree with Laud's dictum that the altar took precedence over the pulpit. The attitude of the hierarchy to lecturers was in fact largely a matter of theological perspective. From a Calvinist standpoint preaching, whether by a beneficed incumbent or a lecturer, was the chief means of salvation. Only an episcopate dominated by Arminians could contemplate with equanimity, and indeed pleasure, a diminution in the number of sermons preached. Similarly Arminian bishops had little compunction in silencing nonconforming lecturers, whereas their Calvinist predecessors had so far as possible avoided this extreme.[19]

This change in attitude was not confined to the treatment of lecturers, but extended to nonconformity in general, and not only did the breaking of the Calvinist theological bond lead to the stricter enforcement of conformity: nonconformity itself acquired a much wider definition. Nonconformist offences now included expounding the Thirty-Nine Articles in a Calvinist sense or any form of predestinarian preaching, objecting to the new ceremonies associated with the transformation of communion tables into altars, and refusal to implement the Declaration of Sports which was reissued by Charles in 1633. The surviving Calvinist bishops found themselves in an alien world, and were distrusted by their colleagues; the Arminian Laud went so far as to put a spy on the tail of the Calvinist Morton. We have already noted that the English Arminians redefined Puritanism so as to include doctrinal Calvinism and this elicited from Bishop Davenant of Salisbury the anguished complaint: 'Why that should now be esteemed Puritan doctrine, which those held who have done our Church the greatest service in beating down Puritanism, or why men should be restrained from teaching that doctrine hereafter, which hitherto has been generally and publicly maintained, (wiser men perhaps may) but I cannot understand.' When however in 1633 the Calvinist Davenant, who was also a sabbatarian, had to discipline the recorder of Salisbury, Henry Sherfield, for destroying an allegedly idolatrous window in a church, doubts were expressed by his cathedral dean as to whether he would take a sufficiently firm line. Hardly surprisingly the 1630s as a whole saw a great increase in the number of prosecutions for Puritanism, an indirect measure of this being the large scale emigration to New England. In addition to creating widespread resentment of the episcopal hierarchy, these persecuting activities generated a Puritan militancy which in the early 1640s was to erupt in the shape of presbyterianism and congregationalism.[20]

Arminian clerics also revealed themselves as very hostile to lay intervention in church matters. This was partly because parliament had proved so antagonistic, and they were in any case completely dependent on royal protection, but there was also a novel sacerdotal element in their teaching whereby the priestly replaced the preaching function. Evidence exists to suggest that one of the factors involved here was a desire to compensate for a sense of social inferiority. Certainly the Calvinist bishops had better blood relations with the gentry and aldermanic classes than did their Arminian successors, and there was some substance to Lord Brooke's derogatory remarks in 1641 about low-born prelates. At the same time the reassertion of sacramental grace lent itself to the view that clerics were almost a caste apart, but because of their magical not their preaching roles. Indeed many English Arminians consciously regarded themselves as engaged in a counter-reforming movement dedicated to undoing the Protestant damage of the Reformation.

While English Arminianism did not automatically result in the theoretical advancement of royal absolutism in the secular sphere, the injunction 'render unto Caesar' might seem a fitting counterpart to the idea of a holy priesthood with consecrated property rights. The Calvinist opposition however conveniently forgot that during the debates on the Petition of Right the Arminian Bishop Harsnett had spoken out in defence of the subject's liberties, and instead they remembered the stance of Archbishop Abbot, in condemning the arguments of Sibthorpe and Mainwaring for unparliamentary taxation. Indeed as early as the 1590s Abbot had taught that 'God is better pleased, when good things shall be commanded, first by the highest in place, and then after it shall be added, by the Lords spiritual and temporal, and by the assent of the commons. And Princes which are gracious do never grieve at this, and wise men do love that style, when all is not appropriated to one, but there is a kind of parting.' Yet a decade or so earlier Archbishop Sandys, a man of similar theological colour to Abbot, had preached that taxation was a tribute due to the King and not a gift freely given. Thus there was an element of accident in the Arminian and royalist partnership. But in practice the religious policy of King Charles meant that during the Personal Rule absolutism and Arminianism became closely identified in the popular mind.[21]

On the future Parliamentarian side there did however exist a positive link with Calvinism, concerning the right of political resistance. Calvinists held no monopoly of such views, but among Protestants they had developed the most explicit body of teaching on the subject. In England by far the most important vehicle of their thought was the Genevan annotated version of the Bible, which among other things had a predestinarian catechism bound up with it. Not always entirely consistent and stopping considerably short of an outright doctrine of tyrannicide, the Genevan commentators were prepared to admit the legitimacy of resistance to magistrates in certain circumstances, especially when the issue was religion. Their medium was Biblical history, notably that contained in the Old Testament, and the use they made of it led King James to insist that the new Authorised translation of the Bible should contain no marginalia at all, apart from variant readings and cross-references. Illustrative of the political tendency of the Genevan annotations is that Ecclesiastes, viii. 3. had been glossed as 'withdraw not thy self lightly from the obedience of thy prince,' and the famous opening verse of Romans xiii, 'Let every soul be subject unto the higher powers . . .' was described as relating to a 'private man', thus in principle leaving inferior magistrates free to act against erring superiors.[22]

Despite the existence of an official rival from 1611 onwards, the Genevan Bible long retained its popularity, being printed latterly in the Low Countries with the fictitious date 1599 on its title page. In origin the Genevan version was the work of a group of Marian exiles. They had included Goodman and Knox, who were both authors of works advocating the right of armed defence, particularly against heretical and persecuting rulers. Although the product of a specific exilic situation, ideas of this type survived the turn of the century, by which date however they were usually confined to discussions about continental Protestantism. Thus in 1603 Robert Abbot, brother of the future Archbishop, dedicated a book to King James which contained a defence of both Dutch and French Protestant rebels. At the same time there existed a competing body of passive-resistance theory, against which the only regular antidote was the Genevan Bible. With the subsequent rise of English Arminianism, Calvinist ideas of resistance took on new domestic relevance; as early as 1632 a Puritan lecturer, Nathaniel Barnard, dared to make the connection in a sermon. After the actual outbreak of hostilities, one of those to be found defending the Parliamentary cause on religious grounds was Stephen Marshall, who has been described as 'the most famous political parson of the Revolution'. Eschewing legal arguments, Marshall cited Biblical precedent and among more recent authorities Bishop Abbot.[23]

Perhaps even without a rebellion in Scotland the finances of the Personal Rule would have foundered on their own inadequacies, and a parliament have had to be summoned. What however until recently has largely gone unnoticed, is the part played in the Scottish disturbances by Arminianism. The Scots at this time are usually thought of as intransigent presbyterians for whom Charles's attempt to impose an English-style prayer book was simply an excuse to throw off the whole episcopalian system. But it has been pointed out that many of the members of the Glasgow Assembly, which in 1638 abolished bishops, had never known a fully presbyterian church. Moreover someone like Robert Baillie, who is traditionally thought of as a presbyterian diehard, was even at that date not prepared to deny that a form of episcopacy had scriptural warrant. Arminianism however appears to have been the deciding factor. The Glasgow Assembly explicitly modelled itself on the Synod of Dort and listened to a series of harangues on the Arminian question. What really seems to have rankled was not so much the office of bishop but that the hierarchy were mostly Arminians. Again and again this charge features in the indictments, and heterodox teaching on predestination clearly is meant. The dual association with unpopular royalist policies in the secular field and with Arminianism in the religious meant that episcopacy went down even faster in Scotland than it was to in England where the system was more indigenous.[24]

The Short Parliament of 1640, called to subsidise the suppression of the Scottish rebellion, did not last long enough for the religious question fully to come out in the open, although 'innovations in matters of religion' were high on Pym's list of grievances. The fact that after the dissolution of parliament the convocation of clergy continued in session and proceeded to enact a series of canons which included a strong statement of royal absolution, all fostered a mounting hostility to the episcopate. Nor was the example of Scotland lost on the English opposition, and increasingly too a presbyterian model in religion became the price of Scottish support. When the Long Parliament assembled later in the year more radical pressures were brought to bear by the London populace, and the Root and Branch Petition of December, which called for the abolition of bishops, in part represented such interests. Even here however it was the woeful results of episcopacy, with Arminianism taking a prominent place, that were stressed rather than the essential unlawfulness of the order. Moreover, Calvinists like Archbishop Ussher and Bishop Morton meeting in committee during March 1641 with Puritan ministers such as Marshall and Calamy looked like agreeing on a common reformist platform. But the basic Arminian intransigence of King Charles, combined with the sheer speed of events, made religious compromises of this kind unworkable. Conciliation was overtaken by the drift to war.[25]

As an old man looking back on the Civil War at the end of the century, Philip fourth Lord Wharton, who had fought against the king, claimed that 'a hundred to one of the Calvinists . . . joined the parliamentarians'.

The process which had brought this alleged situation about was highly complex, and even Wharton would not have seriously maintained that all they were fighting about was Calvinism. At the same time the propaganda put out by Parliamentary army officers in the early stages of the war does suggest a high degree of religious motivation. This declaration of sentiments took the visual form of battle standards flown by the captains of each cavalry troop, who incidentally all claimed to be gentlemen. While Magna Carta and a blood-stained head, probably Strafford's, were occasionally chosen as symbols, the dominating motif was the Bible with accompanying slogans such as 'Verbum Dei', 'Sacra Scriptura' and 'Jehova Nisi'. Also depicted were bishops tumbling from their thrones with the caption 'Antichrist Must Down', a lethal rain of arrows labelled 'Contra Impios' and cloud-wreathed anchors illustrating the assertion 'Only in Heaven'. Comparable propaganda on the Royalist side was of a much more secular kind, displaying the insignia of monarchy or satirising the 'roundhead' opposition. One popular emblem was a pack of hounds all barking 'Pym'. Revealingly, Charles described his opponents as consisting mainly of 'Brownists, Anabaptists and Atheists'. Such was the gulf of misunderstanding that had opened up between the Arminian king and his Calvinist subjects.[26]

In terms of English Protestant history the charge in 1640 that King Charles and Archbishop Laud were religious innovators is irrefutable. The reaction provoked however by the Arminian revolution was of such violence that it could be transformed with relative ease into a call for 'root and branch' remedies, and presbyterianism emerge as the cure of Arminian disease. Thus what had begun as a counter-revolution itself became radicalised.

5. Fear of Popery

ROBIN CLIFTON

I

Among London newspapers and pamphlets published after 1642 no explanation of the Civil War was more common than the assumption that Catholics and Catholicism were in some way to be found at the heart of it. Taking their cue from the House of Commons, which reiterated at every crisis that it was acting 'to maintain and defend . . . the true reformed Protestant religion . . . against all Popery and popish innovations',[1] almost every despatch reporting the progress of the armies described Charles's forces as 'papistical' or 'jesuitised' or 'Romish'. The writers recorded incessantly the crucifixes found on royalist dead, the 'mass-books' found in the enemy baggage, and the supposed frequency of Mass in the King's garrisons. From every town near the Irish Sea enormous and largely mythical reinforcements of savage Irish Catholics were reported, hurrying to join the King. The Venetian ambassador dryly calculated that by the end of 1643 alone, 60,000 men had been added to Charles's army in this way – sufficient to treble or quadruple his actual strength. The number of English papists in London grew with a speed no less phenomenal: in the summer of 1643 *Speciall Passages* assured its readers that 'it is conceived that there were not so many of them when they ruled the Kingdom'. Other papers carried reports of royalists charging into battle with cries of 'In with Queen Mary' and waving flags bearing 'the inscription of the Popes Motto', doubtless buoyed up with the news that Prince Rupert was about to be replaced by the legendary Piccolomini as commander of the King's forces.[2]

Few pamphleteers however took the trouble to show in detail precisely *how* Catholics had started the war. At most they would refer to their 'devilish malice against the intended reformation of the true Protestant religion'; or find 'one disease' beneath the sudden epidemic of conflict in the British Isles – war between Scotland and England, rebellion in Ireland, and Civil War in England – all within the space of just three years. More typical (and requiring less hard fact and dialectical expertise) were general denunciatory pieces against Catholicism. A typical six-week period in September–October 1641 saw the publication of a 'threefold Plot of Treason' against England received from a friar supposedly on the point of death and two non-specific confessions from an apostate priest, while other pamphlets contained details of an alleged plot against London, and a report of a Vatican meeting summoned, it seemed, with the sole purpose of destroying the English heresy. The Pope Joan legend was rehearsed once more and four slightly more sophisticated attacks on popish dogma also appeared.

Crude, repetitious and essentially unconvincing though these pamphlet and newspaper accounts appear to a modern reader, contemporary royalists were plainly afraid that they would be believed. Charles was prevailed upon to ban by proclamation Catholics from his army (officially at least), and to protest upon the Sacrament that his purpose in taking up arms was to defend 'the true Protestant religion'. One of his Secretaries of State noted that 'the Alarm of Popish plots amuse and fright the people here more than anything', and several other important royalists lamented the public consequences of the Catholics all-too-evidently present in the King's camp.[3] Recollecting the situation some time later Edward Hyde believed that his master's association with Catholicism had consequences little short of disastrous:

> The imputation raised by Parliament upon the King of an intention to bring in, or . . . of conniving at and tolerating Popery, did make a deep impression on the people generally, . . . [for] their strength and number were then thought so vast within the Kingdom . . . that if they were drawn together and armed under what pretext soever, they might not be willing to submit to the power which raised them, but be able to give the law both to King and Parliament.[4]

Thus one of Charles's advisers most noted for his sharp analysis and cool judgement in political matters. The reason why royalists like Hyde worried over even the most fantastic tales of Catholic involvement in the war had little to do with the inherent plausibility of such rumours. As the King's supporters well knew, seventeenth-century English Protestants were educated from birth to make certain assumptions about the nature of the Catholic religion and to expect certain specific patterns of behaviour from papists, and it was within the framework of these beliefs that accusations of popish responsibility for the war were heard and believed. The characteristics of this education must be indicated to explain at least in part the otherwise remarkable gullibility of Protestants where their Catholic recusant neighbours were concerned, and particularly to show why so many contemporaries suspected a popish hidden hand guiding events in the British Isles in the 1630s and 1640s.

II

Full understanding of Protestant emotional attitudes towards Catholics at this time must start from the obvious proposition that Protestants were not taught to regard Catholicism simply as an alternative, or even as an aberrant, form of Christianity. In pamphlet and sermon popery was presented as essentially the *debasement* of Christ's teaching, a total and blasphemous perversion of Apostolic practice. As such it was far more repugnant and damnable than any form of paganism. It was debased and perverted because successive generations of believers had each slightly modified the uncompromising message of Christ in order first to permit, and then to licence, their worldly pursuits and pleasures. 'Of all religions, to the carnal man none is so pleasant as Popery is, in which be so many kinds of satisfaction to be obtained':[5] William Perkins, one of the Puritan writers most influential in the early seventeenth century, here expressed a very basic Protestant attitude.

Reformers explained the contrast between early Christianity and the corrupt Catholicism which was its lineal descendant by arguing that the natural weaknesses of Fallen Man led the clergy, the laity and the Papacy gradually to remodel Christian religion to accommodate their several interests and pleasures. The process of accommodation was slow and imperceptible: it occurred not through apostasy on a spectacular scale, but rather by a slower and far more insidious weakening to the pressures of the world and the flesh. 'Nothing in popery [is] so gross', wrote the Puritan Richard Sibbes, 'but had some small beginnings, which being neglected by those that should have watched over the church, grew at length insufferable'.[6]

This was particularly true of one aspect of Catholicism which was for Protestants possible the most appalling feature of that faith – 'idol-worship'. By this was meant not simply the veneration and intercessory prayers addressed to images of the saints and the Virgin, but also the ceremony of the Mass where a priest claimed to create the bodily presence of God. On the use of images and idols first-generation Anglicans were no less intransigent than Puritan writers. The *Book of Homilies* – the very widely used collection of sermons prepared by Elizabethan bishops to be read by clergy too unlearned to write their own – referred extensively to Catholicism's 'idolatry'. The Homily 'Of Good Works' postulated an innate 'corrupt inclination of man, ever superstitiously given to make new honouring of God [out] of his own head'. This weakness led medieval Catholics, as it had led the Jews under Moses and Aaron, to worship idols of wood and stone shaped by man, ignoring God's Commandments. The Homily 'On Idolatry' traced an exact parallel between this desire to go whoring after strange gods and man's restless sexual appetite: just as man will inevitably come to fornication in the presence of a whore, it was argued, so the mere existence of images would tempt him beyond respect for what they represented to worship of the statue or painting itself. Unless they exercise strict self-control men everywhere – in the time of the Jews, the pagan Romans or the early Christians – derive greater satisfaction from worshipping visible gods than the immeasurable Jehovah, obtain more comfort by trying to coerce miracles from these deities by magic than from worshipping the implacable and inscrutable God of Scripture.[7]

Neither the Anglican bishops nor their Puritan opponents believed that man bore the entire responsibility for idolatry. All forms of worship and veneration belong to God solely. Consequently, it was argued, the Devil ceaselessly tries to appropriate that worship which man owes to his Maker alone. The Angel in *Revelations* refused to permit John to kneel before him, saying that Satan desired nothing so much as to see this honour removed from God. In the temptation on the mountain Satan offered Christ all earthly kingdoms if he would worship him. To contemporary writers the most heinous aspect of witchcraft was the worship given by witches to the Devil: this was the ultimate blasphemy against God.

Catholicism's elaborate cycle of observances, its complex ritual and dramatic ceremonial, drew biting criticism from most Protestant writers. All such devices had been added to the original simple practices of the apostles by later generations of priests with no Scriptural justification whatever, making Catholicism essentially a religion devised by man and not ordained by God. This complex ceremonial resulted in part from the laity's weak preference for a spectacular and visible religion, but equally relevant was the clergy's desire for power. Catholic ritual was directed towards elevating and sanctifying the position of the priest *vis-à-vis* the laity, thus confirming his authority over them. In Sibbes's words:

If you ask the reason that raised popery to be so gaudy as it is, they saw the people of the world fools [sic], and knew that children must have baubles, and fools trifles, and empty men must have empty things; they saw what pleased them and the cunning clergy thought, we will have a religion fit for you.[8]

Hence the accusation made by all English critics of Catholicism, regardless of their position within the Church of England, that popish priests deliberately maintained and fostered the ignorance of lay papists on all matters of substance in religion. These false shepherds cynically imperilled the souls of their congregations, encouraging superstitious beliefs and practices to secure the docile and submissive following which would willingly gratify their lust for power and their taste for worldly ease. Emphasis on the clerical appetite for power merged readily with a spontaneous popular anti-clericalism evident in the late medieval world, and which first the Henrician reformers and then the puritan preachers had exploited as a powerful if wayward ally. In many respects Jacobean and Caroline anti-Catholicism perpetuated and re-directed pre-Reformation lay antagonism toward the clergy. The linked views that the Catholic laity were deplorably ignorant of the truths of Christianity, and that they were deliberately kept in this condition by a parasitic and power-hungry clergy are regularly found in anti-popish works, but perhaps most frequently in the descriptions of popery recorded by Catholics who had been converted to Protestantism. These publications exercised an influence wholly disproportionate to their number and literary merit, for they were presented as lively and truthful accounts of the enemy camp written by men familiar with its workings. In fact five examples written between 1612 and 1638 informed their readers of nothing which they did not already believe. Pursuing respectability and new patronage, the authors carefully flattered the most basic and best-known Protestant prejudices and preconceptions about Catholicism.

All five apostates wrote vividly of the ignorance and superstition of papists, and the deceits employed by priests to rule the laity. John Gee quoted a priest who allegedly told him that 'they maintain Ignorance to be the Mother of Devotion'. Such frankness seems suspicious and Gee may sometimes have confused what he heard with what he had read. Thus another story he derived from supposedly personal acqaintance concerned a friar who filled his purse by informing his audience 'that whosoever came up with money to the Altar, and would think of any of his dearest friend, whom he thought to be a prisoner in Purgatory should obtain this grace by that indulgence, that at the very instant of the money's thrown in and clinking in the Basin the soul should leap out of Purgatory'. The parallel with the practices of Tel-fer's celebrated indulgence-selling in Luther's Germany is striking and probably not accidental. James Wadsworth, recollecting several years colourfully mis-spent in a Spanish seminary, described the 'sottish credulity' of Catholics who 'make spells of their relics'. He encountered some priests who brazenly invented miraculous tales for the laity saying 'that otherwise there would be no means to govern them, and especially the women, being . . . for the most part addicted to novelties and mirac-ulous events'. Richard Sheldon furnished further examples of priests who drew upon a well-stocked repertoire to gull the superstitious public; while Henry Yaxlee selected as the most obnoxious feature of Catholicism the blind obedience which it imposed on the laity toward their priests; and the Scot Abernethie ('sometime Jesuit') ascribed his conversion to Presbyterianism in the propitious year 1638 to his realisa-tion that popery was 'a superstitious mass of policy under pretext of religion'.[9]

All writers spent some time proving that Catholicism was destructive of a subject's loyalty to his prince, a theme which recurred more fre-quently in the *Book of Homilies* (as fitted a work of the Established Church) than among Puritan writers. The homilists charged Catholicism with perverting Christ's teaching in respect of temporal rulers, pre-senting this as an example of the process whereby popery had adultera-ted all aspects of the Gospel. To argue that in some circumstances the pope could release subjects from their oaths of loyalty, and thus patron-ise rebellion, confirmed Protestant views that Rome pursued supreme worldly power above all else; and it illustrated the way Catholics adapted and re-fashioned Christianity to suit their own needs, once more show-ing it a religion made by man and not derived from God.[10]

No work expressed the political dangers of Catholicism more clearly than John Foxe's *Acts and Monuments of the Christian Reformation*, popularly known as 'The Book of Martyrs'. Found in churches along-side the Scriptures and the Book of Common Prayer, printed and re-printed in numbers second only to the Bible itself, Foxe's work spawned a host of imitators and provided the material for dozens of Rome-baiting pamphlets. Its popularity derived not from the number or vividness of its martyrdom scenes, but rather from Foxe's skill in work-ing events in the reigns of Henry VIII, Mary Tudor and Elizabeth into a convincing and highly chauvinistic interpretation of the whole of English history. England was the Elect Nation, converted to Christianity

in early Apostolic times (and not at the instigation of a Pope five centuries later), degraded by the medieval papacy so that King John was
forced to surrender his kingdom as a fief to Rome, but with Wyclif and
the Lollards the first country in Europe to protest against papal usurpations, and under Henry VIII the first nation in Europe entirely to
throw off the popish thraldom. The Elect Nation then survived fierce
persecution under Mary, and foreign attack under Elizabeth, and it
could expect further severe popish offensives in the future. Its survival
however was guaranteed by God, for England was to play a leading role
in the final downfall of Rome foretold in the *Revelation of St. John*.
Foxe's work intensified anti-Catholic feeling by supplying it with a
pedigree and an historical *rationale*, linking it inextricably with powerful nationalist feeling so that for well over a century after its first publication one of the marks of English nationalism was anti-Catholicism.

One must observe, however, that the thrust of Foxe's argument dealt
with *foreign* Catholics – the Papacy and Continental powers – and not
primarily with the dangers of home-bred papists. The reign of Mary
Tudor exemplified the dangers to Protestants from Catholics in power,
not the dangers from Catholics plotting as a minority to regain power.
Only at the end of the work, in the pages dealing with Elizabeth, was
Foxe's emphasis on the Catholic danger from abroad varied by reference
to the tools of such foreign powers, the English recusants. When Foxe
was long dead, seventeenth-century readers of his work themselves
gradually assumed that England's chief danger came not from Catholic
invasion but from internal conspiracy. Accepting Foxe's basic thesis of
implacable popish hostility to the Elect Nation they brought Rome's
likely methods up to date. In this context Charles' toleration towards
Catholics, the growth of Arminianism which seemed to open a door to
Catholic doctrines of salvation by works, and above all the war with
Scotland, the Irish rebellion and the English Civil War all seemed the
products of deep popish conspiracy. *Acts and Monuments*, like all
successful propaganda, could continue to explain contemporary events
long after the point at which the book's actual narrative came to an end.

Foxe's concept of the Elect Nation pointed towards a catastrophic
end for its enemies, and in particular for its chief enemy the Papacy.
Anglicans, Puritans and apostate Catholics all shared the deep interest
in eschatology which recent research has found in the most moderate
and reputable writers of the time.[11] They laboured to identify the Pope
with the Beast, the Antichrist of St. John's *Revelation*; to show that the
Catholic church was symbolised by the whore; and that contemporary

Rome was Babylon, the city destined for total destruction. Perkins and Sibbes both wrote at length on the *Book of Revelation* and Henry Burton, mutilated by Star Chamber in 1637, contributed a major work on the subject. The interest of the topic lay not only in establishing the date of the world's end and identifying with some precision what disasters would occur meantime and to whom; *Revelations* contained the answer to an obvious and central objection made by Catholics against Protestants. It was surely inconceivable that God should have permitted successive generations to believe the supposedly false and damnable doctrines of Catholicism for over a thousand years without lifting a finger to save these souls. Protestants drew upon *Revelations* to assert that God had indeed allowed most of the Church, for most of its existence, to have been sunk in apostasy. They argued with William Perkins that 'in this Revelation how often is it said, that Antichrist should deceive all the world . . . and that the Church of Christ should be driven into the wilderness . . . and there remain for a space'.[12] Naturally the Pope was not the only candidate for Antichrist's title – Catholic writers suggested the Turk, or a fabulous beast, or the product of a monstrous birth – but the references in *Revelations* to the city of Rome inevitably meant only one thing to most Protestant commentators. And once the Papacy was identified as Antichrist unrelenting hostility was all that could be expected or offered, and the only safe course towards Catholics was to treat them as St. John recommended dealing with those marked by the Beast: 'Come out of her my people that ye be not partakers of her sins, and that ye receive not of her plagues'.*

III

Protestant writers therefore presented Catholicism as a perversion of Christianity, a system of error and idolatry sustained on the one hand by the laity's ignorance and desire for a pleasant life, and on the other by a clerical itch for power. And having been corrupted once and then miraculously purified by God at the Reformation, what was there to prevent Christianity from once more making that slow surrender to the world? The natural promptings of carnal man – for idolatrous worship, for a life of pleasure untroubled by pangs of conscience, for a religion of miracles – were the same from one generation to the next. Consequently the post-Reformation churches could anticipate the

* Dr. Christopher Hill's *Antichrist in Seventeenth Century England* was published too late to be used by Dr. Clifton (Ed.).

same pressures to compromise true religion as the early Church had surrendered to. The panicky depth of opposition to Archbishop Laud's regime can now be fully appreciated. His policies expressed the same attitudes that had corrupted early Christianity. Whether or not Laud *consciously* intended to lead England back to Catholicism was in the last analysis irrelevant since the emphasis placed by Charles I and his Archbishop upon ceremonial, clerical dress, confession, doctrinal Arminianism, and the authority of a priest over laymen would ultimately and inevitably return the Church to its corrupted, pre-Reformation condition. Puritans resisted Laud's practices with a ferocity often apparently disproportionate to the actual measures he proposed because they saw the issue as one of resisting a fatal drift: not the practice in itself but the end to which it pointed occupied their attention.

Opposition to Laudianism was thus distinct from anti-Catholicism. Laud's changes were an expression of precisely that attitude which had debased the Christian Church, turning it into popery. Laudianism was a step on the road to Catholicism, an instalment of corruption; it manifested a willingness to compromise with the world which if not checked, would eventually lead to Catholicism. But anti-Laudianism did undoubtedly stimulate anti-Catholicism. Firstly because both offered the same target for critics (though in different degrees) – the perversion of true religion. Secondly, because of the two men who framed Laudianism, Charles at least conspicuously chose Catholics as his friends and administrators. Lord Treasurer Portland died a Catholic in 1634; Cottington, another Privy Councillor, declared for Catholicism during an illness in 1636; the Bishop of Gloucester asked permission to keep an Italian priest in his house to celebrate Mass; and the King made no secret of his enjoyment of the company of George Con, the first Papal representative to enter England for nearly one hundred years. The King's principal Secretary of State Sir Francis Windebank was rumoured to be a secret Catholic, and converts increased in the Queen's circle under her husband's apparently benign gaze. Laud's hostility to the conversions, his suspicion of the Papal Agent, and his real indifference to Rome were little known outside the court, and when in 1638 he finally secured a proclamation forbidding English Catholics from attending the chapels of the Queen or the foreign ambassadors, Henrietta publicly defied it by accompanying her recent converts to Christmas Mass.

The strength of Catholicism among such influential people – courtiers, aristocracy, gentry – was a principal reason why contemporaries feared it so deeply. Possibly one fifth of the early seventeenth century peerage were papists;[13] and while no estimate can be given of Catholicism's numerical following among the gentry, contemporaries were clearly apprehensive. Catholicism *was* a religion of the gentry. Converts were particularly sought in this class,[14] and priests invariably came from gentry families because only at this level of society did there exist the wealth and connections to send sons abroad to seminaries for training. On their return priests naturally sought out the society they knew, and were almost to a man sheltered in the houses of recusant gentry where they could be passed off as tutors or chaplains, relatives, or visiting gentlemen friends. Outside London among the common people Catholicism gradually died out where there was no local gentry family to shelter a priest.[15] Seventeenth-century Catholicism was thus nucleated about these centres and the number of gentry among its supporters was correspondingly highlighted. In times of national emergency J.P.s regularly received instructions to disarm 'principal recusants', or those 'that are rich and have most power in the counties where they live'.[16]

This pattern of concentration about specific houses also tended to make Catholicism appear in some areas disproportionately alarming in terms of mere numbers. Although recent estimates have put the number of practising Catholics as low as $1\frac{1}{2}\%$ of the total population contemporaries undoubtedly thought the number far larger. They may not have agreed with Gondomar the Spanish ambassador to James I who put the number at 900,000 or one quarter of the whole population, but they would probably have agreed with the papal representatives who suggested a figure of 150,000 to 200,000. Because their numbers were not spread evenly over the countryside but were concentrated in certain pockets, Catholics in some parishes sometimes were (and frequently appeared to be) more numerous than Protestants. The Lancashire village of Formby was 'almost completely Catholic' and this was also true of Clayton-le-Moors in the same county. Both were entirely controlled by a recusant gentry family. Even a small minority was thus capable of inspiring fear locally. When Lord Vaux of Harrowden 'did claim his house to be a parish by itself' his remark held unpleasant overtones for Protestant contemporaries in terms of numerical concentration and unity of purpose.[17]

Only a handful of such Catholic gentry as Lord Vaux in fact ever attempted regicide or rebellion. But the innocent majority found it virtually impossible to convince other Englishmen of their patriotism because no Oath of Allegiance could be devised which would reconcile the conflicting claims to their loyalty of prince and Pope. No ruler of England would accept anything less than an unconditional declaration of loyalty in temporals, and acceptance of the Crown as the supreme head of the English Church. On neither issue could the papacy make concessions. Rome had not abandoned its claim to excommunicate and depose rulers who gravely offended against religion or natural law, and it still asserted ultimate jurisdiction over the lawfulness of oaths, including oaths of loyalty. Furthermore the King of England could not be recognised as the head of any Church because Christ's successor on earth was the Pope.

For both the government and the English Catholics, however, there was sufficient at stake for several attempts to be made to find a way out of this *impasse*. In the last years of Elizabeth's reign a group of secular priests attempted to negotiate some form of toleration with the Privy Council, but although the latter encouraged them the hopes of both parties were destroyed by hostile reaction from Rome and by the death of Elizabeth, which left no member of the government sufficiently sure of James's attitude to try to renew contacts. The next move came from the government when, in the wake of the Gunpowder Plot, a bill requiring an Oath of Allegiance was passed by Parliament. This was devised to test the loyalty of Catholics, and it complemented the Oath of Supremacy which was designed to establish *who* was a Catholic by offering an Oath which no adherent of Rome could accept.

Perhaps inevitably in view of the conspiracy which was its occasion, the Oath of Allegiance also contained phrases difficult for a Catholic to accept: the Papacy's claim to depose monarchs for example was described as 'impious, heretical and damnable'. In two separate Briefs Rome condemned the Oath and explicitly forbade English Catholics to swear it. Nevertheless many priests disobeyed including the Archpriest George Blackwell (head in England of the secular priests' hierarchy). Several others wrote in defence of swearing the Oath and repudiated the doctrine of the papal deposing power. Among laymen the Catholic peerage set a corrosive example: at least sixteen of the twenty recusant lords alive in 1610 are known to have conformed to government wishes.[18]

But many Catholics refused, and by causing the Oath to be offered to condemned priests on the scaffold the Jacobean Privy Council imprinted upon the public mind a powerful image of Catholic disloyalty. (Between 1607 and 1616, for example, thirteen Catholics were executed, and in each case they were offered the Oath on the scaffold.) The nonjurors' motives were the more suspect because educated Protestants were fully aware that the King of France experienced no such difficulty in obtaining an oath of loyalty from his Catholic subjects, papal deposing power and jurisdiction over oaths notwithstanding. Alluding to an English priest, and to a pair of Scottish Catholic lawyers then teaching in France, the Deputy Lieutenants of Staffordshire reminded the Privy Council in 1625 that many English Catholics refused to swear 'notwithstanding Mr. Preston the priest and Barclay the father and son have with many others defended the taking of the said oath to be lawful'.[19] Charles I believed that the majority of his Catholic subjects wished to swear and spent much time in the 1630s discussing with papal representatives various formulae which were dutifully sent to Rome – and were there entombed.[20] Throughout the seventeenth century the Papacy refused to permit English Catholics to make any declaration of loyalty acceptable to Protestant opinion even though the possibility of any Pope's effectively releasing subjects from their vows of loyalty became increasingly remote.

In any case such a declaration would possibly have been greeted with scepticism, not only because of some Catholic teachings on equivocation (no strict line was taken on this by the Papacy until 1679), but also because serious doubts existed over the relationship between recusants and foreign Catholic powers, Spain in particular. All Elizabethan conspiracies contained a foreign popish power somewhere in the background and Robert Parsons' appeal to English Catholics to support Spain as the Armada sailed was merely the most public and notorious association of internal subversion with foreign attack. Catholics had good reason to feel sympathetic towards Spain: under James I and Charles I the Spanish ambassadors were far the most active in defending their interests at Court. Their gratitude was obvious even to Queen Henrietta Maria who once expostulated that English Catholics 'would think little of heaven itself unless they got it at the hands of Spain'. Spain (and its territories) was a popular place for seminarists to study abroad, and its pensions attracted many English Catholics living in exile. Oliver Cromwell had a particular interest in mind when he spoke to the second Parliament of the Protectorate on the subject of recusants and Spain, but the phrases came easily to him because he was expressing a view which he knew his audience shared: 'The Papists in England, – they have been accounted, ever since I was born, Spaniolised ... Spain was their patron'. English Catholics were 'Spaniolised' in part because, it was felt, they would need outside assistance to uproot

Protestantism in England. For a parallel reason Catholics could also plausibly be represented as supporters, under some circumstances, of any move towards absolutism in England. Parliament was irrevocably committed to Protestantism: consequently, it was argued, only a despotic monarchy could override it and re-establish the old religion. This was obvious to the courtiers and the Catholics who, in the 1630s, cautiously discussed reunion between England and Rome. Indiscreet papal assurances to Charles that reunion would strengthen his prerogative – at least against his subjects – caused forebodings; and a scandal followed the publication in 1629 of the Catholic Sir Robert Dudley's memorandum on establishing military rule in England.[21]

On the eve of the Civil War therefore English Protestants had been told for years that Catholicism was politically seditious, morally evil, and doctrinally damnable. It was indelibly associated with foreign attempts to invade England, with domestic plots to assassinate its monarchs, and – paradoxically – with support under some circumstances for an absolute monarch. Papists would give no satisfactory assurance of their temporal loyalty; their sworn word could not be trusted; they asked for toleration when on the Continent Protestant lives and liberties were being destroyed. They professed a religion which was a superstitious and idolatrous reconstruction of Christianity by the priestly caste to pander to man's worldly pleasures and smother the pangs of guilty conscience. Their final end was plainly foretold in the *Book of Revelation*. The full emotional depth of loathing for Catholicism expressed here must be appreciated before acts of savagery and fear before and during the Civil War can be understood. It was this detestation of popery which led to repeated assaults by Londoners on Catholics leaving the foreign embassy chapels throughout the century; it inspired the jubilant tone which marked the destruction (among other 'relics of popery') of London's Cheapside Cross in 1643; it was expressed in an assertion that papists should be segregated because their living conditions made them particularly likely to spread disease and infection.[22] In a curious decision of 1641 the House of Commons showed its genuine belief that Catholicism was idolatrous. After a number of Catholics had been arrested and claimed privilege as members of the Queen's court (leading to strained relations with foreign Catholic ambassadors who felt an obligation to support their co-religionists), it was proposed that Henrietta Maria should submit a full list of the members of her court to Parliament. These people would be permitted to worship without molestation and in this way tensions with foreign powers, which Parliament could ill afford, would be removed. Henrietta was saved from her dilemma by the scruples of the Lower House itself which upon reflection concluded that such a list of people licensed to attend Mass would make Parliament an accessory to their sin of idolatry.[23]

Protestant horror of Catholicism can therefore be demonstrated and explained. But was there any real *fear* of papists? Statutes against Catholics can be enumerated; the works of papist-baiting pamphleteers can be cited; but neither reveals whether ordinary Proestants in Jacobean and Caroline England ever felt themselves in real danger from their Catholic neighbours. This can only be established by their actions, not from what writers were saying. On two occasions, in 1605 and 1679, hysteria was certainly present, and to these may be added the belief in 1666 that papists had started the Fire of London. But three brief periods of alarm spread over a century – or three generations – do not suggest that the fear of Catholics was a very common factor in English politics; and if the tension was as acute on these occasions as contemporaries alleged, it is odd that the fear should have broken out on average only once in a generation. And so far as the causes of the Civil War are concerned these episodes are not particularly helpful, for two of them took place too late in the century to be relevant, and the third in 1605 occurred so long before the war that it was a memory of very early childhood to almost all of the men who began the fighting.

Alongside these major disturbances, however, another and much less known series of alarms can be traced. Sometimes affecting only a single town or village, occasionally spreading over an entire county, they typically took the form of rumours that Catholics were making preparations to rise and massacre all Protestants in some particular region. They were characteristically local in nature: talk of a papist conspiracy on a *national* scale can be found but the area imagined to be under threat was seldom larger than a county, and frequently as small as a parish. The House of Commons in 1610 took notice of 'the great confluence of Recusants' into London, warning that this gave cause 'to doubt some imminent danger'; and two years later Princess Elizabeth and the Elector Palatine were married to the accompaniment of 'many rumours . . . spread abroad' that 'Papists were to have made a massacre' using for the purpose a special shipment of arms from Spain.[24] In 1615 the Bishop of Durham received worrying reports of suspicious Catholic activity in the north, and a very widespread alarm in 1625 was explicitly compared by contemporaries to fears felt in 1605 and 1588 – the number of strangers visiting Catholic gentry in 1625, one witness said, exceeded 'those which fore-ran the attempts of the Spanish invasion and the Gunpowder treason'.[25] Northamptonshire and Bristol were shaken by alarms in 1630 and 1636 respectively, and when a Spanish fleet appeared in the Channel in 1639 carrying troops for the Netherlands 'It was thought by many that these Wallons and Irishes . . . were intended to be used against us', and the ghost of the Armada sailed once more.[26]

These cases come mostly from the records of the central government and search among local sources would very probably uncover further examples. Even so, known rumours of papist plots in the years from the Gunpowder Plot to the Short Parliament are sufficiently numerous to demonstrate very real Protestant fears. Normally buried under the day-to-day business of living, these tensions could erupt and paralyse a whole community when their dormant existence was stirred by the appropriate combination of circumstances. The elements of this combi-nation – and the depth of anti-Catholic fears which a really powerful stimulus could evoke – are seen most clearly in the years 1640–42, the period when the immediate causes of the Civil War were set in train. In three years the number of known panics over 'Catholic plots' was six times that for the preceding four decades. Alarms over these supposed insurrections took place in the five largest towns of England – London, Norwich, Bristol, Newcastle and York; there were panics in at least three dozen other communities ranging in size from Oxford, Colchester and Salisbury to hamlets such as Pudsey and Bingley in Yorkshire, besides numerous other disturbances where precise location is impos-sible because the source refers only to a county.

The alarms occurred in a very clear chronological pattern. Five distinct concentrations can be seen between April 1640 and August 1642, each coinciding with a period of major political crisis. The first outbreak of alarm and panic followed the dissolution of the Short Parliament on 5 May 1640. Rioters in London included among their proposed targets the Catholic Queen, her chapel priests, the Papal Agent, and sundry recusant gentry and peers. Two small girls threw Colchester into uproar when they reported the presence of strangers – assumed to be Irish arsonists – to the mayor.[27] Word passed in London of Charles' supposed intention to use a popish Irish army to restore order in both of his unsettled kingdoms, and troops in Berkshire, Hertfordshire, Gloucestershire, Wiltshire and Northamptonshire mutinied against Catholic officers amid scenes of riot, desertion and (on at least two occasions) murder.[28]

The next cluster of anti-Catholic disturbances coincided with the petitioning campaign for a Parliament in September 1640 and the first six weeks of that Parliament's life in November-December of that year. As in the summer an excited population found popish enemies devising its ruin. In London during September unusual numbers of Irishmen were noticed in the capital, as well as in the north of England. These alarms give substance to popish dangers referred to in the London petition for a Parliament, circulating at this time. It spoke of 'The great concourse of Papists and their Inhabitations in London, and the Suburbs . . . where they have more means and opportunity of Plotting . . . against the Religion established'.[29] Parliament received several warnings of Catholic plots in the last two months of 1640 – warnings which it took the more seriously after a Catholic who was probably mentally unstable stabbed and seriously wounded a J.P. as the latter took a list of suspected papists to the House of Commons. Concern over recusants' arms was widespread in these months. Three dozen muskets were found in Chancery Lane, and from Berkshire, Gloucestershire, Monmouthshire, Lancashire, and York came similar reports or rumours about papists' weapons; while in Lichfield Catholics were allegedly preparing for a particularly sanguinary event using not swords and guns, but axes and hatchets.[30]

The early summer of 1641 found relations between Charles and Paliament at their worst point since April 1640. On 5 May Pym told the Commons what he had learned of attempts by courtiers (some of them close to the Catholic Queen) to create disaffection among officers in the northern army. At this time the King was hesitating over signing Strafford's attainder, finally abandoning his servant on 8 May. Henrietta Maria considered fleeing London but was persuaded of the danger of appearing even briefly in the streets. Rumours of popish plots accompanied these events: worshippers leaving Catholic embassy chapels were mobbed in London, and street-rioting in the capital between 5 and 8 May was directed especially at the Queen, her courtiers and her popish mother. The Venetian ambassador reported that in the countryside Catholics found their homes under attack from 'the peasants'.[31]

The violence ebbed during the remainder of the summer, but the uneasiness stirred in autumn by Charles's preparations for a visit to Scotland – all too clearly to recruit support there against his English Parliament – rose to crisis pitch once more, as news was received at the beginning of November of rebellion and massacre in Ireland. The news stimulated a series of rumours and panics in England which continued through the winter, lasting until February 1642. These anti-Catholic disturbances thus coincided for a third time with a political crisis, as Charles's relations with Parliament rapidly deteriorated during November-December 1641 and he was led to the Five Members gamble. Public alarm over Catholic plots reached its peak in these months. Tales of 'a plot intended to be done by the Papists upon the Protestants' swept Leicester, Lichfield and Ashby-de-la-Zouche as well as Kidderminster and four neighbouring villages in November, causing night-long watches in towns and, in the smaller villages, the flight of whole populations to strong points taking 'provision thither with them, and in great fear'.[32] The Mayors of Berwick, Carlisle, Newcastle and Hull wrote independently to the Commons of their fear of 'Papists which were come thither out of Scotland and out of some part of England and had much Arms in their Custody'.[33] Influential landowners in Lancashire and in North Wales – some of them royalists – expressed deep and genuine fears over Catholic plots.[34] In parts of Staffordshire and Yorkshire Protestants were afraid to go to church unarmed, or without first inspecting the vaults; Norwich and Guildford experienced fires allegedly started by papists; and in Liverpool a Catholic was arrested after saying that 'the Protestants should shortly have a blow and the papists should have crosses or the like on their hats that they thereby might not be killed'.[35] Rumours that Catholics were storing arms spread in London, Portsmouth, Colchester, near Raglan Castle in Monmouthshire, Oxford, Maidenhead, and in the neighbourhood of Eltham in Kent, while a recusant was detained near Southampton for possessing a suspiciously detailed map of England.[36]

Alarms continued spasmodically through the spring and summer of 1642, but only reached a peak again when King and Parliament parted irrevocably and the war began. Prompted by a conviction that the town authorities were too dilatory and would 'suffer their throats to be cut' by Catholics, a Southampton cobbler attempted in September 1642 to organise an armed band 'to endeavour the disarming of the Papists' in the countryside nearby. No such official negligence was reported from Bristol where the population were reported to 'watch in arms day and night to prevent the surprising of the City by the Irish rebels'.[37] After anti-Catholic rioting in Essex and Cambridgeshire the House of Commons was obliged to send two local M.P.s to the area and to issue a declaration before order was restored.[38] Though refraining from such

drastic counter-measures the populations of towns and villages in Lancashire and Cheshire believed their region was 'nev[er] in great[er] fear nor
in more danger than now it is' because of the strength and activity of
local recusants.[39] Once fighting began, however, the alarms became at
first spasmodic, and then in the course of 1643 died out almost entirely.
For the remainder of the decade and during the 1650s preoccupation
with papists no longer centred upon their rumoured conspiracies to rebel
and massacre Protestants. What drew attention was the belief that the
flourishing sectarian groups were but 'Jesuits in disguise', a misconception shared as widely by royalists as by Parliamentarians.[40]

IV

Fears of Catholic plots to murder Protestants and overthrow the established government and religion were clearly acute and widespread in the
years 1640–42. They can be found over almost the whole of England and
the total of those occurring in villages and provincial towns nearly
equalled that for the capital itself. Their number, and the often hysterical reaction of Protestant to these rumours, demonstrates vividly the
deeply rooted fears of the majority towards papists. The question
whether the panics were deliberately stimulated by Parliament's supporters (as several contemporaries alleged) or whether they were
spontaneous does not affect their usefulness as an index of popular anti-
Catholic feeling: without a widespread willingness to believe in conspiracies no forged letters or inspired rumours could have produced
results. Anti-Catholicism alone did not cause the war, but it has probably been underestimated by historians as a factor leading men first to
distrust the King, and then to join his opponents as the political crisis
worsened. The panics recorded here are the emotional background
against which the political impact of Charles's friendly relations with
popery are to be weighed. The King had refused to intervene on the
Protestant side in the continental war; he had married a Catholic and
tolerated the popish services of her priests; he had winked at court
conversions, discouraged and all but ended the prosecution of priests,
and exchanged gifts and civil messages with the Pope. He had welcomed the first Papal Agent to enter England since the Reformation.
Unavoidably some of the Catholic phobia rubbed off on him. It is
highly significant that the King's supporters invariably blamed Parliament for starting the panics; implicitly they assumed that public
excitement over popery could do nothing but harm to the monarchy.
One curious feature of the rumoured plots is remarkably revealing. In

the reigns of Elizabeth and James I the monarch was assumed to be the prime target for any Catholic conspirators, and the tradition continued with two rumoured papist plots against Charles in the 1630s. But after 1640 not one of the pullulating 'conspiracies' made any reference to regicide: popular apprehensions settled upon Parliament and the protestant nation itself as the likeliest victims of popish conspiracies. Catholics, it was all too clear, would only lose by removing Charles. Final evidence of the extent to which an identity of interest was assumed between the the court and Catholicism can be seen in a common reaction to the Irish rebellion. Edward Hyde, Edmund Ludlow and Robert Baillie each, and from very different standpoints, recorded the country's immediate conviction that the Queen certainly, and the King possibly, had encouraged the massacre.[41] Such suspicions made trust between the King and his subjects impossible and without trust no compromise in the constitutional crisis was feasible. Anti-Catholic feeling was the more influential politically because of the tendency, already noted, for panics to reach a peak at times when relations between King and Parliament were at crisis point: it became a political factor on precisely those occasions when far-reaching decisions had to be made.

In other ways too anti-Catholicism influenced the political crisis. It supplied a convenient stalking horse for Parliamentarians wishing to alter the balance of the constitution without admitting to their followers, or possibly even to themselves, that this was what their criticisms of the King led to. To repeat slogans about opposing 'popery and tyranny' – in the manner of the Commons' Protestation of May 1641 – was a useful alternative to basing claims upon precedents and an 'ancient constitution' which events were clearly leaving well behind. The plausibility and effectiveness of this double-think obviously depended upon the strength of popular fears of popery. And quite apart from setting men against the King and providing his opponents with ideological camouflage, the 'popish plot' panics between 1640 and 1642 heightened the general sense of crisis, making large numbers of the common population feel personally threatened and in danger. Even where it did not directly affect the course of events anti-Catholicism increased tension, creating suspicion and fear, and so helped drive the situation on to conflict.

For many contemporary writers the essence of the conflict was in fact a collision between true religion and popery: here, for them, was the reality underlying disagreement between King and Parliament. Superficially irrational, this interpretation was in fact a logical and obvious extension of Foxe's persuasive explanation of English history as the record of God's latter-day Chosen People. After leading other European nations in attacking the Papacy's usurped power, England had marked time for nearly a century under Elizabeth and the first two Stuarts. In this time the seat of true religion had moved elsewhere – to France, Germany and Switzerland – while the Elect Nation had lived under a lame religious compromise. What could the disturbances of 1640 and 1641 mean but that God was once more moving among his People, that the work of Wyclif and Henry VIII was to be continued and possibly completed by this generation?[42] Men who thought in such terms would contemplate any extreme if compromisers or traitors attempted once more to block the work of God. They would regret Civil War but it would be understood and accepted as one of the Elect Nation's inevitable tribulations. But to ask whether Protestants held by this apocalyptic vision helped to make anti-Catholicism a cause of the war shows the very general nature of their influence. Any major disturbance was seen as part of the conflict between God's people and those of Antichrist. Great upheavals had been foretold in *Revelations*, great upheavals were occurring now, and consequently there seemed no necessity to demonstrate more precisely how Antichrist was working in this case. Similarly they could assert that the crisis in 1641 fell into a pattern stretching back to the Gunpowder Plot, the Armada, the Reformation and the Lollards without feeling any need to furnish detailed proof. They repeated and strengthened a popular feeling that in some way Catholicism was at the root of the trouble, but relatively few of the general population probably shared their beliefs in greater detail. Until sects and unlicensed preachers expanded during the war years millenarian views were the property of well-educated and literary men. Moreover the very local – and ineed parochial – character of most of the panics over Catholics noted here suggests that few of those genuinely frightened by talk of popish conspiracy really thought in terms of a massive international operation under Rome's control to destroy the Elect Nation.

v

The limited influence of millenarianism upon the outbreak of war leads to a related but larger issue. Of the intensity of anti-Catholic fears revealed in panics there can be no question. Why then did these fears issue in relatively so few alarms? Any why were relations between Catholics and Protestants in most places and over most of the century so peaceful? Protestants at times sincerely believed that papists were about to murder them – but for most of the time they displayed strikingly little inclination to harry Catholics financially, to confront them with the penalties of refusing the Oaths of Allegiance and Supremacy, or to hunt out and execute priests. Studies of the enforcement of the recusancy laws present a picture of curious laxity: executions of priests and Catholic laity declined from 187 in the reign of Elizabeth to 26 under James, and to 3 between Charles I's accession and 1640. Twenty-two were executed during the 1640s and 1650, though many more were held in prison, this action against Catholics can scarcely be termed a reign of terror. Lord Protector Oliver Cromwell actually intervened to prevent the execution of priests in Scotland and a historian of Scottish Catholicism considers that Cromwell's victory in 1650 marked the turn of the tide for toleration there.[43] When government officials attempted to arrest priests they were often defeated by collusion among Protestants to save their Catholic neighbours from the central government's attentions: local sympathies were stronger than religious divisions. Protestants willingly participated in fraudulent transfers of land to preserve intact the estates of Catholics threatened by fines or sequestration.

How can this behaviour be reconciled with panics among the common people, or with the hysterical alarm and near despair expressed by writers? It may be objected that the volume of recusancy fines, like the number of priests captured and executed, reflected not the emotions and prejudices of the public, but the number and efficiency of a small group of administrators and government agents who had to enforce the laws. In other words professionalism, and not public fear and hatred, largely determined how Catholics as a group were treated. There is obvious force in this argument–prosecution rates for any offence usually tell as much about the enforcement agency as they do about public attitudes to the offence in question – but it would be a mistake to press it too far. The practice of informing for profit was central to the enforcement of most laws in the seventeenth century, and this involved the general public in prosecutions far more than is the case today. If priests went unhunted, if recusants were not prosecuted, this was at least in part because people with essential local knowledge were not interested in selling it. And there remains the evidence of fraudulent conveying of recusants' estates, and their persistent under-valuation by Protesant neighbours, to show widespread Protestant toleration of the papist enemy.

An explanation of this apparently contradictory behaviour can be found by asking which Catholics were feared, and which were tolerated. Toleration was associated with the very strong regional or county feeling in the seventeenth century. Catholics who were near neighbours, close relatives, or good friends of Protestants formed part of the 'county community', and if they practised their religion with some discretion, they could expect the usual assistance given to a county family having trouble with the London government. By contrast, many alarms centred upon Catholics who were strangers locally, often because they were refugees or vagrants. When a disturbance centred upon Catholics known to the locality they were almost invariably recusants living just beyond the town affected – there are a dozen cases of this, involving towns as large as Norwich, Chester and Portsmouth, and villages as small as Ampthill (Bedfordshire), Bingley (Yorkshire) and Sherborne (Dorset). Where the Catholics suspected of conspiracy fell into neither category, the reason for alarm was usually some striking and alarming departure from their customary behaviour: hurried and furtive consultations between groups of recusants, or their purchase of arms or food in quantities far larger than their immediate families could have used or consumed.[44]

Local factors therefore partly explain why Protestants could live peacefully with recusants, but could also suspect them from time to time of plotting a massacre. A further influence was the condition of national, and international, politics. Alarms regularly coincided with political crises between 1640 and 1642; the Popish Plot of the 1670s climaxed a decade of growing suspicion about Charles II's policies; and panics accompanied the Revolution of 1688. Many disturbances before the Civil War also occurred at these times of tension. Panics occurred at the time of the Gunpowder Plot, and in 1610 after the assassination of Henry IV of France; worsening relations between King and Parliament, and a more active foreign policy, underlay alarms in 1625; and a Bristol panic of 1636 was linked with reports of the new liturgy intended for the Scottish Church.[45] The regularity through generation after generation of this coincidence between political tension and anti-Catholic alarm suggests a fear of popery so ingrained and intense that, at popular level, political developments were often understood, not in terms of the interest groups and political principles distinguished by later historians, but in terms of a simple popery/no-popery dichotomy.

This does not however necessarily increase the role of anti-Catholicism as a cause of the Civil War. The scattered nature of panics in the four decades before the war indicates that no-popery existed as a latent force; buried beneath the day-to-day business of living until a crisis burst upon the country. Invoked as a partial or complete explanation, religious antagonism *then* became a political factor in its own right. During 1641 and 1642 it was the more powerful because of the King's known indulgence toward Catholicism. Its political impact was felt not so much as an original cause of the crisis between Charles and his subjects, but rather as a factor which greatly worsened existing tension and increased the probability that the situation would end in warfare. Such a view implies that anti-Catholicism counted for more politically between 1640 and 1642 than it did in the 1630s and for the mass of the population this is probably true.

Anti-Catholicism became dangerous to the Court because of a twofold gap in comprehension between the latter and the country at large. The anti-Catholic mythology had largely been created during a period of war with Spain. But by the seventeenth century the situation had changed. England was no longer under direct attack; instead it was trying to influence a continental war to regain the Palatinate for the Elector Frederick, son-in-law to James I. With a negligible army at their disposal James I and Charles I could achieve this object only by diplomacy, and since Spain (the key to the situation) could not be coerced they had to try to save continental Protestants by a policy of friendship toward their greatest persecutor. But the country was unable to understand this paradox. They saw only a government which tolerated domestic papists and made leagues with the arch-enemy of Protestants abroad. A suspicious population was thus ready to believe the worst when Charles and Laud encouraged Arminianism, and when the King began to restore relations with the Papacy, hoping to end an inherited and obsolete quarrel which offended his sense of religious decency.

The reason for this change in internal policy was – again – simple. From the last years of Elizabeth's reign the Privy Council had begun to realise through its spies' reports that the vast majority of Catholics posed no danger at all to England's security, that they had given up hope of a Catholic restoration, and that they probably wished to come to terms bartering loyalty for toleration. The number of Catholics who took the Oath of Allegiance (even after Rome had condemned it) confirmed this impression, and the government's lessening sense of urgency is seen in the decline in the number of Catholics executed for treason in the seventeenth century. But most of the Protestant population had no knowledge of the documents and negotiations which had slowly changed the government's attitude, and they remained frozen in a deep Elizabethan distrust of papists' loyalty. Advocates of a more Calvinist church settlement were appalled by the policies pursued under Charles, although for some time they were a minority because they were not talking about the present but really issuing warnings about the future. Only when there was war with Scotland, rebellion in Ireland, and political deadlock in England were they taken seriously. The crisis came and the population looked as usual for its popish enemies. But because of Charles's actions in the 1630s enemies were especially sought inside England and at the highest levels of government. The emotions which under Elizabeth had unified and strengthened the nation against foreign attack were now turned inwards and helped to shatter it.

6. Two Cultures?
Court and Country under
Charles I

P. W. THOMAS

I

'AND never Rebel was to Arts a friend', John Dryden pronounced with great finality in *Absalom and Achitophel* in 1679. Faced with the threat of Monmouth's reckless yielding to the temptation of Shaftesbury's eloquent, Satanic prompting, he could not refrain from recalling the great upheaval of English society in the middle of the seventeenth century. The Great Rebellion, for Tories of his generation, was a reminder of the madness that insurrection and innovation, challenging established values, might yet at any moment conjure up. They cherished the memory of a divided, deluded society as a cautionary tale apt for their own crises.

Their habit of equating 'Wit' and 'Fool' with Tory and Whig belongs to the cooler world (wary of holy enthusiasms, rhapsodical fanaticism, and all the paraphernalia of 'godly thorough Reformation') that bantering scepticism and common sense had helped to create: it is not remote from our sort of party politics. Yet plainly it was also a legacy of the not far distant conflagration when King and Parliament, Orthodoxy and Dissent (in its many forms) contended so fiercely. Their language reverberated still with meanings and associations that we may not at first hearing catch.

Dryden, in his Preface of 1682 to *Religio Laici* deliberately carried the quarrel back beyond the Revolution:

> *Martin Mar-Prelate* (the Marvel of those times) was the first Presbyterian Scribbler, who sanctified Libels and Scurrility to the use of the Good Old Cause . . .; to their ignorance all things are Wit, which are abusive; . . . Thus Sectaries, we may see, were born with teeth, foul-mouth'd and scurrilous from their Infancy . . .

That touches deep convictions about politics and literature which we must investigate.

II

Looking back we still sometimes imagine we see a Parliament of prudes in 1642 sanctimoniously bolting and barring the theatres; statues and stained glass falling before the Apostolic blows and knocks; the royal patron decapitated and his great collection of art treasures put up to auction; we behold the Universities, those 'old standing judges of good Poetry' as Humphrey Moseley the publisher called them in 1651, ignominiously purged; and men of letters scurrying for cover in the provinces or abroad. The picture is one of rampant, insane utilitarianism putting the Muses to flight as it overturns the Court, despoils the Church, and tramples through the groves of Academe. There stands the great Leviathan of the Republic, presiding grim and godly over a wasteland.

Of course, that is all rather one-sided. We may set against it the memory of Andrew Marvell, richly gifted, moderate, discreet, serving the Protectorate and writing one of the most civilised odes in the language to celebrate Cromwell's return from Ireland; or Milton, whose learning and brilliance were a byword in Europe, composing his great epic of English humanism.

We may even, on closer examination, perceive ways in which Puritanism transcended the boundaries of sect and party: asceticism was not the monopoly of nonconformity, and we confidently talk today of Anglican Puritans, citing the affinities between the fine spirituality of Richard Baxter and Jeremy Taylor, or reflecting that Laud's 'Diary' is a thoroughly Puritan document.[1] At the same time we observe that Presbyterians and Independents – often lumped together in propaganda – were frequently at each other's throats. Prynne, Burton, and Lilburne were all Puritans but they represented in the end quite different points of view. Their careers, as Presbyterian, Independent, and Leveller respectively, display the essential diveristy of nonconformity and its rooted principle of divergence. In them we trace how Puritanism grew beyond its concern with ceremonies and the sins of the flesh – for assuredly it had deep convictions about these matters – to demand root and branch political and legal reform.

Yet the simplifications of caricature were even at the time more graspable than the very complicated 'facts'; and in the event they become a sort of fact and had a real impact on events. Prynne, a moral Puritan who insisted that he was conformable to Church and Crown, became perforce a political Puritan, and so a godly hero or a deluded meddler, depending on your point of view. In his writing and in his 'martyrdom' a quarrel was polarised. We shall not be able to dispense after all with the term 'Puritan' nor with the prejudices that were attributed to it. But we may hope to come to understand them and their role more fully.

Ben Jonson unforgettably established the type on stage: his caricature of Puritanism in *Bartholomew Fair*, acted in 1614 and printed in 1631, displays the features which Cavalier propaganda so lovingly dwelt on. Zeal-of-the-Land-Busy, originally a lowborn tradesman, has risen by exercising his gift of prophetic utterance to heights of hypocrisy and indulgence: denouncing the 'vanity of the eye', 'the lust of the palate', and all 'carnal provocations' he stops his ears and averts his gaze in the Fair, but smells his way to the food instead. Ale is Satan's drink, though he imbibes it liberally; and as for 'long hair, it is an Ensign of pride, a banner'. He spouts the cant of Revelation, seeing 'the broken belly of the Beast' in a drum and an 'Idolatrous Grove of Images' in the hobbyhorse seller's stock-in-trade of musical instruments, toys, and gingerbread. With a visionary eye on the millennium he bursts in during the puppet show inveighing against 'Stage-players, Rhymers, and Morris dancers, who have walked hand-in-hand, in contempt of the Brethren, and the Cause'. He abominates the dressing up of male as female, and vice versa, on the stage; and in a scene of high farce the puppet is assailed because it has 'no Calling', no vocation – 'your old stale argument against the Players', as the puppet retorts! Unrepentant even in the stocks Busy rejoices in his affliction and foretells the destruction of 'Fairs and May-games, Wakes, and Whitsun-ales', sighing and groaning and gaping in due form for the reformation of these abuses. For prophecy is *his* calling; and he recognises no 'other Learning, than Inspiration'. Like Dryden's MacFlecknoe fifty years later, he is 'a fellow of a most arrogant, and invincible dulness', kept ever in 'seditious motion' by the conviction (which Shakespeare's Malvolio, 'a kind of Puritan', shares) that the future will be his.

Jonson expresses the growing anxiety of the early seventeenth century over militant nonconformism. To see how his caricature took shape we must carry the story a little further back to the challenge of Elizabethan Puritanism, which was contained, and in particular to the controversies of the 1580's. All the differences which in the decades prior to Civil War hardened into faction are there expressed. But the Elizabethan settlement, punitive to extremists, was sufficiently tolerant of the broad middle range of dissent. That accommodation made national unity possible, and is reflected in some of the major literary achievements of the period. Spenser could speak from reasonably close to the centres of power and, with the support of influential patrons, in tones distinctly Calvinist at times. At the same time his is a truly national ideal that embraces all the aspirations of Renaissance courtly man. His *Faerie Queene* (1596), written 'to fashion a gentleman or noble person in virtuous and gentle discipline', celebrates that unity of Church and State, of Court with Country, of 'grace' with 'policy', that the Queen's Council embodied. It concludes with a prayer breathing a millenarian faith, 'O that great Sabbath God, grant me that Sabbaths sight'. Little wonder that many Puritans in the Interregnum recalled this as a golden era. But Spenser does not need to look yet to revolutionary politics to achieve his vision. He found, as did his patron Sir Philip Sidney and Sidney's editor and friend the Chancellor of the Exchequer Fulke Greville, that his aspirations as man and artist were at least acceptable to the State.

Nor did they affront the prevailing spirit of Calvinism as it was formulated by its most notable English champion William Perkins (1558–1602). The current of reform and asceticism which spread its ripples through Europe from the source in Calvin's Geneva was in him calmly and painstakingly assimilated into English Protestant nationalism. It was his achievement to establish over the whole range of human life a scrupulously detailed, practical code of conduct. He is critical therefore not merely of Romish ritual in church but of all ostentation and ceremony. Mixed dancing, those 'frisks of lightness and vanity', cosmetics which make women 'seem what they are not', long hair in man ('a foreign trick'), any dress which does not suit a man's vocation, and especially the 'new fangled attire' that makes women 'like to an image in a frame, set bolt upright' – all are condemned in terms that shrewdly imply the idolatry of *haute couture* and the vanity of trying to appear what one is not. Carnal distractions from one's calling must be removed; and into his net Perkins swept 'vain love songs, ballads, interludes, and amorous books'. Yet as always he was discriminating and uninflammatory: 'This is the thing we are carefully to shun in the reading of Poets, yet so, as mariners do in navigation, who forsake not the sea, but decline and fly from the rocks'.[2]

In practice Spenser showed that even the erotic impulse and the language of love songs could serve a holy ideal. His celebration of matrimony in *Epithalamion* (1595) is a major achievement of Puritan Platonism in which the senses, human feeling, and spiritual fervour triumph together. The problem which he solved there was not new:

mistrust of passions and affective language was routine in Renaissance thinking. But Calvinism undoubtedly fortified that suspicion of outward show and merely carnal pleasures which is a major preoccupation of *The Faerie Queene*. This is not to say that the poem merely versifies Calvinist dogma, though the destruction of the Bower of Bliss has been interpreted as an act of iconoclasm. In fact Spenser is making a very important distinction between false beauty, which is just carnal, and true beauty which involves spirituality also. For the new poetry which Spenser and Sidney launched was sensitive to the need to establish the moral value of art and to justify poetry as a fit Christian vocation. The Calvinist Fulke Greville, editing Sidney's pastoral romance *Arcadia* (1590), defended the book's good doctrine, albeit somewhat uneasy over its fictitious garb; it afforded 'not vanishing pleasure alone, but moral Images, and Examples . . . to guide every man through the confused Labyrinth of his own desires and life'. Greville was perhaps the most distrustful of all the Calvinist poets, and elsewhere, in stricter ideological mood, he denounced all human Arts as 'beams of folly'. Yet he proceeded even then to defend their practical utility with equal conviction. Fundamentally his position is much like Bacon's: he was alert to the ways in which 'feigned history' and the 'craft of words' could seduce, and wary of affections that might colour and confound true understanding: but he argued pragmatically that poetry, properly disciplined, could perform public service by furnishing images of magnanimity, morality, and delectation.[3]

The Puritans were heirs to the humanist position, in fact. But the poets especially seized on the ancient notion that poetry had something of divinity in it too. Here conventions of artistic inspiration might be reconciled with the Calvinist idea of being called, with the belief that God could speak through man. Christian poets, with discipline and grace, might serve the revelation of truth. Aesthetic pleasure could be a fit vehicle for moral illumination. Thus far Puritanism and Art did not conflict.

One point on which Perkins had touched was proving, nevertheless, uncomfortably divisive. He mistrusted stage plays above all as 'most commonly dangerous representations of vices and misdemeanours' which ought not to be spoken of. Spenser's jibe at 'painted faces' and 'the courting masker' in *The Ruines of Time* (1591) suggests how widespread this sort of anxiety was becoming. Sidney in his *Apologie for Poetry* (1595) was forced to admit that there were unworthy poets, and 'naughty Play-makers and Stage-keepers'. Unlike Perkins, and for that matter Greville, he did not however eschew drama. Properly purified, even it could be a worthy instrument.

Sidney's antagonist Stephen Gosson had no time for such nice points. He devoted *The School of Abuse* (1579) and the even more strident *Plays Confuted* (1582) to a doctrinaire onslaught on the whole business. 'Garish apparel masks . . . , Dancing of jigs, galliards, morrises, hobby horses'; 'amorous Poets', and all such 'peevish cattle', but above all 'Stage Plays', were nothing but the 'doctrine and invention of the Devil' to lure the carnally minded. He had read his Lactantius and trotted out all his objections: the eye, that susceptible organ, is beguiled by spectacle while the 'sweet numbers of Poetry flowing in verse do wonderfully tickle the hearers ears'. Such a combined assault on the senses was scarce to be resisted. Puritans of his temper might allow music of the right sort (since it afforded abstract images only); they could accept paintings if they were not lascivious; they could accommodate poetry; theoretically they might even accept drama. But in practice – and the spirit of pragmatism was strong – the dangers were so great that it seemed better to avoid temptation.

Gosson was in no doubt that such 'Italian devices' (he was thinking chiefly of masques) had 'poisoned the old manners of our Country with foreign delights'. To 'the hazard of their souls' and in a 'riot of their expenses', men had deserted 'the old discipline of England'. As a display of chauvinism, bourgeois thrift, prudence and fundamentalism, it is remarkable. The objections to display, to acting as a sort of lying, to the imitation of vice are conventional enough: but Gosson – though he at one point mentions 'good plays and sweet plays', his own among them – makes of the drama a matter almost of political offence by denouncing it as the 'Ratsbane to the government of commonweals'. His prayer, that 'some Hercules in the Court' might cleanse the land as the 'godly preachers' of London had urged, sounds ominously like a reproach to a negligent administration.

With varying degrees of vehemence and skill this Puritan assault on the theatre (usually combined with attacks on extravagance and idolatry, especially of the Romish sort) was maintained through the last decades of the sixteenth century. The case for the defence was basically Sidney's argument that it was foolish to equate fiction with falsehood and that plays could both teach and delight. Thomas Lodge and Thomas Heywood among others conducted the defence; but it was necessarily less emotive than the prosecution – at least for the time being.

We stand however on the threshold of a changing world; ahead lies a complicated shift of temper at the centre, which was to affect the whole range of life. As long as the Court tolerated a variety of manners in worship and doctrine, as long as the Crown was not exclusively identified with the vices of plays and players and extravagant indulgence in the pleasures of carnal arts, the broad Calvinist hostility to ritual and ceremony was not seditious. In the 1580s, despite Gosson's hint, the Court could not be made the scapegoat. Nor, for that matter, was criticism of the theatre ever exclusively Puritan or 'extra-mural'. Among the orthodox clergy, too, many were uneasy: they knew that the Church Fathers and Christian tradition were on the side of the 'godly'. Laud would go no further than arguing rather halfheartedly against Prynne that plays were not necessarily evil. There was a surprising amount of agreement between Puritan and Anglican in this matter. But in practice and in time the Puritans' habit of associating criticism of the stage with ecclesiastical and other grievances was to strike most woundingly. It was as a subversive challenge that, some fifty years after Gosson, William Prynne's *Histriomatrix* would be received when it revived the issue in the most inflammatory way.

The explanation of this lies not just in Prynne's contentious stubbornness nor in some monstrous, unslakeable thirst after righteousness. It involves a decline in the public theatre and an increasing inclination at Court to patronise an art remote from the sort of concerns that the Spenserian-Jonsonian consensus insisted on. Of course, this did not happen overnight. Spenser and Sidney were dead, and their loss (in terms of enlightened patronage and the justification of poetry and drama in a Christian society) was important. But Jonson flourished, upholding neo-classical didacticism in his brilliant comedies for the public stage. Shakespeare too survived into the reign of King James, subtly adapting his drama to the changing audience, and the great Folio edition (1623) of his works belongs here. We might interpret this as some indication of a continuing vitality, perhaps even of a thriving drama. Yet the inclination of many Jacobean playwrights to pile on the melancholy, bawdiness and horror suggests jaded palates. There was plenty for Puritans to object to. Ben Jonson himself rounded on popular plays for their 'ribaldry, profanation, all licence of offence to God, and man', to say nothing of absurd plots and trivial themes. He shared the view that drama had failed to uphold unequivocally 'the doctrine which is the principal end of poesy, to inform men, in the best reason of living'. For all his mockery of ranting Puritans Jonson believed that art must rest on an unequivocal moral commitment.

Courtly taste also reacted against the coarseness of popular drama; but only to demand of art (as Jonson in the fullness of time discovered) a sort of conformity and propriety that was doubly irksome. The carnal pleasures proffered in the fashionable private theatre for the delectation of noble sophisticates and aspiring worldlings became more exquisite and ambiguous; and they framed political and social assumptions that were increasingly exclusive. This art was dutifully doctrinal but for many in the country it offered the wrong doctrine. All this, with a mounting extravagance, in the end aroused even moderate men of middle station.

Puritans meanwhile cannot have failed to take note of Jonson's caricature of their hopes, mocking them in the sight of the ungodly vulgar. His being drawn further into the orbit of the Court where he hoped for a more discriminating audience is unlikely to have eased their antipathy. Even the mounting pressure of censorship on the theatre (and only the King's Players were strong enough to survive the plague and close-down of 1625) did not help, since the Court was more than ever bent on cultivating its own entertainments in private. And if Puritans studied the offerings of those darlings of Jacobean and Caroline intellectuals, Beaumont and Fletcher, they found plays which, as Coleridge observed, carried 'even *jure divino* principles . . . to excess'. They were to become to the Cavaliers an epitome of the noblest artistic and political ideals; while Dryden, though looking back with profoundest wonder on Shakespeare's genius, significantly applauded them for bringing the conversation of gentlemen on to the stage.[4] Such fashionable art confirmed the *élitist* tendencies of Stuart rule.

Militant Puritanism was not, in our sense, a popular mass movement: men like Prynne probably shared the genteel objection that Shakespeare had too much respected the mob; but their alternative was not a more refined drama. To the zealous, their eyes on the dawning millennium, it was all (from Shakespeare to Davenant) a dark distraction. Their objections in the end articulated what many dimly felt about the growing isolation, exclusiveness and repression of the Court. Even men of unstrict temper could reflect on the difference between a literature that had been the authentic voice of patriotic high seriousness and Protestant nationalism, and one that, however refined, seemed to speak for narrow snobbery and an effete indulgence. For too many the art the Stuarts encouraged mirrored the moral, social, and political defects of its philosophy.

III

With the advantage of hindsight we can relate that decline to a change for the worse in Church and State which eventually made containment and reconciliation impossible. The reasonableness and integrity of Perkins's case for Calvinism had been met with the answerable magnanimity and flexibility of Hooker's *Ecclesiastical Polity*. Now the enlightened moderation of Bacon, who envisaged a broad church unity encompassing divers forms and ceremonies, was brushed aside. Country and City, the old aristocracy, the property owners, the magnates, merchants and industrialists did not care to pay taxes to subsidise the salaries and pleasures of court parasites. Almost inevitably they leaned towards Puritanism.

The early Stuarts for their part, failed fully to understand the nation they had come down to rule – witness James's constant toying with the grandiose dream of reconciling Protestant to Catholic in Europe through the magic of dynastic marriages. The public rejoicing when Prince Charles and Buckingham returned empty-handed (save for some paintings) from their theatrical excursion in false beards in pursuit of a Spanish wife should have enlightened them. Yet Charles I, stubbornly devoted to the silliest aspects of his father's policies, was to take a French Catholic wife. She proved a liability.

Popery, painting and playacting – could anything be more calculated to stir the anxieties and resentments we have been discussing? The new Court espoused them all.

Charles's household was more gentlemanly: James's robust humour, to which the Jonsonian anti-masque paid tribute, and his bad manners were replaced by more cultivated behaviour. The new King was a connoisseur: his collection of paintings took Rubens's breath away when he came here in 1629 expecting to find a culture as barbarous as the climate. Such sophistication, such aesthetic sensitivity amazed him. But Charles was prepared to take a deal of trouble and spend a lot of money on these treasures. Men like Buckingham's protégé, the diplomat-adventurer Balthazar Gerbier, were equally eager to conduct tortuous negotiations to acquire art works. In 1628 Charles outbid Richelieu, lifting the Mantuan Collection from under his nose. Van Dyck, whose elegance and ostentation perfectly matched the king's, was ensconced in grand style at Blackfriars to paint his flattering dream of a wise, sensitive, dignified monarchy. Rubens himself, the most expensive painter in Europe, was engaged. His ceiling at Whitehall is beautiful; and the sensuous allegory of the 'Blessings of Peace' richly proclaims a pious aspiration. We may however wonder at the wisdom of patronising the great propagandist of the Counter-Reformation, or of doing deals with Cardinal Barberini who helped Charles import treasures from Italy, hopeful of winning a proselyte.

The king's military expeditions into Europe were even less propitious. Perhaps the fact that Gerbier, who made machines for masques, was employed to devise mines to blow up the dyke at La Rochelle sufficiently characterises that episode. It was little better than a charade. This and the earlier Cádiz adventure were felt, outside the Court at any rate, as betrayals of national pride and pious duty. The King, however, rested on the lesser Europeanism of international art dealing.

In 1637 he did make a gesture to the popular desire for England to assume her old role: he launched the *Sovereign of the Seas*. The ship's decoration was aptly assigned to the dramatist Thomas Heywood (one of those who had defended the stage against Puritan criticism). He published a careful explanation of the allegorical significance of his designs, to the satisfaction, no doubt, of a Monarch who to the last had an eye for the theatrical.

Fittingly it is in the fantastic and elaborate court masques of his reign that the King most lived up to Jonson's rather unfortunate advice that a prince should be 'studious of riches and magnificence in the outward celebration or show'.[5] Out of the combined arts of poet, painter, musician, choreographer and architect, the masque fashioned a mirror in which the Court most loved to behold itself.

The pieces were essentially ephemeral, commonly performed but once; and the audience was small and select. But the cost of costumes, scenery and the wonderful machines was prodigious. Even under James the effects were astonishing: '[The curtain] falling, an artificial sea was seen to shoot forth, as if it flowed to the land, raised with waves, which seemed to move, and in some places the billow to break ... The *Masquers* were placed in a great concave shell, like mother of pearl, curiously made to move on those waters and rise with the billow.' Thus, Sir Dudley Carleton in 1605. Bacon, twenty years later, very sensibly dismissed such affairs as 'but Toys'. But what expensive toys!

Jonson, the greatest writer of masques, later regretted the 'jewels, stuffs, the pains, the wit' wasted on 'the short bravery of the night'. He strove for twenty years to make the masque moral and doctrinal as well as pleasurable: he dared in his robust honest man's way to lecture the Court, even to remind it of the realities of people's dissatisfaction.

If the masque commands respect as a literary form, this is, *Comus* apart, Jonson's achievement. His fate is significant, however: the court of Charles would not tolerate his reminders of actualities; it wanted something more decorous, polite, Italianate than he would give; it wanted, above all, something spectacular but reassuring. In a word, the courtiers desired pageantry. Inigo Jones, with whom Jonson had long but uneasily collaborated, was their man. He did not think masques were anything more than 'pictures with Light and Motion'. He could and would devise the magnificence they desired, build scenes and devices to the measure of their dreams.

Tamer collaborators, like Aurelian Townshend, William Davenant and James Shirley, were enlisted to aid him. Jonson was left to condemn, in his *Expostulation with Inigo Jones*, the shallow profligacy of it all:

> Painting and Carpentry are the Soul of Masque!
> Pack with your peddling Poetry to the Stage
> This is the money-get, Mechanic-Age.

Forced back to the public theatre he fared little better: his play *The Magnetick Lady* written in 1632 attracted Laud's disapproval, ostensibly because the players used oaths.[6] One cannot help suspecting that the portrait of Parson Palate, 'our Parish Pope', had something to do with it. Jonson was obviously depressed not just by his advancing years and infirmity but by the whole prospect of schism and faction in Church and State. He lashes equally Arminians and Puritans and the 'Luke-warm Protestants' between, to say nothing of the tribe of Doctors, Lawyers and Courtiers. Neither 'common approbation' nor 'genteel ignorance' could please him now: he is hardly confident that his art can heal. In *The Magnetick Lady*'s excessive reliance on the apparatus of choral explanations of its own meaning it appears that the poet can no longer express himself directly to his society through a dramatic action. He falls back, as in other of his late plays, on an almost stubborn appeal away from the expectations of the bulk of his audience to theoretical precept. All those tacts and conventions, the sense of some broad agreement (with and within the audience) about ends and means, those shared expectations which underwrite the finest Elizabethan and early Jacobean plays and poems, seem to be dissolving in his hands. Jonson's play may still outshine the efforts of lesser contemporaries; but it remains sadly significant of a loss of common purpose.

His departure had meanwhile deprived the Court of the one writer of stature whose ideals (of gravity, 'plain down-right wisdom', and pure neat language instead of 'false and affected eloquence') were those of the great humanists, Cheke, Ascham and Sidney. The scene was left to poetasters and dutiful University wits, most commonly anxious to versify and glamourise official ideology. Even Laud and Strafford feared the king was too susceptible to flattery. Those masquing 'Shows! Shows! Mighty Shows!' now offered little else.

Frank and pusillanimous hedonism reached a new height in Thomas Carew's lines of 1632. Demurring at the chance to write an elegy for Gustavus Adolphus, great hero of international Protestantism and revered by the surviving Elizabethans on the Council, he urged

> But let us that in myrtle bowers sit
> Under secure shades, use the benefit
> Of peace and plenty, which the blessed hand
> Of our good King gives this obdurate Land.
> Let us of Revels sing, and let their breath gently inspire
> Thy past'rall pipe.
> Tourneys, Masques, Theaters better become
> Our Halcyon days; what though the Genevan Drum
> Bellow for freedom and revenge, the noise
> Concerns not us, nor should divert our joys.

Two years later in his masque *Coelum Britannicum* he went further: the existence of 'obdurate' folk is not even hinted at as the three nations bend the willing knee in 'cheerful loyal reverence'.

It was into this dream world that William Prynne, defying censorship, came crashing with his immense, unignorable encylopaedia of complaint. His *Histriomatrix the Players Scourge or Actors Tragedie*, of 1632–3 voluminously annotated the Puritan code of secular and religious conduct. Its one thousand pages comprise the most exhaustive statement of Puritan asceticism. Such an exclamatory attack on idolatry and ritual in all its guises could not but set the Court by the ears. 'This man', sneered Lord Dorset, the most vindictive of Prynne's judges, 'will be frighted at a three-cornered cap, sweat at a surplice, sigh to hear music, swound to the sign of the cross . . .' Indignation knew no bounds, nor in this case did obsequiousness: his lordship capped his observations with a nice compliment to the Queen 'in whose praise it is impossible for a poet to feign, or orator to flatter'. That was well the wrong side idolatry. It could only confirm fears that in its life and letters the Court had dispensed with all Christian restraint. The full weight of traditional opposition to the cult of personal beauty and seductive pleasure was

behind Prynne's scourging assault – for it was too late for the calm tone
of a Perkins. He runs through the gamut of vanity: 'long false curled
hair and lovelocks' are a 'vile and abominable abuse . . . much now used
in this our Realm'; they are 'an effeminate unnatural amorous practice,
an incitation of lust, an occasion of Sodomy': 'coranto frisking gallants'
and 'lewd lascivious dancings' indulge the most 'beastly' pleasures and
draw young men from study and young women from their household
duties when they should be 'keepers at home, not gadders abroad'; and
the whole apparatus of 'comedies, tragedies, Arcadias, amorous histories,
poems, and other profane discourses' are so many scandals in the face
of God. Prynne did not reject poetry as such: he allowed that one of the
Fathers could pen 'a poem of Christ's passion only to be read, which to
act were most profane'; he himself composed six lines attacking Laud
and praising God when he returned from his ordeal in the pillory in
1637.[7] But he would not countenance the sort of love lyric courtiers
addressed to their mistresses.

Above all, of course, he objects to plays and masques: they portray
vice, they dress men as women and vice versa, they display 'lustful
gestures, compliments, kisses, dalliances, or embracements', and their
scenes and costumes are nothing but an 'overcostly gaudiness, amorous-
ness, fantastiqueness, and disguisedness'. The campaign against women
actors had been launched from middle ground by Sir Benjamin Rudyerd
and the third Earl of Pembroke. Boldly Prynne pressed home the attack:
his reflections on the acting of a play at Blackfriars in 1629 by 'some
French women, or monsters rather' and his terse index entry 'Women
actors, notorious whores' were taken as a frightful insult to Henrietta
Maria. The king himself, in earlier days, had starchily reproached the
Queen's frolicsome gambolling as 'degrading ceremonies'. Her love of
dancing and dressing up had however survived his disapproval; and
a public attack was different from a private rebuke.

It was commonly believed that Prynne had in mind her acting in the
long pastoral drama, *Shepherd's Paradise*, written by a Catholic, Walter
Montague, and played at Court in January 1633. She delighted in the
sports and merry games, the fresh fair maids and wanton shepherds
common in the mode; and Montague's piece began a court craze. In
January 1634, for example, Fletcher's *The Faithful Shepherdess*, which
had failed in the public theatre in 1609, was revived with the help of
scenery by Inigo Jones and costumes by Henrietta Maria. It went down
well and was subsequently acted with applause in the Blackfriars private
theatre.

Unmistakably, and with fanatical courage, Prynne had flung all the age-old accusations about the idolatry of drama and Popish ceremonial in the face of King, Queen and Bishops. Never had the Court been so vulnerable, with its worship dictated by a High Church martinet and its pleasures presided over by a French consort, indulged in her extravagance and her Catholicism. Prynne did not omit to note that many of the players were Papists.

He had other cavils too. Shakespeare's plays were printed on better paper than Bibles; and playbooks, pouring from the presses in torrents, found 'better vent than sermons'. When preachers were harried and free use of the press denied the devout, such licence was intolerable. Prynne counted, despite 'late penurious times', no fewer than five 'devil's chapels' in London with a sixth theatre under construction. Such 'over prodigal disbursements' were more than enough to have financed that holy war that Protestant honour demanded. They were 'intolerable in a Christian frugal State'.

Little wonder Prynne was charged with trying 'to withdraw the peoples affections from the King and Governments'. If men believed his jeremiad, as one of his judges pointed out, with what heart would they pay subsidies and duties in future? That was a key question and exposes the root of the matter. Prynne had contrived to focus in his attack on the theatre the growing opposition to the Court's foreign policies, its ecclesiastical exactions, and its financial methods. He drew together all the practical and spiritual objections of bourgeois thrift and Puritan asceticism. *Histriomatrix* was not a manual of piety but a political indictment of the Crown.

Collision with Laudian bureaucracy, equally disinclined to turn a blind eye to anything, was inevitable. If Prynne was no Perkins, Laud was certainly no Hooker. His reaction was swift and ruthless: William Cartwright and Jasper Mayne (two young sprigs of Laudian academicism) with Peter Heylin, historian and divine, were set to hound the troublesome meddler; and to exact poetic justice in full measure James Shirley was commissioned to write a masque, *The Triumph of Peace*, for Prynne's own Inns of Court to produce at prodigious expense. The Court needed soothing: Carew's sycophantic *Coelum Britannicum* followed; and in 1638, just to show a lofty contempt, Davenant's *Brittania Triumphans* was acted on the Sabbath.

While men like Prynne, Bastwick, Burton and Alexander Leighton courageously endured their punishments for speaking out of turn, the Court acted in its old ways. Henrietta Maria still cultivated her *précieuses* fashions, and maintained her baroque entourage of Catholic chaplains, negro servants, monkeys, dogs of all sizes and one small dwarf. 1636 saw the publication, doubtless to her taste, of *The Female Glory*, a work in praise of the Blessed Virgin; and in 1637, for the first time since the reign of Bloody Mary, a Papal Agent was welcomed at Court.

The Laudians still did not care for a missionary European role; and when at last Charles took up arms it was in a parochial cause and against the Calvinists in the North. The first expedition ended in humiliating truce at Berwick in 1639; but the Monarch, optimism buoyed by the enchantment of a Twelfth Night masque by Davenant, prepared to march again in 1640. His half-hearted army was easily defeated at Newburn. Perhaps the contribution of Sir John Suckling best characterises the whole feckless enterprise. Suckling, gambler, rakehell and writer of licentious verse, patron saint of the Roaring Boys and 'greatest gallant of his time', raised a troop of horse for the First Bishops' War. At a cost of some £3,000 he decked them out in white doublets, scarlet breeches and scarlet coats, hats and feathers – the costumes were no less gorgeous than those used in his play *Aglaura* in 1638. So caparisoned he led them into battle. Suckling was no coward; but his band was surely more for show than for fighting. This piece of theatre and the incompetent execution of the whole royal manoeuvre suggest how far the acting out of fantasies had become a function of Personal Rule. For poor Suckling, forced into exile after the final fiasco of the Army Plot in 1641, all the gallantry and glamour ended in suicide in Paris.[8]

All too plainly royal patronage had failed to sustain at the centre a culture (using the word in its proper, widest sense to embrace social and political *mores* as well as those of art) of unequivocal moral and intellectual vigour. It mistook flexibility for weakness and a governing clique for the nation; it confused true and spurious eloquence, so that men of real ability like Falkland and Clarendon did not have the King's ear; it cultivated an attenuated self-regarding sort of high seriousness that was in the end no match for the tough dedication of its opponents. It managed to construct a mythology of itself that was deeply divisive.

In the Root and Branch Petition of 11 December 1641 this was finally challenged on all fronts and decisively identified as the work of Antichrist. All that tolerating of sports on Sunday and that dressing up in Popish vestments, all that bowing to Popish images and ceremonies was positively heathen. So was 'the swarming of lascivious, idle, and unprofitable Books and Pamphlets, Play-books, and Ballads, as namely

Ovids fits of love, . . . to the increase of all vices, and withdrawing of of people from reading, studying, and hearing the Word of God, and other Books.'[9] The petitioners saw a New Jerusalem just ahead and nothing was too great or too small for their attention. These men, no less than Laud, knew what was good for the people.

It seems indeed as if a militant radical culture was bent on sweeping away all trace of the Court, down to its very last poem or play. That was how Royalists interpreted the Ordinance of 1642 which closed the theatres and crowned the long campaign to stop that subversion of godliness. John Cleveland jested from Oxford a few years later that 'the only playhouse is at Westminster'; and *Mercurius Anti-Britanicus* about the same time joked that the stage would return to its proper home at Blackfriars only when the citizens went back to their 'old harmless profession of killing Men in Tragedies without Manslaughter'. Samuel Butler in *Mercurius Mennippeus* spelled out the lesson:

> We perceive, at last why plays went down; to wit, that murders might be acted in earnest. Stages must submit to scaffolds, and personated tragedies to real ones . . . No need of heightening revels; these Herods can behead without the allurements of a dance. These tragedians have outvied invention.[10]

In their zeal to cast out fiction and falsehood, he implies, the rebels had committed the worst confusion of all and unmasked themselves as of the Devil's party. This was twisting the old objections to plays with a vengeance. From the other side things looked different: in the Cavalier raking in 'the dunghill of ruined stages' the journalist Marchamont Nedham detected the corrupted airs of Inigo Jones and the masquers, and the noxious features of 'his grandfather Ben Jonson, and his Uncle *Shakespear* . . . and his cousin-germain *Fletcher*, and *Beaumont*, and nose-less Davenant, and Friar *Shirley* the Poets'.[11] There could scarcely be a blunter polarisation of views about literature and politics. Even in the matter of hair, which can as we know inflame passions, the opposition appears. The jeers at Cavalier lovelocks were not allowed to go unanswered: never trust a man if you can see his ears, was the advice of one Anglican divine to his fellow.[12] Short hair became, in propaganda, the badge of the Puritan: witness Cleveland's Sir John Presbyter 'With Hair in Character and Lugs in Text', or Butler's 'long-ear'd Rout', or even Dryden's finally polished cut at the Presbyter who 'pricks up his predestinating Ears'.[13] Powerful prejudices accumulate around seeming trivialities.

We know of course that Milton, though cropped at the insistence of a strict tutor when he was ten, wore his hair long in maturity, as did Cromwell. But in the embittered climate of the late 1630s and 1640s nice distinctions were easily disregarded. Henry Parker had good cause to protest, in his *Discourse Concerning Puritans* of 1641, that the name was being used to discredit 'men of strict life and precise opinions, which cannot be hated for any thing but their singularity in zeal and piety'. 'Scarce any civil honest Protestant' could avoid the slur. Milton in his *Reason of Church Government* (1642) and Sir Benjamin Rudyerd on the day, in November 1640, that the Long Parliament assembled, made the same point.[14] Moderate Anglicans might equally protest that all orthodox churches, all bishops, ritual and ceremony were being tarred with the brush of Popery. In vain they proposed in 1641 the sort of reform that Bacon advocated in 1604. It was too late. Propaganda with its cries of 'Popish Arminian fry' or 'Anabaptist, Brownist scum' was in the saddle. Hooker's faith in 'visible solemnity' and Bastwick's objection to 'the bondage of the figure and shadow'[15] could no longer coexist, even uneasily. Idolater confronted Iconoclast.

There were it seems two warring cultures. But it is more accurate to talk of a breakdown of the national culture, an erosion through the 1630's of a middle ground that men of moderation and good will had once occupied. Fulke Greville's heir, who largely shared his views, was perforce a leading revolutionary. The case of Anne Bradstreet, the Puritan poet who fled from Laudian tyranny to America in the 1630s, is similarly instructive.[16] The 'heroes' of her Pantheon were that 'fleshly Deity' Queen Elizabeth, the poets Du Bartas, Spenser and Sidney. At the same time, in *A Dialogue between Old England and New* written in 1642, New England rejoices in the spirit of root and branch:

> Let's bring Baals vestments forth to make a fire,
> Their Mitres, Surplices, and all their Tire,
> Copes, Rochets, Crosiers, and such empty trash.

The lesson is clear: Puritanism, except in cases of extreme fanaticism, did not demand that the slate be wiped clean of everything upon it. Their objection was not to literature, not necessarily even to plays of the right sort, but to what they felt was the pollution of the high seriousness and moral earnestness of the mainstream of English humanism.

The Court behaved as though the Golden Age had arrived through the miraculous intercession of the divine Stuart. To the godly it looked a thoroughly carnal kingdom, more like Babylon than the New Jerusalem. The future demanded that it, and all its idolatrous bric-à-brac, be brushed aside.

IV

The picture of a decadent Court, its art an index to a deep malaise, is not just hindsight. Many saw the issue so at the time; and Milton confirms the diagnosis.[17] In his life's work, as poet and pamphleteer, he endeavoured (as did others) to recover the strenuousness and dedication of the earlier phase of the English Renaissance. Could we follow him closely through the years of retreat at Horton in the late 1630s and on his journey to Rome and Geneva, we would see growing his realisation that poetry's true theme was Christian revelation. 'Church-outed' by the Laudian prelatical bureaucracy, he found his calling as a Christian and a writer to be the same. Returning to England he proclaimed his programme to use letters to 'inbreed and cherish in a great people the seeds of virtue, and public civility to allay the perturbations of the mind, and set the affections in right tune, to celebrate in glorious and lofty Hymns the throne and equipage of God's Almightiness and what he works.' Some thirty years later, when so much had changed, he still endeavoured to reveal 'What makes a Nation happy, and keeps it so',[18] though by then it was a theme for epic tragedy.

Not only the Restoration, but a secularisation that set in well before that, overtook the Millennium. Puritanism had always appealed strongly to bourgeois fanaticism and in the end it produced a remarkable laicisation of life. When the vision of a New Jerusalem was hi-jacked by extremists and made a creed for cranks, even Milton's sort of vocation came to look a bit old-fashioned. All inspirations and enthusiasms were suspect. The poet himself in *Paradise Lost* (1667) seemed aware that it was late in the day for his sort of flight. In Book IX he invokes his

> . . . Celestial Patroness, who deigns
> Her nightly visitation unimplor'd,
> And dictates to me slumbring, or inspires
> Easy my unpremeditated Verse:

He is sure of his mission, less so of the time:

> . . . higher Argument
> Remains, sufficient of it self to raise
> That name, unless an age too late, or cold

Climate, or Years damp my intended wing
Deprest, and much they may, if all be mine
Not Hers who brings it nightly to my Ear.

He had, as we shall see, come to share some of the prevalent concern for everyday practicalities, without surrendering the prophetic role. Like Hobbes, whose very different apocalypse had terrified the time, Milton lived on into a serene old age when he would be, as John Aubrey put it, 'cheerful even in his gout fits and sing'. Still believing in inspired inner witness, he sat quietly at home receiving the homage of men who came from far and wide to see the blind poet, the apologist who had bested the great Salmasius. Wryly he gave young Dryden permission to 'tag' his lines, to fit them to the new fashion of couplets prevailing in the smart world of professional letters. He had his own ideas about poetry.

All this is illuminated by Milton's response to the tragic events of 1649. Though at first the 'rebels' did not aim at the king, it came to that at last. The Royalists found the one martyr they needed, and proceeded to enshrine in *Eikon Basilike* the memory of his taste, grace and sanctity. Such an opposite and widely cherished image of what had been expunged could not go unanswered. Milton's crushing reply *Eikonoklastes* sums up so much of the tension over *mores* we have been looking at that it compels attention.

Here, at first sight, the greatest Puritan poet displays the Prynne-like antipathies we might expect of one who (in *Of Reformation*, 1641) had flayed the luxury and waste of ceremonial episcopacy. He berates the vanity and theatricality of courtly taste: regrettably, Charles found Shakespeare a fit companion for his hours of imprisonment; shockingly, on the very scaffold he was so foolish as to pop a prayer from *Arcadia* into Juxon's hand. Milton was never contemptuous of Shakespeare – indeed his own poetry suggests that he was more at ease with him than many of the Cavalier *literati* and than Dryden himself. He called *Arcadia* a 'vain amatorious poem' finding it 'a book in that kind full of worth and wit, but among religious thoughts and duties not worthy to be named, nor to be read at any time without good caution'. Events between Greville's time and his had deepened suspicion but not to the point of outright rejection. Milton's concern was, like Anne Bradstreet's, that *Arcadia* might 'infatuate fools'. In the king's case it confirmed dilettantism. What appalled was Charles's lack of proper seriousness: 'It can hardly be thought upon without some laughter that he who had acted over us so stately and so tragically should leave the world at last with such a ridiculous exit . . .' The frontispiece to *Eikon Basilike* spoke volumes: William Marshall's engraving of the martyr king is a 'conceited portraiture . . . drawn out to the full measure of a masking scene, and set there to catch fools and silly gazers'. These Those 'quaint emblems and devices, begged from the old pageantry of some Twelfth-Night's Entertainment at Whitehall will do but little to make a saint or martyr'.

This 'idolised Book, and the whole rosary of his Prayers', the final gesture of a King and his 'deifying friends', expressed everything the Puritans objected to as fictitious and fabricated. Marvell's *Horatian Ode* admiringly draws out the 'memorable scene': the 'armed Bands' surround the 'Tragic Scaffold' clapping their 'bloody hands' at the exquisite, self-possessed performance of 'the Royal Actor'. It is a subtle, ironic reply to those Cavalier allegations about acting murders in earnest to imply that the King's addiction to artifice and gesture has brought him here. More solidly real, to the poet, is the sight of Cromwell's 'acting', inspired not by a fiction but real knowledge – he has the capacity 'to act and know'. This man, reserved, austere, reluctantly emerged from his rural retreat to answer his true calling, which was to labour with 'industrious valour' and 'wiser Art' than the Stuarts had for the living God. To his natural 'Arts' without which a nation, 'A Pow'r', cannot subsist, Marvell knows his own art must be answerable. It is a realistic and mature comment on the relationship between life and letters. One is reminded of Milton's recognition in 1640 that his own literary ambitions must wait upon the completion of more pressing practical tasks. That too was no denial of art but a recognition of priorities, of a man's responsibility to the whole of life.

The writer must convey to us 'things useful to be known'. This Baconian conviction, noted in Milton's *Commonplace Book*, lies behind the constant emphasis of Puritan letters on solid knowledge and plain expression. It was, we see from the eloquence and wit of *An Horatian Ode*, the reverse of crudifying. Milton in Book IV of *Paradise Regained* makes the crucial distinctions between the Ancients' purely carnal wisdom (amounting to 'dreams', 'fancies', 'fabling', 'smooth conceits') and the 'plain sense' of Christian revelation. Manifestly he did not despise the Ancients but poetry must put Christianity first and last. Truth is not, it teaches us, a matter of fine style, of 'swelling Epithets' merely: it belongs to 'songs' expressing 'moral virtue', and 'The solid rules of Civil Government' in 'majestic unaffected style'.

> In them is plainest taught, and easiest learnt
> What makes a Nation happy, and keeps it so.

Eikonoklastes' tart remarks about 'a masking scene' must however take us back to the 1630s. Surely Milton had not forgotten his own masque, *Comus*, that 'high ritual in Arcadia, with Plato and Spenser as priests and all mythology in attendance' as his biographer W. R. Parker describes it?[19] Milton did not openly acknowledge *Comus* when it was published in 1637, and it may have met his father's disapproval. Possibly it was written partly in protest against *Histriomatrix*: Milton was still young and destined for a Church career; and, as the early projecttions of *Paradise Lost* in dramatic form and *Samson Agonistes* prove, he never rejected drama. In the *Reason of Church Government*, in fact, he argued against purists that the State should sponsor the theatre. *Samson* was the sort of play he had in mind. Carefully he states that it is a tragic poem meant only for reading, which would have pleased Prynne; but he is prepared to challenge comparison with classical and modern Italian plays. It is ironic that this unmistakably Puritan piece (if it does not predict a nation's Sabbath, it proposes an ideal of personal integrity and witness that distinguishes God's people) seems now a more illuminating, serious drama, profounder in its political realism and psychological insights than anything Dryden was able to write for his fashionable live audience.

But *Comus* too was no ordinary composition; this Masque was written for the provincial aristocratic household of the Earl of Bridgewater at Ludlow, where spectacle was impossible. The Earl's family were devout and of a Calvinist inclination. So Milton wrote something very different from Carew's *Coelum Britannicum* in which the two Egerton boys had actually appeared at Court. That was no place to commend virginity in; but Ludlow was different, and *Comus* celebrates the virtue of chastity. It is a drama of the will, teaching the distinction between aestheticism and morality, but delightfully, as 'sage and serious' Spenser would have wished.

The villain, Comus, embodies the grossest enchantments of sensuality – for Milton was not one to follow Perkins's inclination to bury such things. Comus's eloquence is 'glosing courtesy' like Satan's in *Paradise Lost*: his words flow, to borrow a phrase from the *Reason of Church Government*, 'at waste from the pen of some vulgar amorist or the trencher fury of a rhyming parasite'. True poetry, in this masque. is spoken by others. There is no essential contradiction between *Comus* and *Eikonoklastes*. Even the reproach that Charles had written of his wife 'in strains that come almost to sonneting' does not prove a desire to emasculate poetry. Far from suppressing the sensual and sentimental element in sexual relationships, English Puritanism exposed it to the full force of its habit of scrupulous analysis.[20] The practical insight, refinement of feeling, and sophisticated psychology that was achieved is shown by Daniel Rogers's *Matrimonial Honour* (1642). The conviction that marriage should be a mutual joy, a sharing of physical and spiritual experience, goes back to Perkins. It was a positive ideal of family life as the ground on which worldly and religious duties met.

Hence the objections to the amorous effusions of 'libidinous and ignorant Poetasters'.[21] An ethic which deeply respected women and the family could hardly applaud the erotic fantasies or the idealisation of extra-marital love in the writings of a Suckling or a Waller. Though some have been tempted to talk of the life-affirming hedonism of Cavaliers faced with Puritan prudery, the facts are against them. The Platonism cultivated at Court too easily declined into a mere gallantry in which a contempt for women was (as so commonly happens) disguised by an extreme outward courtesy towards them. Cavalier romanticism came, irresponsibly, to think of affection chiefly in the narrow context of wooing or seducing. It trickled down into the frivolous cynicism with which too much Restoration Comedy and hordes of blades treated marriage; until it was finally degraded in the condescending well-bred brutality (against which another great humanist, Pope, protested) of things like Halifax's *Advice to a Daughter*, which flippantly asserts that husbands and infidelities are mere *bagatelles*. The actuality of the domestic tenderness of Milton, of Colonel Hutchinson, of Richard Baxter, of Bunyan or of Cromwell puts all that to shame.

Jonson had found that the ideals of domesticity and hospitality which he celebrated in *To Penshurst* prevailed little at the centre. In Puritan literature they were reasserted; and their greatest monument is not in the works of the sons of Ben but in *Paradise Lost*. The picture of Adam and Eve's relationship breathes the spirit of Puritan marriage: here is the shared work of 'joint hands', the hospitality, the unaffected domesticity of household tasks, the family prayer at morning and evening; here too, in the frank eroticism of some of the descriptions of the naked Eve, is the ready recognition of physical joy as part of a spiritual and intellectual sharing. The hymn 'Hail wedded love' in Book IV of the epic is wholly Puritan and wholly of Renaissance humanism too. One is forced to admit that beside this the charming Cavalier love lyrics of a Richard Lovelace are as a tinkling cymbal.

Milton was not the only Puritan poet who could acknowledge sexuality. Anne Bradstreet's humble muse voices a tender desire for her absent husband in 'As loving hind that (Hartless) wants her Dear'. Of course Puritanism did not monopolise this sort of experience; but in those successful Puritan marriages and in the literary evidence is warrant for describing the ideal in life and letters as, characteristically, an achievement of seventeenth century Puritanism.

It marks a recovery of Spenser's vision of human love and perfectibility. Here again, however, some change is apparent: we find it in turning from his elusive allegory to the more exact definitions of *Paradise Lost*. Milton's epic has clarity and toughness, distinctness of purpose and execution. He had lived to see the dawning millennium fade; and Adam and Eve's marriage is tested by mutual betrayal. Their love-making after the Fall is degraded to a barbarous mutual rape: it is a wholly unceremonious, unlovely lust. The shattered ideal is not however the end of things: the great epic which ranges freely through all the perspectives of time and space closes on the image of a man and woman, thrust from Paradise, going forward hand in hand to work out their salvation in the world together.

This proposes (dare one say it?) a more homely, practical image than high seriousness could have achieved before the Revolution. The grand struggles of good and evil, God and Satan, finally concern Milton at that point where they touch a human couple. So, too, Christ, at the very end of *Paradise Regained* (1671) 'Sung Victor', returns quietly 'unobserv'd' home to his Mother's house. It is a simple, deeply moving action. Poetry here achieves that modest, passionate, unostentatious expression that was a goal of Renaissance critical theory.

The note recurs in Marvell's fine observations of Cromwell's qualities – 'That port which so Majestic was and strong', that 'piercing sweetness' in the gaze, and 'the wondrous softness of his Heart'. This man embodies Milton's literary ideal of a 'majestic, unaffected style'. At one time the Protector looked like the promised leader – 'If these be the Times then this must be the Man' was Marvell's typically circumspect reaction. But he was never idolised by these poets. Marvell's *A Poem upon the Death of O.C.* (1658) describes the corpse:

> I saw him dead, a leaden slumber lies,
> And mortal sleep over those wakeful eyes:

> All wither'd, all discolour'd, pale and wan,
> How much another thing, no more that man?

He launches into a significantly Spenserian lament:

> Oh human glory, vain, Oh death, oh wings,
> Oh worthless world of transitory things!

But that is not the end of it:

> Yet dwelt that greatness in his shape decay'd
> That still though dead, greater than death he lay'd:
> And in his alter'd face you something feign,
> That threatens death, he yet will live again.

It is the portrait of mortal, redeemed man: eloquent, admiring, affectionate, it has no false glamour, no sentimental idolatry. This, to adopt a phrase of Milton's, is neither fustian nor flattery.

The man of God at the centre, who had his portrait painted 'warts and all', and the able scrupulous men who rallied to his service had displaced the false allurements of dilettantism and extravagance.

V

Far from leaving a wasteland as Restoration propaganda alleged, the Interregnum left behind it achievements too numerous to describe in painting, engraving, miniatures, architecture, music, biography and autobiography, journalism, devotional literature, education, science, and all the Baconian useful arts – for Bacon, whose influence before 1640 was negligible, became a major inspiration of the period. The Protector was not a patron in Charles's way; but he employed able lieutenants, had an eye for men of progressive views, and attracted talented writers to his government. John Hall of Durham, Marchamont Nedham, George Wither, Pepys, Dryden, Marvell, Milton – it is a formidable civil service. Cromwell's was a more enlightened, tolerant, intellectually adventurous and less monolothic regime than may popularly be imagined.[22] It genuinely endeavoured, in its political and intellectual concerns, the recovery of England's European and overseas role, to restore, in fact, what it regarded as the best features of the Elizabethan settlement: in their different ways Milton's writing and Cromwell's policies were both shaped to that end.

Their dreams were frustrated. The Protectorate foundered when the essential divisiveness of sectarianism was exposed by Cromwell's death.

Sadly it bequeathed no lasting civil or ecclesiastical institutions permanently embodying its ideals.[23] Yet the Puritanism which for a while triumphed had (though not single-handed and not always wittingly) affected a great shift in the national temper. The Court, last of the great Renaissance princedoms against which root and branch had reared itself in 1640, went for ever; and that can be a matter for regret on aesthetic grounds only if we think of art as a commodity, something glamorous to be bought and sold, not as an expression of the condition of a whole society. The world that emerged from the long crisis was remarkably changed. The Merry Monarch, versed in the arts of survival, was not tempted to indulge his father's magnificent presumptions or his lavish patronage: equally he looked for no pious martyrdom; no apocalyptic gleam lit his eye. His new Court was neither the eldorado many an old Cavalier deliriously greeted in 1660, nor the promised land the godly generation had once envisaged.

The King, mindful of his past and of Parliament at his elbow, was ready to smile on worldly, circumspect, businesslike, urbane men and women of all persuasions, and of none. Significantly in 1663 a war-weary generation, and the young bucks to whom ancient dogmatism and high-flying rhetoric were anathema, acclaimed Samuel Butler's burlesque poem *Hudibras*. Pouring cold water on all those holy enthusiasms that had heated the nation to a blaze, Butler brilliantly caught the mood of the new era. In these years, with all their faults, a sort of middle ground was recovered, where men of wit and common sense, fearful of extremes, might meet.

Dryden's cool indictment of Rebellion as antipathetic to art with which this essay began, expressed, like his unruffled replies to Jeremy Collier's attacks on the stage, something of that new and necessary temper. Yet from our safer distance we may venture against it a very different speculation. Perhaps the Millenarian era in some ways fostered a climate sympathetic to poetry. Its conviction of the interpenetration of present and eternal, visible and invisible, helped sustain the role of the imagination: the promptings of the Holy Ghost joined with Platonic ideals of poetic insight. It was at best a spiritualising, invigorating force. One is certainly aware that, in the cooler rationalistic air of the post-Restoration period, poetry was frequently hard put to it to justify its essential reliance on intuitive powers, on the 'gift' of genius which, as Dryden argued, was born not made.[24] Be that as it may, in the Interregnum and its aftermath English life and letters (and the Cavaliers too were braced by the impact of Revolution) recovered some sense of shared purposes and commitment to centrally important problems that a self-indulgent patronage had vitiated. Assuredly, the Civil War was not fought over poems, plays, romances, masques and ballads, any more than it was just about economics; but in the concern with these things a sense of a deep and complicated crisis was expressed.

To portray the 'Great Rebellion' as an assault by a counter-culture is, as we see, too simple. Yet in one respect Dryden's remark was right: art and politics, literature and history do not exist in separate compartments of the mind. The Civil War was about the whole condition of a society threatened by a failure of the ruling caste both to uphold traditional national aims and values, and to adapt itself to a rapidly changing world.

allied purposes and could not serve to exemplify important problems that
called for urgent resolution. But whatever. Essentially, the Civil War was
not simply, to poetic players, romances or bloody bibles or balladshaw more
that it was, not of ideology or economics, but that it concern with those tell relat
sense of a deep and complicated crisis was expressed.

To portray the Great Revolution as an assay by a counter-culture is,
as we say, too simple. Yet more at parts of Dryden structure too well in
far and politics literature and history in poets actual peace compost-
ments of the mind. The Civil War was about the whole caudal of a
society in one hand by nature of a rebellion, cast forth to uphold traditional national arms and values, and in defent itself to a modelly shruling
world.

Section Three

7. Economic Issues and Ideologies

PENELOPE CORFIELD

I

CIVIL war is rarely recommended as a recipe for economic growth, though Rousseau once argued this case in a spirited footnote to the *Social Contract*. Few advocates of unfettered competition take their logic so far. Certainly this viewpoint was not canvassed in England in the years before the outbreak of Civil War in 1642. The number of people who actively desired the war was small. Many of the participants probably shared instead the puzzlement and distress expressed by Sir Thomas Knyvett at the prospect of armed conflict: he thought it was 'a lamentable condition, to consume the wealth and treasure of such a kingdom, perhaps the blood too, upon a few nice willful quibbles'.[1] Neverthless Civil War did break out. This then raises the question of whether there were economic issues at stake among these 'quibbles' which proved so intractable. Was the war fought over issues of economic policy? Did the conflict also represent a clash of economic ideologies, royal paternalism against the *laissez-faire* doctrines of the Parliamentarians? This essay seeks to review the debate on these questions.

There are always difficulties in discussing the issues of one age in the terminology of another. This becomes immediately apparent when considering seventeenth-century attitudes towards 'the economy'. It is difficult to know whether men utilised this concept at the time. Economic questions were not discussed in isolation from political, religious and social issues, although a broad distinction was sometimes made between 'commonwealth matters' and 'matters of state'. The use of the term 'the economy' to refer to the collective material resources of the country was indeed just coming into currency from the mid-seventeenth century onwards, by extension from its earlier connotations of domestic management. But when Oliver St. John in 1637 spoke of 'the law of economics', he was using the term in a political context, referring to the King's duty to protect the realm. Nor did a systematic study of the workings of the economy begin until the late seventeenth century, with the writings of Petty, Locke and North; and economics as a subject of enquiry emerged only slowly thereafter.[2] A full century later, the economist was still to some people the sinister herald of a new and degenerate age, as Burke proclaimed in 1790: 'The Age of Chivalry is gone! That of sophisters, economists and calculators has succeeded, and the glory of Europe is extinguished for ever'.[3] The study of economics was thus still in its infancy in the mid-seventeenth century. The Civil War was not fought between rival schools of economists.

In this period too men's expectations from government economic policy were much more limited than they have become in the twentieth century. There was no concept of the fully managed or planned economy, simply because governments then lacked both the knowledge and the power to undertake the systematic direction of the economy. This does not mean however that economic life was unregulated. Nor does it mean that the government was thought to have no role to play in economic matters. On the contrary, appeals for action were loud and frequent, especially in economic recessions; and numerous statutes and proclamations attested to the willingness of governments to respond. But this fell far short of economic planning.[4] The genesis of most intervention was defensive and *ad hoc*, designed to meet problems as they arose, and policy was frequently influenced by short term financial and political preoccupations. There was furthermore a large gulf between legislative intention and administrative enforcement, as there was in many other spheres of government activity. In practice, Tudor and Stuart England was not a much-governed society. The major government initiative in economic planning in the early seventeenth century was the ill-fated Cockayne project in 1614–17, which proved a disastrous and unmitigated failure. This demonstrated the dangers of clumsy and ill-prepared government intervention, and did not encourage repetition. Hence controversy centred around specific issues rather than rival programmes for the economy as a whole.

Certainly the economic background of the time presented plenty of problems. The English economy was still an underdeveloped agrarian one, with no built-in tendency to sustained growth. The century before the Civil War had seen a number of important developments but, as often happens, change had brought many intractable economic and social problems in tow. The period is sometimes loosely described as one of 'growth', 'expansion' or 'advance', but such expressions without further qualification are misleading. They imply that the economy was more prosperous and flourishing than was in fact the case. In the sixteenth and early seventeenth century, England had experienced a considerable growth in population, from about two-and-a-half million (or less) in

1500 to over four million in 1640. This was quite rapid growth for the time, though it is not so impressive by twentieth century standards. In an agrarian economy, population expansion is far from an unmixed blessing. It produces a growing number of people to feed, clothe and house, without necessarily generating sufficient economic growth to cater for the increased demand, as the current problems of the Third World countries demonstrate. The English economy before the civil war was therefore in many ways under pressure, burdened as well as stimulated by demographic change.

The expansion of demand had produced some important innovations in the agricultural system. It stimulated new techniques of farming, encouraged enclosures in place of the open field economy in some parts of the country, and fostered a general expansion of the acreage of land under cultivation. By these means, both the total volume of production and productivity per acre increased. At the same time, there was a general land-hunger, which pushed up land values, rents and entry fines. The expansion of supplies lagged behind the growth of demand, producing a century-long price inflation (though monetary factors may also have augmented this). These economic circumstances worked in favour of those who were producing to sell and against those who consumed. Landowners, farmers and freeholders flourished, though even theirs was a highly competitive and precarious world. Success was not automatic but depended on good luck and skill in estate management. But equally, on the reverse of the coin, there was considerable hardship, poverty and distress lower down the social scale. In this sort of economy, population change is one of the major regulators of the standard of living among the lower classes. By the 1590s, contemporaries were expressing fears that the country was over-populated. There were frequent food shortages, accompanied by popular disturbances, though there was no famine. In areas of extensive enclosure, small tenants and cottagers dependent upon access to common lands were facing hardship. And all those on small incomes suffered from the rising price of foodstuffs, which constituted a large part of the budget of the poor. Landless labourers and others dependent upon wage earnings also experienced a worsening standard of living, since wage rates lagged far behind the rise in prices.[5]

The economy found it difficult to absorb the growing population into the work-force. The majority of the working population was employed in agriculture, which was not generating demand for labour at the same pace as the increase in population. Indeed, in some areas the process of farm amalgamation and conversion from arable to pastoral use may have reduced local demand for labour. Nor was there an expanding industrial sector into which the surplus agricultural work-force could be absorbed. It is true that some industries were stimulated by the expansion of demand. A notable example was the vigorous growth of the coal-mining industry, producing for both industrial and domestic users. There was also a considerable amount of domestic building, to fill an obvious need. And some consumption industries, such as brewing, soap-making and glass-manufacture, were also stimula-ted. The total volume of production probably increased, through simple mutliplication of the number of producers. On the other hand, it is unlikely that *per capita* production increased at all, though in the absence of reliable figures for many industries it is difficult to be sure.

The major problem faced by industries at this time lay as much in the lack of effective demand as in any shortage of skilled labour or capital. Export markets were not fast-growing, and at home there were no expanding mass markets of urbanised industrial workers. While there were some striking examples of individual urban growth, notably in the case of London, this was not a period of marked urbanisation in the country as a whole. And within the towns, the urban poor did not wield any great purchasing power, since income levels probably remained low, while prices were rising steeply. It is rather paradoxical to argue, as does Christopher Hill, that in this period there was at the same time 'a savage depression of the living standards of the lower half of the population' and also a considerable expansion of consumer purchasing power within the domestic economy. A certain amount of demand was generated by the landed elite, and by merchants and tradesmen in the towns. This stimulated production of luxury and semi-luxury goods, and encouraged an extension of consumer services and the professions. But some, at least, of the demand for luxury goods was catered for by fashionable imported goods (though the exact proportion is un-known).[6] Mass domestic demand thus did not provide the basis for sustained industrial expansion, and certainly not for industrialisation. The bands of vagrants who roamed the countryside and clustered in the towns, to the anxiety of central government and local justices alike, testified to the difficulties of finding employment. In the same way, at another level of society, the number of gentlemen's sons who went into the professions rather than into the business world, also pointed to a sluggish and inexpansive industrial sector.

To some extent these economic problems were not new ones. There are some parallels between England in this period and in the late twelfth and thirteenth centuries, another period of population growth. But in the sixteenth century there were other developments taking place which were novel. They were engendered by fundamental changes within the international economy of the day. In the course of the sixteenth and seventeenth centuries, the focus of international trade moved away from the Mediterranean towards the Atlantic seaboard countries, as a result of the opening up of New World markets and the establishment of new trading routes to the East. In the long term, these changes proved of incalculable importance to the growth of the English economy, and laid the basis of the country's emergence as a major trading and colonial power in the late seventeenth and eighteenth centuries. Some important developments had already taken place in the years before the Civil War. From being on the fringe of the developed world, England had begun to play a more integral part. In the sixteenth century, control over English trade came increasingly into the hands of English merchants, in place of Italians and Germans. The range and variety of goods produced for export began to expand, although textiles were still the major export commodity. The tendency to export goods in a finished or semi-finished state instead of as raw materials continued. This was a sign of increased economic independence, though Holland was still a major finishing centre for English textiles. From the late sixteenth century onwards, there was a growing interest in overseas exploration and colonial settlement. This increased the range of commercial activities and colonial settlement, and inaugurated the re-export trade in colonial products. New avenues of advancement and speculation were opened up and some vast fortunes were made by these means.

The impact of these changes, however, took some time to become fully effective. The expansion of English overseas trade in the century before the civil war was still spasmodic and highly vulnerable to disruption. The total volume of trade, which is difficult to calculate precisely, may not have increased much in the sixteenth century, although English control over this trade did. European markets, which still took the great bulk of the country's exports, were not especially buoyant or expansive in the late sixteenth or early seventeenth centuries. Nor of course was England their only supplier. Overseas markets for English textiles were very sluggish in the late sixteenth century and, after a brief boom in the early years of the next century, were again depressed from the 1620s onwards. A commission, which was set up in 1638 to investigate the causes of the decline in trade, reported a gloomy picture of stagnation at home, and strong competition abroad.[7] This background helps to explain the prospecting zeal brought to colonial ventures and the search for new markets. There was a growing sense of competition in international trade which became a marked feature of the late seventeenth century; and many English merchants and statesmen evinced a mixture of hostility and admiration for the successes of their near neighbours, the Dutch.

By the early 1640s therefore the English economy was not on the verge of take-off into a modern growth economy. Some striking developments had taken place, more notably in agricultural techniques than in industry, and some changes of great long-term importance had begun, with the early steps towards the acquisition of an overseas colonial empire. But the constraints on expansion still remained immense. This was not a burgeoning economy restrained only by the bonds of restrictive government economic policies, though some royal policies may well have had harmful effects on economic development. Seventeenth-century experience did not suggest a happy faith in the unfettered powers of the market. It was not until over a century later that Adam Smith synthesised the confidence of a growth economy into the classic doctrines of *laissez-faire*.

There were in fact many occasions for anxiety in the years before the Civil War. The economy was highly vulnerable to short-term crises, which were characteristically haphazard (rather than cyclical) in their incidence. A run of bad harvests, an outbreak of epidemic disease, a collapse in overseas markets, or any of these in combination, could disrupt economic activity and produce unemployment and hardship. The 1620s and 1630s were particularly uneasy decades: against a general background of depressed European trade, there were commercial crises in the early 1620s, the late 1620s and the late 1630s; there were bad harvests in 1621–3, and some of the worst of the century in 1630 and 1631; and there were serious outbreaks of plague in 1625, 1636 and 1638. Crises such as these produced considerable controversy and debate, notably that over the causes and cure of the trade depression of the early 1620s. Writers and pamphleteers showed not only concern for the state of the economy but also a lively sense of the potential opportunities facing the country. The atmosphere was far from one of passive fatalism. The political crisis of 1640 and 1641, which preceded the outbreak of war in August 1642, also coincided with an economic depression, especially in trade and industry – albeit a less serious one than that of the early 1620s. 'The decay of trade is in everybody's mouth', wrote Henry Robinson in 1641. London was badly hit. Unemployed tradesmen and apprentices in the City petitioned parliament for relief in January 1642. To a large extent the depression was itself the product of the political uncertainty.[8] Against this background, economic problems naturally intruded into the political arena.

II

Already by the end of 1641, when the Royalist and Parliamentarian parties emerged, a considerable constitutional revolution had taken place, pushed through against the wishes of the King, by the virtually unanimous forces of the political nation represented in Parliament. The Civil War came about afterwards, when the ruling class divided amongst itself over how far the revolution was to go. This was the first of many subsequent divisions on the winning side. A party of constitutional Royalists rallied to the King. They included men like Hyde, Falkland and Culpeper, who earlier had been keen critics of Charles. The Civil War thus did not begin as a class war, though as the fighting progressed and as other issues emerged it took on more of those characteristics. In the first Civil War, there were country gentlemen, lawyers and merchants on both sides. Hence it is not surprising to find that Royalists and Parliamentarians alike shared a number of fundamental assumptions, as well as differing over a number of specific issues.

Stuart monarchy stood for definable, though often inconsistent, economic policies. Three major considerations came into play. Underlying all was a fundamental social and economic conservatism. The Crown, as head of the social hierarchy, had a vested interest in social stability and was anxious to prevent any changes which might prove disruptive. Secondly, since the economy was not static, the monarchy had to take into account the emergence of new sources of wealth in industry and commerce. Here the Crown's policy was to ally itself with the largest business interests, which had the greatest vested interest in the preservation of the *status quo*, and which were moreover prepared to pay for privileges and protection. Finally, the short-term formulation of policy was dominated to a large extent by financial considerations. The chronic indebtedness of the early Stuarts and their desire to find sources of income that were outside the control of Parliament led to intensive exploitation of economic regulation for fiscal purposes. The outcome was a policy which was often devious, tactless and ineffectual. By the end of the 1630s, the crown had alienated many of the vested interests that it had itself helped to create and maintain.[9] The first two Stuarts failed to sell favours intelligently to build up a nucleus of support, and had isolated themselves from those who were otherwise the 'natural' allies of the Crown. This is a theme which recurs in every aspect of royal policies.

In their agrarian policies, the Stuarts probably shared the broad objectives held by Tudor monarchs. They wished to prevent social dislocation through too rapid a course of agrarian change, a policy which can broadly be termed paternalist (though this should not be confused with real sympathy for the poor). In the sixteenth century this had led to some legislation against depopulating enclosures and against the conversion of tillage into pasture, which often accompanied enclosure. The Tillage Act of 1597, which applied to twenty-five counties, had by implication sanctioned conversion of land use in the rest of the country, acknowledging that in some economic circumstances it might prove beneficial. Under James no real attempt was made to put the Elizabethan legislation into operation. Indeed in 1608 Parliament passed the first, very limited pro-enclosure Act, in favour of six Herefordshire parishes, though this was not followed up by any others. The Crown however began to exploit the sale of exemptions from the Tillage Acts in favour of individual landowners. This proved a useful source of income, and in 1618 a formal Commission for selling exemptions was established. It was not a popular policy; by 1621, after a run of good harvests, Parliament was prepared to repeal the Tillage laws, but was prevented by an abrupt dissolution. In 1624 the 1563 Tillage Act was formally repealed and the Act of 1597 allowed to lapse.

After the bad harvest of 1630, however, the government of Charles I was stimulated to concern for the poor by its fears of social disorder. The Privy Council blamed the depopulating encloser for the dearth and high prices: 'it being a great occasion of fear in the common sort of people that such conversion being suffered will occasion more scarcity hereafter'. In 1630 therefore Charles I established a Commission for Depopulation to seek out and fine landowners whose enclosures had brought about a loss of houses or land under tillage. But this became very quickly another method of selling exemptions. The policy, described by Beresford as 'a mixture of paternalism and pick-pocketry' had become much more of the latter than the former. It achieved the worst of all worlds. It was deeply unpopular with landowners, without achieving any social gain. As Pym commented: 'If really it be a nuisance that is compounded for, 'tis an hurt to the people; if no nuisance, then 'tis a grand prejudice to the party.' There is no evidence to suggest that the Commission did anything to halt the process of enclosure and changing land use. Indeed throughout this period many enclosure agreements were given formal recognition in Chancery after collusive suits undertaken for this purpose.[10]

Another landowners' grievance was the Crown's policy of levying fines for ancient forest land which had subsequently been brought into cultivation. This was a purely arbitrary charge for a technical infringement of the royal prerogative, which Charles was exploiting for financial reasons. It added to the fiscal burden on the improving landowner, and as such was greatly resented.

Opposition to royal agrarian policies had a long parliamentary history and the Parliamentarian party in 1641 was heir to this tradition. The Grand Remonstrance, which contained a roll-call of opposition grievances, tersely denounced 'the enlargements of forests, contrary to the *Carta de Foresta*, and the composition thereupon' and complained that 'the conversion of arable into pasture, [and] continuance of pasture, under the name of depopulation, have driven many millions out of the subjects' purses, without any considerable profit to his Majesty'. These brief references concentrated upon the practical and financial implication of royal policy, since this was not the time for extensive theoretical justification. But some of the arguments put forward can be seen from previous parliamentary debates. The Tillage laws were opposed on grounds both of theory and of practice. The practical arguments centred on the positive advantages to be gained from enclosures, such as increased food production and improved agricultural productivity. They also stressed that blanket legislation on a national scale was undesirable, since it failed to take into account variations in local farming conditions. Others argued on theoretical grounds, defending the rights of landowners to choose their own methods of farming. This viewpoint was expressed by Raleigh in debate in 1601. In advocating the repeal of the Tillage Acts, he urged: 'And therefore I think the best course is to set it at liberty, and leave every man free, which is the desire of a true Englishman.' Yet other advocates of enclosures and improved farming techniques argued for positive government intervention to promote change. In 1641 for example the reformer and pamphleteer Plattes urged the Long Parliament to set up a College of Husbandry and to levy 20% death duties on landed estates to finance improvements, with heavy penalties against those who refused to co-operate.[11] In the event, the Long Parliament was too preoccupied with short term political problems in the months before the Civil War to take any positive action. No general enabling legislation to permit regulated enclosure was passed, though the proposal had been canvassed earlier in the century. Nor did Plattes's more drastic proposals find support. The end of attempts to regulate enclosure was a silent one. It was achieved in 1641 by the abolition of the prerogative courts, which were the Crown's agencies of enforcement. A solitary attempt after this to legislate against enclosures was made in 1656 by Major-General Whalley, but the bill was rejected as 'against property'. Henceforth enclosures proceeded by agreement sanctioned by privately introduced Acts of Parliament.

The Parliamentarians in 1641 were not acting in the name of *laissez-faire* economics, despite Raleigh's words on freedom. They were clearly concerned to free men of property from arbitrary fiscal impositions, levied in the name of paternalist control. But this was not part of a general philosophy of free trade. There is no sign that they wished to end all government intervention in the internal economy. While these landed gentlemen and property owners opposed regulation of their own activities, they did not cease to wish to regulate others themselves. Demands couched in the name of 'freedom' can often sound more libertarian than they are. As John Selden commented on the Parliamentarians' attack on the Bishops: 'This is the juggling trick of the parity: they would have nobody above them, but they do not tell you that they would have nobody below them.'[12] Thus the Parliamentarians proceeded in 1645 with further reforms in the gentry interest. They abolished the unpopular Court of Wards and converted lands held from the King by feudal tenure into freehold. But it was left to the Levellers and other radicals to attack copyhold tenure. A later petition in 1652 commented: 'how great an inconvenience and how disagreeable and inconsistent it is, for a free State to maintain by their Laws any arbitrary power as is used now by Lords of Manors in several places, upon Copyholders of inheritance, forcing them to pay uncertain fines at their pleasure'.[13] But appeals such as this went unanswered.

On some issues the interests of Crown and landowners coincided. Policies to iron out some of the inelasticities of the agrarian system and to prevent social disorder were generally accepted among the ruling class. Indeed the provision of poor relief and the setting of price and wage levels depended for their execution upon the local Justices in the countryside and upon the urban Corporations. The Crown acted as general supervisor and in time of crisis it took steps to prod the local authorities into action, as it did for example in 1631 with the issuing of the Book of Orders. This policy did not indicate any new concept of governmental benevolence on the part of the Crown but indicates rather the gravity of the situation in 1630 and 1631. Supple also suggests that the government was anxious to avoid any popular clamour for the recall of parliament.[14] Nor did the impetus for these schemes come solely from the Crown. Some local Justices and many urban oligarchies themselves took the initiative in providing local programmes for poor relief and for setting the poor to work. Policies such as these were stressed particularly by Puritan pamphleteers, with their emphasis on work discipline. Such attitudes were far from symptomatic of an invincible hostility to government intervention.

Opposition was however aroused when traditional offices appeared to be used by the Crown for the collection of arbitrary fines. The office of the Clerk of the Market for example was widely unpopular for this reason. The Clerk, a royal appointee, was responsible for the collection of purveyance, which was never popular, and for the general regulation of weights and measures in the markets. The intention of this latter regulation was to protect the interests of the poor consumer. But it was alleged in a petition of 1637 that the Clerk was abusing his position and simply levying fees without actually examining any weights and measures.[15] The King tried to stem hostility in 1639 by prohibiting the Clerk from taking fees but failed to appease trading and commercial interests. The Long Parliament acted promptly in 1641 and legislated to restrict the activities of the Clerk, while local Justices and the Corporations took over his function of regulating weights and measures. But the attack was confined to a few cases of abuse. Many regulations remained on the Statute book into the eighteenth century, applied with greater or lesser zeal in different parts of the country, as local conditions seemed to demand. In the mid-eighteenth century propagandists began to argue that the mechanisms of the market would work satisfactorily without regulation and that price controls could be abandoned – a change which reflected the growing integration of regional markets into a national one. It was not until 1828 that the Statute for setting the Assize of Bread was finally repealed,[16] though it had probably long been circumvented in practice.

III

The regulation of industries also generated controversy. The Crown generally favoured the maintenance of the traditional companies and guilds, which supervised the standard of goods produced and operated some degree of control over recruitment into the industry. Enforcement of these regulations was left to the companies and hence was not operated uniformly. In times of expansion, controls tended to be by-passed or ignored, though in slumps they were applied more rigorously. It ensured a reasonably flexible system, which allowed some degree of local autonomy within a general framework of regulation. This sort of supervision commanded widespread support among the ruling oligarchy, though the crown, as adjudicator in the event of disputes, was unable to please all interests. But the major controversy was that over monopolies.

From the late sixteenth century onwards, the Crown found that it could exploit the granting of monopolies for the production or distribution of individual commodities, and by this means provide itself with an extra-parliamentary source of revenue. Monopolies could be defended as a legitimate device for the protection of new commodities in need of development. But as the range of goods that came under monopoly licence was extended, it became increasingly obvious that the Crown's motives were not economic but financial. It was in fact a clumsy attempt at a purchase tax on consumer goods. Successive parliaments from 1571 onwards had protested at this policy and in 1624 an Act against Monopolies was put on the statute book. Charles I was therefore contravening the spirit, if not the letter of the law, by continuing this policy in the 1630s, using a loophole in the law by making grants to companies rather than to individuals. Again the Crown incurred considerable unpopularity for only little gain. Even in financial terms, the Crown derived very little benefit from monopolies, since most of the profits accrued to the patentees. This was a point made by Pym in debate in 1641, and by Clarendon in his *History*, where he noted: 'Projects of many kinds, many ridiculous, many scandalous, all very grievous, were set on foot; the envy and reproach of which came to the King, the profit to other men'.[17]

The Crown was on doubly dangerous ground here, since parliamentary opposition made common cause with popular feeling on this issue. Monopolies were strongly resented by the consuming public at large, who blamed monopolists for rising prices. These sentiments were felt most strongly in the towns, where monopolists, especially those of Catholic persuasion, became scapegoats for the general unpopularity of the regime in the 1630s. Charles I revoked a number of patents in 1639 in an attempt to allay the criticism but without success. The Long Parliament took quick action in November 1640, issuing a general statement against monopolies and ordering the exclusion of all monopolists from the House. They also set up a committee to look into all outstanding grants. They were encouraged by continued popular clamour. The Root-and-Branch petition for radical religious reform, which was presented to Parliament in December 1640 by inhabitants of London and the counties around, had also included an additional clause attacking monopolies and patents.

The Long Parliament, however, was cautious. It did not proceed to any general legislation against monopolies, but called in individual patents one by one. Nor did it instigate a general attack on the regulated companies and guilds, despite the fact that the Grand Remonstrance had arraigned 'the restraint of the liberties of the subject in their habitations, trades and other interests'. It was left to the Levellers in the late 1640s to take up the campaign to open up entry into the regulated companies and to democratise the guilds.

The organisation of the London soap industry provides a case history. In August 1641 the Long Parliament annulled the patent of the highly unpopular Catholic-dominated Westminster Soap Company. This left the industry in the control of the traditional Company of London Soapmakers, who had previously been ousted by the Westminster Company. The Soapmakers were a closed company, though more open in their recruitment and more efficient in their organisation than their defeated rivals. They were then challenged in turn by the independent soapmakers of London. The Long Parliament ordered a bill to be drawn up against the Company in 1642, but did not proceed any further. The issue eventually went to law and was finally won by the London Company in 1656 after protracted legal battles. It is true of course that the Parliamentarians after 1642 had the immediate problems of the war to pursue. As Christopher Hill has noted, 'the New Jerusalem was under attack before it was even built'.[18] But the manner of proceeding against monopolies in 1641 does not suggest a very strong opposition on the part of the Parliamentarians to the principle of regulation in itself.

The same point can be made about the position of Coke, the great common lawyer, whose ruling, with his fellow judges, against monopolies in the test case of *Darcy versus Allein* in 1602 had thrown the weight of the common law on the side of the opposition. Judgement was given against Darcy's playing-card monopoly on grounds as diverse as reference to the Bible, to the fifteenth-century jurist Fortescue, to precedent and to the common weal. Two different discussions have centred around Coke's decision in this case: firstly whether he was here re-interpreting the law, and secondly, whether he was doing this as part of a general predilection for *laissez-faire* economics. It seems probable that Coke was in fact amending and liberalising the law on this issue.[19] One of the perennial strengths of the common law has always been its ability to adapt with changing circumstances. But this does not necessarily mean that Coke's motives were those of a free-trader. This attributes to Coke a far more consistent and logical economic philosophy than seems to have been the case. He was not primarily an economic theorist. There is no evidence to show that he opposed all forms of economic regulation or government intervention in the economy. On the contrary, there is evidence that he positively supported some forms of regulation. For example in the 1630s he declared his approval of laws for setting wage rates and considered that not to implement these could be detrimental 'to the common law and the wealth of this land'.[20] Coke's undoubted influence with the parliamentary opposition in the early seventeenth century lay not so much in his devotion to abstract economic theories as in his emphasis on the duty of the common law to curtail the claims of an arbitrary prerogative.

IV

A further arena of conflict lay in the regulation and promotion of overseas trade. In some respects the interest of Crown and merchants were similar. The Crown derived an increased revenue in customs from an expanding overseas commerce. All kings were also tradesmen, as Selden observed. But the Crown had other political considerations to bear in mind. Nor were mercantile interests homogeneous, so that it was difficult for the Crown to please them all. The early Stuarts tended to ally themselves with the largest commercial interests, notably a few great London traders who were well established and could advance loans to the Crown. These included merchants such as Crispe, Garway, Hickes and Salter. This in itself provoked hostility and opposition from small merchants and newcomers, as well as from the outport merchants who envied the commercial dominance of the capital. But even this policy was not carried out consistently. The Crown was prepared in certain circumstances to jettison its traditional allies. The most notorious example of this was the Cockayne scheme, in which James broke with the Merchant Adventurers in favour of Cockayne and his allies known as the 'King's Adventurers'. Here formulation of policy seems to have been dictated by James's gambling instincts, fed by the desire of a few merchants to take over the valuable overseas trade in English cloths. There was a certain economic rationale to the scheme, which was designed to bring the finishing stages of textile production into English hands. But there was no sound preparation behind the project, which failed completely. This disaster intensified the trading problems facing English merchants.[21] After this, the Crown was more cautious and returned to traditional ways. The Merchant Adventurers were allowed to buy back their exclusive trading privileges. Under pressure from Parliament in the early 1620s, however, the crown was forced to open up terms of entry into the trading companies, including the Adventurers. But left to his own devices after 1629, Charles I allowed the Adventurers to buy back their privileges again in 1634. Even then he was still prepared to sell exemptions to interlopers and to rival groups.[22] This sort of behaviour upset everybody. It created serious business uncertainty and alienated those upon whose support the crown might otherwise have counted.

The Parliamentary opposition had long called for the opening up of these traditional trading companies in the name of 'free trade'. In 1604 the outport merchants and interlopers together had attacked the dominance of London merchants. Outport merchants were relatively well represented in Parliament, and their cause won considerable landed gentry support. In 1606 partial success was obtained by an Act to open up trade with France, Spain and Portugal. Some of the heat went out of this debate in the following decade which saw a trading boom, but the issue revived again in the depression of the late 1610s and early 1620s. The demand for 'free trade' was taken up vigorously by the Parliament of 1621. The privileges of the Merchant Adventurers, the East India Company and the Muscovy Company all came under attack. It was in this debate that Sir Edward Coke declared: 'In all Acts of Parliament, freedom of trade is held the life of trade.'[23] The Parliament of 1624 continued the attack. A bill for 'free trade into all countries' was unsuccessful, but terms of entry into many companies were liberalised. It is notable however that in 1640–2 the attack on the conditions of entry into the trading companies was muted, although Charles I had reversed Parliament's policy in the 1630s. The Parliamentarians in 1641 did not seize the chance to pass any general legislation to reform or to throw open entry into the companies. In 1643 the privileges of the Merchant Adventurers were confirmed, and the fine for admission doubled. Here financial necessity seems to have dictated policy; the Adventurers had just advanced a loan of £30,000 to Parliament.

The demand for a free as opposed to a regulated trade had been prompted by economic depression. Critics argued that the regulated companies were holding back foreign sales by keeping prices artificially high. They showed a growing realisation that England could not expect its goods to find automatic vent in the competitive European markets. And they argued that the prosperity of the Dutch was based on their liberal trading policies. Defenders of the companies, on the other hand, pointed out that if a few merchants could not find sales it was unlikely that many would be able to succeed. As the Duke of Newcastle later mournfully observed; 'I have heard much discourse of free trade what great advantage that would be to the Commonwealth ... But I could never hear it well resolved'.[24] But the debate was not couched in terms of two alternative economic ideologies. Those arguing for 'free trade' did not display an implicit faith in the self-regulating capacities of the market. They were arguing for liberalisation of the terms of entry but not the abolition of the companies. Nor did they demand complete freedom in all areas of the economy. Free trade in the seventeenth century meant what it said: it did not imply a demand for free agriculture or industry. It was not until the nineteenth century that the term acquired the wider connotations of *laissez-faire*. In the 1640s it was left to the Levellers to take the logic of the Parliamentarians' position one stage further and demand the abolition of the trading companies. Lilburne attacked with special venom 'the prerogative-patentee monopolising Merchant Adventurers'.[25] But the Levellers were unsuccessful. It was only in the later seventeenth century that the exclusive powers of the trading companies were eroded, as the state began to provide naval protection for merchants and consular advice for English tradesmen overseas, and as England's commercial position strengthened.

The debate illustrated the concern that was felt over England's foreign trade in the early years of the century. Here again the first two Stuarts disappointed many. For diplomatic and financial reasons, they tended to prefer pacific foreign policies. This pleased some mercantile interests, especially the better established ones. A bellicose policy was not automatically successful. A war, even when initially popular, could become disliked with time, as Elizabeth I had discovered in the late 1590s. But many felt that under the early Stuarts passivity had degenerated into supineness. This was felt especially strongly by merchants with trading interests in the far-flung and vulnerable trades to the American colonies and the Far East. The government's failure to seek revenge from the Dutch in 1623 for the massacre of English traders at Amboyna in the East Indies was resented, as this left the Dutch in control of the lucrative spice trade. The Crown was also passive in the New World, doing little to encourage the drive towards colonial acquisition. In 1629 Charles I bargained away to France English claims to Canada. In the competitive international conditions of the 1620s and 1630s, merchants began to feel the need for more aggressive and positive policies from the state in the interests of trade. These desires were left unsatisfied by the early Stuarts. Instead merchants felt harassed politically and burdened financially for no concrete return. These grievances were included in the Grand Remonstrance. The levying of tunnage and poundage duties without parliamentary consent, the payments of Ship Money, and the arbitrary compositions raised by the king were denounced, while at the same time Charles was blamed for failing to stamp out piracy.

The parliamentary opposition in the early seventeenth century had by contrast shown itself eager to promote the interests of trade and colonial development. Under pressure from Parliament in 1622 the king had set up the first Committee of Trade. It marked an initial step towards the creation of a specialised government body for trading matters, and was the ancestor, by indirect descent, of the later Board of Trade. The Committee of 1622, composed of both Members of Parliament and Privy Councillors, was short-lived. It suggested some remedies for the commercial depression, which were taken up by the Parliament of 1624, but by the mid 1620s it had become defunct. It was followed by another short-lived Commission for Trade in 1625. Subsequently Charles I in 1630 set up a permanent sub-committee of the Privy Council with general responsibility for supervision of trade and a similar Commission for the Plantations followed in 1634. But this Commission was more concerned to sell privileges in the New World than to encourage expansion. On the other hand, many of the leading Parliamentarians had played a prominent part in colonising companies in the 1630s, notably in the Massachusetts Bay Company and the Providence Island Company. In the early years of the political crisis, some steps were taken towards furthering colonial expansion in the Americas, despite the preoccupations of domestic affairs. Before the Long Parliament went into recess in September 1641, both the Lords and Commons set up standing committees for the West Indies, the Lords' Committee being chaired by Warwick and the Commons' by

Pym. Little, however, was achieved during the years of the Civil War.[26]

The Grand Remonstrance also called in general terms for policies to improve England's commercial position. It demanded action to prevent the outflow of gold and silver from the country, to encourage domestic manufactures and to promote a favourable balance of trade. It also advocated the improvement of the herring fishing industry, which would provide employment for the poor and act as 'a plentiful nursery for mariners'. Demands such as these were not of course uniquely Parliamentarian. Francis Bacon, a staunch defender of royal prerogatives, had advocated in his *Essays* rather similar policies. This point has sometimes been used to prove Bacon's modernity and concern for trade and industry, despite the fact that elsewhere in his writings he warned against excessive expansion of sedentary trades, as harmful to the military strength of the country.[27] But probably it simply showed that any intelligent observer could see what was needed. The problem was to find a government that could satisfactorily put these suggestions into practice.

The problem ultimately came down to one of lack of confidence in the King and his ministers. At least one of Charles's advisers in the 1630s had seen the advantages of positive economic policies. Strafford in Ireland was anxious for political reasons to strengthen the Irish economy. He wrote to the King that the Irish 'seemed only to want foreign Commerce to make them a civil, rich and contented People: and consequently more easily governed by your Majesty's Ministers . . . and the more profitably for your Crown, than in a savage and poor condition'.[28] In fact the practical effect of his policies was probably minimal, since he was working in adverse economic conditions. But his activities generated intense suspicion among his opponents, and were made an article of charge against him at his trial in 1641. His motives were feared and his methods disliked as too authoritarian. As he was one of the most active, so Strafford was the most feared and hated of the King's ministers in the 1630s. Charles I may well have had cause to wonder whether an increase in trade did indeed render subjects more 'civil and contented'.

V

Thus the divisions between Royalists and Parliamentarians in the first civil war did not reflect a conflict between two rival economic ideologies. Certainly the Parliamentarians were highly critical of many aspects of

Stuart policies. They feared actions which appeared to override established property rights. They resented arbitrary financial expedients. They disliked the Crown's attempts to back industrial and commercial monopolies. But they also blamed the Crown for sins of omission as well as commission. Their demands for more vigorous policies in the interests of trade and colonial expansion implied more state action, not less. In the same way, the comprehensive programme of economic reforms advocated by writers such as Robinson and Hartlib also implied considerable government intervention, though in practice few of their more ambitious proposals were adopted.

There is indeed no reason to assume that a developing economy automatically engenders demands for *laissez-faire* policies. In the economic circumstances of the mid-seventeenth century, it was not surprising to find demands for state protection and promotion of the interests of trade and commerce, especially for overseas trade. And advocates of this point of view naturally tended, in the political circumstances before the Civil War, to look towards Parliament rather than to the King for implementation of these policies. Parliament was not only better able to raise the money needed, through taxation, but was also a publicly accountable body. The King on the other hand was not accountable and in his efforts to find an extra-parliamentary source of revenue had resorted to arbitrary measures, which threatened property rights and undermined business confidence. After the civil wars, successive governments from the Rump onwards, whatever their political complexion, gave much more attention to the interests of trade and colonial development in their foreign policies. It was the Rump government, too, which in 1651 promulgated the famous Navigation Act, in the interests of English shipping. This Act marked the culmination of some thirty years' concern for the development of English maritime strength. It also laid the basis of the 'old colonial system', in which English shipping eventually enjoyed a monopoly position within the nascent overseas Empire.

Issues of economic policy therefore certainly helped to shape allegiances in the early years of the revolution. Economic grievances contributed to the political isolation of Charles I in 1640. Economic interests also throw some light on the emergence of parties in 1642. In some ways it is surprising that the King found a body of supporters to fight for him at all. The emergence of the Royalist party was motivated essentially by social conservatism and fear of the implications of political and religious change. This reaction was strongest among the landed upper classes. Men like Hyde and Falkland supported the King, not for his personal qualities, and certainly not for his past policies, but as head of the social hierarchy. The Royalists in general were people whose social position was dependent upon and guaranteed by the existing status system. The King's party included some great merchants, customs farmers and ex-monopolists, whose economic interests were tied in with the Caroline regime. It did also attract some down-at-heel adventurers, hoping for social advancement from the king. But the Royalists were to a large extent composed of large land-owners and big businessmen, who were prepared to back Charles's show of force against the Parliamentary regime. It is indeed arguable that by 1642 it was Charles I who was in revolt against the established order of things, albeit a very newly established one, which had been pushed through against his will. The prelude to the wars was Charles's attempt at a *coup d'état* in January 1642.

On the Parliamentary side, however, there remained those who felt more threatened by the activities of the King than by the dangers of social revolution. The Parliamentary party of course contained many landowners of considerable social standing and wealth. Its leadership, especially at the start of the wars, was drawn from this social background. It included men like Hampden, Barnardiston, and the Earls of Warwick and Essex. But contemporary observers agreed that the Parliamentarians also derived considerable support from the towns and from the indus-trial areas of the country, especially the clothing areas. Their accounts probably tended to exaggerate the unanimity of these interests, and they certainly glossed over some of the intricacies of urban politics. In many towns, internal power struggles took place before allegiances were settled. The most conspicuous example of this was the contest within London, where at a crucial stage of the revolution in December 1641 the opposition party gained control of the Common Council. Nor were all the industrial interests solidly on the side of the Parlia-mentarians. A great local landowner like Henry Hastings, for example, could call out an army of a hundred miners from his colliery in Derby-shire, as he did in June 1642 when he attacked the county magazine at Leicester for the King.[29] But, by and large, commercial and manu-facturing interests seem to have been opposed to the King. The social position of merchants, tradesmen, and clothiers was not guaranteed by the social structure. In many ways the status and recognition ac-corded to merchants, for example, was not commensurate with their wealth and influence. Some clothiers, too, resented their lowly social standing.[30] These men had nothing to gain from the King and much to lose from his arbitrary policies. Those with liquid assets were highly vulnerable to the depredations of an impecunious monarchy. The Crown's relations with the City of London illustrate this clearly. The affair of the Londonderry lands provides an example. In 1610 the Crown had coerced the City into taking out a charter for the development of lands in Ulster and into investing money there, but in 1631 Charles I had revoked the charter and fined the Corporation. This was tactless and provocative. Eventually Charles tried to reverse his policy and in November 1641 he promised to restore the Londonderry lands to the City as soon as the Irish civil war should be solved. This however was rather a feeble concession, and it came too late. Other actions of Charles I in the early months of the political crisis had thoroughly frightened the business community of the capital. In July 1640 he had seized a stock of bullion from the mint in order to force a loan from city merchants. In the same month he had threatened to mint a new brass coinage to meet his financial needs, and discussed the idea of a devaluation. Projects such as these emphasised for many the dangers in an unfettered prerogative. Clarendon summed up these criticisms with a modest understatement: 'the City of London was looked upon too much of late time as a common stock not easy to be exhausted and as a body not to be grieved by ordinary acts of injustice'.[31]

At the start of the war, the threat from the King to the security of the business community may well have seemed greater than the dangers of social subversion and lower-class discontent. In the years from 1640 to 1642, the political activities of the urban lower classes – in so far as they were concerned in the crisis at all – were solidly behind the Parliamentarians. The attack on the monopolists and against commercial privileges gave the alliance a common cause. The urban mob may have unwittingly been deceived by the apparent liberality of the opposition rhetoric against Charles. They were not yet organised into their own political party, as they were to be later in the years from 1646 to 1649. Holles in 1642 likened them, apparently without any great sense of disquiet, to 'a sleepy lion'. Indeed the eventual emergence of the Leveller movement did much to crystallise the later social conservatism of the Parliamentary regime. By contrast, peasant discontent in the countryside was widespread in the early 1640s. There was a spontaneous, if disorganised, campaign to throw down enclosures in these years. This naturally heightened the social fears felt by landowners.

Economic interests were of course far from the only factors influencing men's actions and allegiances in 1642. The outbreak of Civil War involved many complex issues. No one shared the conviction, voiced later by Rousseau, that civil strife could benefit the economy. But conflict over economic issues also played its part in shaping the origins of the war. Hobbes commented in retrospect that some had hoped that, by defeating a King, the English might emulate the commercial successes of the Dutch after they had ousted the King of Spain.[32] The Parliamentarians in 1642 were not republicans. But they shared a growing feeling that the unpredictability of Stuart kings was bad for business confidence and for trade.

8. Politics and Political Thought 1640-1642

M. J. MENDLE

I

THE BODY POLITIC: HABITS OF THOUGHT

IF politics is the art of the possible, then political thought made politics a difficult activity in the years before the civil war. The aspirations of the political nation were not hopelessly utopian. The men of 1640 wanted a solvent king and frequent, financially responsible parliaments. They wanted an adequately financed church, reformed to suit the spiritual and social needs of the laity. They wanted quiet tenants and peaceful towns, and knew they would get neither if the common people were aggrieved. Taken in themselves, these aims were quite unexceptionable.

But the political thought of the day did not allow the various political hopes to be taken individually. Every aspect of public life was seen as part of a single whole. The parts of the kingdom flourished only when the whole flourished. The whole worked well only when each part worked well. The age had its special language for it, the metaphor of the body politic. It was simply an extended analogy between the state and its parts, and the human body and its limbs and organs. The King was the head. The Lords, and the Commons, the clergy, and the 'people' were organs or limbs – significantly there were no conventional associations with specific parts of the body in the seventeenth century. Still, without any of them the body politic would die or be crippled. Conversely, without the head to lead and inform, the parts were helpless. They were unintelligent, and without wills of their own. It was monstrous, to use the favoured word, for organs to behave like the head; it was also treason.

The analogy stressed that the King was indispensable. As John Pym said in November 1640, the King was 'the fountain of justice, of peace, of protection; therefore we say, the King's Courts, the King's Judges, the King's laws; the royal power and majesty shines upon us in every public blessing we enjoy.'[1] The monarchy was so pervasive, its power so necessary that anti-monarchism seemed foolish. In this sense, royalism was identified with patriotism, and both with constructive opposition. Sir Edward Coke and William Prynne thought of themselves as the king's friends. The situation was not without its irony. When attacking Strafford or Laud for their 'usurpations', the opposition thought themselves more 'royalist' than the king.

The analogy made one point perhaps a little too well in 1640. The houses of parliament existed only when the King allowed. His writ of summons and his power of prorogation and dissolution were absolute. Along with the power to make war and peace, they were the most treasured of his special powers for the common good, known as prerogatives. The Lords and Commons could no more make themselves move without the King, than the body could without the head.

Organological attitudes figured significantly in the muddled politics of 1640. First, political consequences grew out of the stress on the mutuality of interests. Each part had an interest in ensuring the well-being of the other parts, as well as an interest that no part thrived at its expense. This was true of ideals as well. For both there was a presumed state of balance. Politics consisted of constant efforts to keep all in due proportion. For example, the prerogatives of the King had to be set against the liberties of the subject. It was also a balancing of the body politic to measure the claims of religion and justice against the social upheaval they seemed to entail.

The result was a distinctive mixture of highmindedness and self-interest in politics in the years before the civil war. Arguments of principle and appeals to conscience were common in the debates of the Long Parliament. At the same time, the theory of the unity of the body politic legitimised the easy conclusion that any settlement or policy which harmed one's own interests was necessarily against the public interest. These inhibitions against sacrifice and effective action (which were bound to injure some interest) favoured neither a settlement nor a rupture. Instead they encouraged the state of suspension that made the parliament of November 1640 a long parliament even by the outbreak of war. Doubt, passivity, and frequent but impermanent swings of opinion characterised politics in 1640–2.

Secondly, politics were burdened with the historical pessimism of mid-17th century organology. The current age was seen as a decline from the glorious reign of Elizabeth. The most excessive Elizabethan self-congratulations were accepted at face value, and the earlier reign was presumed to be packed full of the virtues lacking in 1640: unity, good will, trust, a common religious and national purpose. By contrast, in 1640 most politicians thought that very substantial reforms were necessary before England could again approach the brink of perfection. Of course, the historical view made the problems of 1640 appear intractable because they were so deeply rooted in a decline dating from the reign of James I. A paradoxical corollary was that the more the organological predictions of doom came true, the less likely were the head and organs to heed the appeal for unity and trust which the organological measures were supposed to encourage.

The idea of the body politic was strained. The moderate and benevolent policies it favoured seemed impotent. But hostile and violent remedies were suicidal. The political failure of the common law was spectacular. Perhaps nothing was more characteristic of the men of 1640 than their love of the common law. They presumed the common law to be the distilled wisdom of immemorial custom. They thought that because such laws were automatically just, the body politic simply needed to listen to its judges, whose great knowledge inspired them with legal truth rather as the Old Testament prophets were inspired with the Word of God. The law then, was supposed to link the parts of the body with the head. The 'laws in a commonwealth are like the sinews in a natural body, by which the hand, foot, and other parts of the body do readily move, by the direction of the head'[2] – a formulation which subtly suggested that the legal way was the only way the limbs of state could possibly be moved.

But the law had proved an unreliable ally. The opposition had lost nearly every major legal case since the turn of the century. Both the judges and the King sometimes took the phrase 'King's Judges' rather too literally. Even if pressure was discounted, the judges had shown the law to be what each of them chose to make of it: 'in such confusion do our Judges leave us [that] either side takes that for granted, which by the other side is utterly denied.'[3] With the loss of faith in jurisprudential politics, and for the same reasons, went the hope that the monarchy could be considered limited or moderated by a law independent of the human agents who interpreted and executed it.

Obviously there was need for fresh thinking. But habits of thought are not dropped or acquired overnight – or even in two years. The men of 1640 were as intelligent and educated as any generation of political Englishmen would be until the nineteenth century. They were also xenophobic and intellectually conservative. They thought it dangerous to stray beyond the conventional wisdom of the body politic and the common law into speculation 'fit for civilians, historians, or the pen of a divine'.[4] These intellectual quicksands were the home of the 'rash spirits' and 'incendiaries': Jesuits and Presbyterian fanatics, regicides and absolutists.

The English therefore had a head and a body and endless disputes about the law, and nothing to tell them how to proceed when disputes refused to solve themselves. The most promising of the tainted political notions was the idea of mixed government by the estates of the realm. It was not intrinsically radical; in time it would serve the King. But historically it was highly suspect. The Presbyterian radicals Thomas Cartwright and Job Throckmorton used it; so had Parsons the Jesuit. This was enough to damn the idea, but it was not all. Kinglessness had come to lurk in the shadows of the perfectly good and traditional word 'estates'. The 'estates' of the Netherlands had revolted from the Habsburgs, and in 1640 it was the 'estates' of Scotland against the King. Thus mixed government was publicly ignored in the early seventeenth century. Perhaps the great puritan peers and their associates took solace from the theory in their dark and brooding years of the late 1620s and the 1630s, but they kept their thoughts largely to themselves. Its public reappearance in 1640 showed the seriousness of the situation.

The English theory of mixed government combined two distinct ideas, and superimposed both on the tangible institutions of King, Lords, and Commons. The first was the classical-Renaissance idea of mixed government. According to it, there were three pure forms of government; the rule of one, the rule of a few, the rule of many. Conventionally, though not always, these forms were called monarchy, aristocracy, and democracy. These pure forms were inherently unstable, the vices of one form naturally suggesting the virtues of the next in an endless cycle. Stability however could be achieved by mixing the three forms into one government.

This rather formal theory was merely an academic curiosity by itself. It became relevant and socially dangerous when linked with a radical revision of the old notion of the estates which was used for this purpose. Traditionally there were three estates – the Lords Temporal (the lay peers) and the Lords Spiritual (in the seventeenth century, the bishops) in one Upper House, and the Commons. These three estates were under the King, as the body is under the head. There was, however, one unchallenged aspect of government where the King was not the head of the body, but merely one among equals. King, Lords, and Commons each had to assent to legislation. That is, each had a veto.

The new theory generalised outward from this single but critical fact to form a theory of English government. Convention and propriety were turned on their heads as the king came to be regarded as an estate like the others, and the Lords Spiritual lost their separate status, though not their seats in the Lords. It was possible to qualify or limit the implied equality by adding that the King had tasks which the other estates did not, and had special powers accordingly. But the emphasis was on equality.

The final step was to associate the government of the three estates with the prized mixture of monarchy, aristocracy, and democracy. Thus the King-in-Parliament was made the most important part of the constitution. The King-out-of-Parliament took a subordinate place. By contrast, in the body politic the King's special powers and abilities for the common good – his prerogatives – gave him the highest expression of his headship. Each view by itself was a sort of heresy. Each view pointed to facts true in themselves but not by themselves. Both views could be qualified to speak in the same moderate voice. But when the King's propagandists argued for his prerogative in the language of mixed government, they found themselves in the same sort of paradoxes and contradictions as the parliamentarians fell into when they insisted, despite repeated royal denials, that the King's actions were not really his but those of his evil advisers.

The problem for the men of 1640 was that the kingdom needed both kinds of government. The attack on the exercise of prerogative power in domestic affairs, particularly in financial matters and in the avoidance of parliaments, was as justified as it was bitter. But the country could not do without prerogatives. They were intended for the common good. Most of them were for the sake either of justice or of national security. Both tasks were divine; both were sworn to by the King in his coronation oath. The prerogatives for national security were by definition necessary – without them the kingdom was open to invasion or subversion, trade depredation or insolvency or other economic and financial disasters. Prerogatives were very often emergency powers, and frequently secret powers as well, when foreign affairs were involved. So it seemed self-defeating to have these powers but to subject them to the public, slow, and occasional ways of Parliament, and to link reason of state (the seductive phrase which meant 'defence of the national interest') to vengeful taxpayers and priggish lawyers.

Most narrowly stated, the objection of the leading men of the opposition (who wanted and respected power) was not to prerogatives themselves, but to their fraudulent use as tricks to improve the domestic political advantage of the King. Prerogatives were indispensable. The seductiveness of the idea of mixed government was that it allowed one to forget this hard truth in favour of the argument that the mixed way was superior – more stable, more harmonious, and more just. The theory of mixed government either licensed the worst sort of irresponsibility, or it urged the assumption by the whole of the duties of the head.

The mischievousness of the theory was not confined to the relations between King and Parliament. The body politic, it will be remembered was strangely disorganised. The Church, the Lords, the Commons, the people were rarely associated with specific parts of the body. It would have been very difficult, as well as tactless, to work out suitable correlatives. Before 1640 in many ways it was also irrelevant. The main points of contention were between the King and his (undifferentiated) subjects. There was not yet enough friction between the Lords and Commons to be of constitutional significance. The question of the relation between the Commons and the people did not arise. The religious issue only burst forth with something like the old Elizabethan intensity in the parliament of 1628–9. A simple head and body were adequate.

By 1640 the Church issue was burning. The King had tried, significantly though unsuccessfully, to meet his financial and military needs through some *ad hoc* meetings with the lay lords alone. The people were clearly aroused about religion, and their zealousness did not go unadmired by their social betters. Almost as if to prove the prejudice against it correct, the notion of the estates clumsily revealed the new tensions and constitutional ambiguities of the body politic.

The exclusion of the Lords Spiritual from the estates was as startling as the parallel inclusion of the King among them. People asked why, if the bishops were not a separate estate, did they sit in the Upper House? They sat in virtue of an office, not in respect of an hereditary dignity as lay peers. Lay peers represented themselves and no others; did bishops represent the clergy or did they sit on the same basis as the lay lords? Was it possible for one House to be one estate, yet be composed of two orders of men who sat for different reasons? On the other hand, did not the clergy need a voice if the bishops' votes did not give them one?

It was a cliché that the Commons were the representative body of the kingdom. That is what the name implied. The common people who swarmed about the houses of parliament surely thought the Lower House was *their* house. According to the notion of mixed government by the estates, the Commons ought to have been the democracy. But was it really so? In 1600 Thomas Wilson thought the 'knights, esquires, gentlemen, lawyers, professors and ministers, archdeacons, prebends, and vicars' were the 'nobilitas minor'. Sir Thomas Aston in 1641 thought popular pressure upon parliament outrageous because the 'Parliament, the Primates [bishops], the Nobiles, with the minores Nobiles, the Gentry, consult and dispense the rules of government; the Plebeians submit to and obey them.' Wilson and Aston had an incontrovertible social point to make: by continental standards the Parliamentary gentry of 1640 were minor nobility. They were not about to give up their social ascendancy, or the political authority it implied. On the other hand, the gentry's claim to nobility was utter nonsense according to English law. It was also true that many members of the Commons were elected by the free votes of their social inferiors, and felt morally bound to represent them.

But the relation between the people and the Commons was not only social and constitutional. What if 'the stirring up of the people of all counties, of all sorts, high and low, rich and poor, of both sexes, men and women, old and young, bond and free' was truly the 'work of the Lord'? Each man had to answer this question for himself. 'God forbid,' said John Pym when the people were intimidating Lords spiritual and temporal, 'that the house of Commons should proceed in any way to dishearten people to obtain their just desires.' 'The insurrections of the apprentices (as all ungoverned multitudes) are of very dangerous consequence,' worried another, who added 'but God, who works miracles, can out of such violent actions bring comfortable effects.'[5]

II

A NARRATIVE OF POLITICS AND POLITICAL THOUGHT

The men who came to Westminster in 1640 were subjects bound by God, affection, and common sense to obey and preserve the royal power that protected and preserved them. They were bound by their responsibility to themselves and to those who sent them to prevent that same power from abusing them. They were statesmen and civil creatures threatened, so they thought, by a church hierarchy asserting independent civil power. They were Christians and laymen obliged by God, King, and country to serve and nurture the same body spiritual which they could not do without, or do with either, as it then stood. Self-interest and the divine imperative of order made them careful of the rights of the greater and lesser 'nobles' and of the King as well. Another sort of religious imperative made them, or some of them, acutely sensitive that *vox Dei* might be *vox populi*, and that neither might be wholly or always compatible with their narrow personal, parochial, and social interests. Sir Benjamin Rudyerd aptly said the Long Parliament assembled 'to do God's business and the King's, in which our own is included'[6]; one narrative of events and attitudes before the outbreak of war can be constructed out of the shifting relations between these three interests, and between each of them and the *vox populi*.

(i)   English Mixed Government and the Scottish Troubles

The English Revolution is famous for its political tracts. The 'badly written and badly printed' little pamphlets of the enormous Thomason Collection at the British Museum as well as the handsome *Leviathan* seem as close to the heart of the period as the attempt on the five members, the battle of Edgehill, or the execution of the King. Surprisingly, in the two years following the summoning of the Short Parliament there are no more than a dozen of these (not including printed speeches in parliament, petitions, or the bottomless pit of writings on church government). Why was there so little constitutional theorising until mid-1642 when, before the shooting began, 'a war did begin between the King and Parliament with their pens'? There are several answers; the first in time was that there was an English reluctance to see the constitutional implications of the Scottish revolt. We emphasise reluctance, because there was no significant development of constitutional theory in the period 1640–2 and because a recent influential account has suggested that the opposition were taught their mixed constitution by the King in 1642.[7]

There were two important constitutional statements in the Short Parliament. In the Commons, John Pym pushed the language of the body politic further than it was intended to go. His careful 'model' of the grievances of the commonwealth compared Parliament to the soul of the body. The soul is suspiciously similar to the head. The several versions of his speech continued his thought in different ways. In one the parliamentary soul was simply and boldly the 'intellectual part, which ought to govern the rest'. Another was less high but more explicit. It spoke of the 'three great faculties and functions of Parliament, the Legislative, the Judiciary, and Consiliary power'. The last touched upon the King-out-of-Parliament as he then was. 'Execution does animate the law', said Harbottle Grimston making the same point in November 1640. Pym had placed powers of the same kind, though not necessarily of the same magnitude, in parliament as, following convention, he put in the King in November, when he spoke of the King's responsibility for justice, peace, and protection. Thus Pym defined the Parliamentary way: the powers of the King-out-of-Parliament were coming to look suspiciously circumscribed.[8]

The opposition in the Short Parliament foundered because the King was able to maintain his position in the Lords that, on this occasion at least, supply should precede redress. The Lords' support for the King was not disinterested; it would probably be a mistake to think them any less constitutionally aggressive than the Commons at this time. Without a parliamentary supply, many of the peers could easily see themselves being 'touched' again for money by the King, always an unpleasant occasion for them. So it was a member of the Commons who gasped at the 'remarkable passage' in the Upper House on Thursday, 16 April 1640. Laud tried to have the whole house adjourned until Saturday, because he and the bishops had to attend Convocation. Meeting opposition from Saye and then from Brooke the bishops retreated, desiring it 'not of right, but of courtesy'. This was also unacceptable. The house made a special point of adjourning because the Lord Keeper Finch planned to be ill, and not otherwise. Passions flamed, so on Monday it was put to the question (it seems by the bishops) 'whether the bishops make a distinct state in the kingdom, . . . the house deny, the house say that it is the King, the Barons, the Commons; the bishops would then make four states, or exclude the King.' There is every reason to endorse Gardiner's gloss: the 'words . . . did not touch the bishops alone. The notion that Parliament was the soul of the body politic had been welcomed by the Lords. The King was no longer to reign supreme, summoning his estates, as Edward I had summoned them to gather round his throne. He. was to be no more than a first estate, called on to join with the others, but not called on to do more.'[9]

Lord Saye's views on the estates were already well formed, to judge from a letter of the following July, and if a man's conduct may be a guide to his thoughts, from his forthright refusal earlier to fight for the King – even in the perfunctory way of his peers – against the Scots. His certain advocacy of the three estates of King, Lords, and Commons, instead of Lords, Bishops and Commons was the likely immediate occasion of a slur made the next day by Joseph Hall, the Bishop of Exeter and advocate of episcopacy by divine right. Hall objected that the Viscount 'savoured of a Scottish Covenanter'. The Covenanters in the General Assembly had abolished episcopacy. In Scottish terms this was not only a change of church government but the abolition of an estate in the civil government; to protect their position they prepared for war. The General Assembly of the Kirk, under the Covenanters, at this time was behaving rather like a Parliament – not surprisingly because Scottish Parliaments usually did not, and the one convened had been successfully prorogued. The Venetian Residents in London and the Hague thought the Scots were about to establish a government upon Dutch principles, as they put it, tactfully, to the Senate and Doge. The Scots, like the English, had a legal and, more importantly, a religious case; both naturally took precedence over the constitutional extremities to which they were compelled. Still, 'Never was there such a stamping and blending of rebellion and religion together,' said a fine old Englishman of the Covenanters, who would 'have none but Jesus Christ to reign over them.' The English peers were not about to rebel, or to abolish episcopacy, or to drum the bishops out of the Upper House, but they would not allow their House to be tied up for as long and as often as the bishops – the King's bishops – chose to go to Convocation.[10]

Very similar words were used in the Long Parliament. Sir John Strangeways asserted that the bishops were one of the three estates. Edward Bagshaw, a professed supporter of primitive episcopacy, shortly denied it. It 'was said . . . that Episcopacy was a third estate in Parliament, and therefore the King and Parliament could not do without them: this I utterly deny, for there are three estates without them, as namely the King, who is the first estate: the Lords Temporal the second, and the Commons the third: and I know no fourth estate.' In May at a debate on the bill to exclude the bishops from the upper house, Saye again implied the bishops were no estate. And out of Parliament Henry Parker wrote of 'our English Parliaments, where the Nobility is not too prevalent, as in Denmark, nor the Commonalty, as in the Netherlands, nor the King, as in France . . . And . . . all the three states have always more harmoniously borne their just proportionable parts in England than elsewhere.'[11]

It is not a bad career for the dubious and troubled proposition that there were three estates of King, Lords and Commons. Boxing the bishops' ears was good sport, and necessary too. Certainly if in future bishops were removed from the Lords, and if all Church affairs required parliamentary consent, it would be pointless to consider bishops as an estate.

And in fact, just a few days after the Lords assented to the exclusion of the bishops in February 1642, Sir Thomas Wroth, a once and future gentleman radical, spoke of the three estates consisting of King, Lords, and Commons. But bishop-baiting and a little constitutional posturing towards the King after eleven years of prayers and tears were one thing, and attacking the king and kingly government rather another. Mixed government by the estates of King, Lords, and Commons was as amenable to any one of these three purposes as another. In 1640–1 though, the Scottish troubles tilted the language of mixed government towards the most radical of the possibilities. After the Short Parliament, the constitutional turn of events was impossible to ignore. By the autumn of 1640, even the pugnaciously baronial Saye was silent about the constitutional implications of reducing the King to being merely one of three estates, although his intellectually self-made 'Allies-man' (so Parker styles himself in a later pamphlet) allowed himself, anonymously, to be more forthcoming.

After the dissolution of the Short Parliament, the Covenanters combined in roughly equal parts the fear of God and the fear of Strafford. Both fears pushed them into increasingly radical positions. Having first fought through the General Assembly of the Kirk, the Covenanters now adopted parliamentary garb. They summoned the Scottish parliament all by themselves, that is, by invoking the King's 'special authority' against his own will. They transacted their business without him. Then they settled in Newcastle to see if Charles and his tatterdemalion army meant to stop them. Most of it had been predicted well before in a repulsive royalist pamphlet which Secretary Windebank made sure was available before the Short Parliament began: 'by such fair ways as you can, be instant to take from him his *negative voice* in Synods and Parliaments, which is a thing so essential to sovereignty, that it standeth and falleth with it. For he being destitute of this pillar, if in Parliaments by plurality of voices it be carried, that you will not *have this man reign over you*, of necessity he must be gone. Secondly, see if you can take from him the *power of making laws*, and let the Parliament and Synod be the *Lawmakers.*'[12]

This is the direction in which talk of the three estates appeared to be leading in the autumn of 1640 and in 1641; it would have been treason were the king in any position to make it so. Calybute Downing took it upon himself in September 1640 to explain to the Honourable Artillery Company of London some biblical and some very recent Scottish history. When 'all truces, treaties, and pacifications [had] treachery under them . . . their first war was defensive, driven the next day into an offensive.' The 'States of a Kingdom, either assembled in a representative body, or virtually concurring in a common resolution, for the common good, and . . . only hindered from assembling by the common enemy . . . may go very far before they can be counted rebels, or be mistaken.' Charles, we should not be surprised, went to look for Dr. Downing, who quickly disappeared into the accommodating arms of his patron, the formidable earl of Warwick.[13]

True, there was one important difference. The Scots stuck to the formula that the king was no part of the estates, while the English tactic was to bring him in. But in the terms of the mixed constitution (which was the rationale for the English revision of the estates) the Scottish and the English situations hung alike on a veto system, or a counting of votes, or of the few and the many against the one – if it came to that.

This point had not yet arrived for the men of 1640. Until summer 1641, when Charles settled with the Scots, the political position of the parliament was precarious, for it was under the protection of two opposing armies. Each army was to protect the godly but unrebellious Englishman from the other. So too the attitudes of the men at Westminster were contradictory. The Scots were embraced for their godliness, their zeal, and their refusal to succumb to the evil councillors, Strafford and Laud. But arguments based on the notion of estates and evil councillors and a great show of godliness did not conceal the fact that the Scots had knocked the head out of the body politic. It was too much for the English, as indeed it was too much for an increasing group of Covenanters. Doubts about the acts led to doubts about the men who took them. The Covenanters, by all acounts, and not least their own, were zealots. Zeal, like 'Thorough', was righteousness in action. Again like 'Thorough', in a great man zeal could be taken, or mistaken, for arrogance; in a base man, or a clergyman, for cheekiness. Whatever were the English reform-minded gentry to make of the leading Scottish divine who told the king's commissioners at Ripon that the English had done very well in their negotiations with the Covenanters (in which they agreed to pay the Scottish army of occupation £850 per day) because it was better to give than to receive ?

In late 1640 or early 1641 Henry Parker implied that the King was the stomach of the body politic – probably he did not mean to say what he did. John Pym did not speak about the parliamentary soul in November. Between April and November 1640 the resolve of the opposition leaders hardened, but their constitutional rhetoric softened. The worst, from the English viewpoint, of the Scottish business had intervened. Henceforth religion was made to carry weight it had not in the Short Parliament. Not until mid-1642 were the major constitutional questions publicly debated. By then, as Parker realised, 'there was no difference . . . betwixt that case of the Scots, and this of ours', by then Parker was clear in his own mind about the relation of the head and the body:

> the head naturally doth not more depend upon the body, then that does upon the head, both head and members must live and die; but it is otherwise with the Head Political, for that receives more subsistence from the body than it gives, and being subservient to that, it has no being when that is dissolved, and that may be preserved after its dissolution.[14]

Parker wrote in reply to the King's *Answer to the Nineteen Propositions*, the classic (though not the first) statement of constitutional royalism in the language of mixed government by the estates. The 'experience and wisdom of your ancestors hath so moulded' this government out of a 'mixture' of monarchy, aristocracy, and democracy 'as to give to this kingdom . . . the conveniences of all three, without the inconveniences of any one, as long as the balance hangs even between the three estates, and they run jointly in their proper channel'.[15] Events had overtaken theory – by mid-1642 the King's propagandists revived formulae which offered little to them or Charles's aggrieved but loyal opposition in 1640-1. The assumption of military authority by the Lords and Commons in the King's name, against his expressed will, settled three issues in a stroke. The royal veto was swept aside. The military powers of the King – historically undoubted prerogatives – were disposed of as the two houses saw fit. Finally, the body was set to resist the forces of the King. By this time, the English situation resembled that of the Scots. To meet this situation, the King's advisers resurrected the theory of mixed government to plead the case of the royal beggar, unjustly and illegally robbed of his negative voice and his right to the 'government', the executive and traditional prerogative powers. By then it was too late. From February 1642, when the King was offered the militia propositions, to the raising of the royal standard in August 1642, the question was more 'could war be avoided' than 'would there be war'. The wills of the King (with an expanding group of gentlemen and peers at his side or willing to join him) and the Lords and Commons (still of unquestioned institutional integrity, despite reduced attendance) were joined in open contest. An arms race ensued, with the predictable consequences.

(ii) *The Early History of Zeal: the Long Parliament until Summer 1641*

How did the English situation become that of the Scots ? The moratorium on brave words did not stop constitutional manoeuvring in the Long Parliament. If anything, constitutional jockeying increased, but until the Grand Remonstrance in early December 1641 it was almost entirely carried out inside Parliament. Reluctance and the momentum of religious politics both inhibited forthright constitutional thought. Ecclesiastical questions were at least partly constitutional; some would have said wholly constitutional. However most men, even while they resisted divine right claims for a particular form of church government because these smacked of theocracy, were concerned nonetheless with the 'godliness' or 'comeliness' of church order or form of worship, with passion and attachment unbecoming in purely civil issues.

In fact men allowed themselves licence in matters of church policy which they never tolerated in other matters. The Laudians have innovated on us, said one M.P., so let us 'innovate upon them'.[16] The common people were expected to defer in civil and indifferent things to their betters and masters – but if Protestantism had any meaning, it was that they deferred to God in religion, if God and man were in conflict. The zealousness of well and base-born anti-episcopalians was matched by the episcopalians and liturgical traditionalists. Conscience was not a puritan monopoly. When both sides agreed, the religious nation swept aside virtually any opposition. Moreover, religion was the one area where the Scots could be received openly as friends and patrons. Upon the points of agreement – that the bishops of the day were too powerful, rich, and worldly, and that Laud's theology and liturgy were (to make a long story short) 'popish' – Charles was bound to give in. Conversely, the religious nation could be divided with equal intensity by social tensions, tensions between the clergy and the laity, and by theological differences as varied as human temperaments.

Zeal could exceed itself; religion could misfire. The men of 1640, with a few exceptions, sensed how far they could push, or be pushed, in civil matters before King and Parliament were irreconcilable. They were not as steady or experienced in religious politics. The possibility existed from the beginning that they would end at each other's throats over religious and ecclesiastical issues. Charles knew that the ill-will generated could serve more than his religious aims. Religious dissension could do his political and constitutional bidding for him. From the time religious and ecclesiastical splits seriously damaged parliamentary unity to the time when that unity was, after a fashion, restored at dreadful cost, constitutional thought was suspended. Until the forms of unity were restored neither King nor opposition knew if they had to go it alone, or if they would get away with it. The period before the breakdown may be described as the first time of zeal; the second, gradually developing in the summer and autumn of 1641, is the time, to adapt Clarendon's phrase, of lost innocence.

The opening speeches of the Long Parliament were all for zeal, though not precisely the zeal Burgess and Marshall had in mind in their fast sermons. But it was sincere and men could live by it. Sir Benjamin Rudyerd, the 'Silver Trumpet', flourished 'Whosoever squares his actions by any rule, either Divine or Humane, he is a Puritan. Whosoever would be governed by the King's laws, he is a Puritan.' A fine figure, and an old one, it had come to occupy a privileged place in parliamentary rhetoric, for it was in substance the same as the one used by Francis Rous, John Pym's step-brother, in the Short Parliament, by Sir Robert Phelips in 1629, and by Job Throckmorton, whom we may credit with first rights on the trope, in 1587. Henry Parker put it marvellously in another form: 'If thou art not an Antipuritan of the worst kind, I am not a Puritan . . . if thou art a down-right Protestant, and no more, I am the same, and no more . . . if thou art [a violent Antipuritan], hate me as a profest Puritan, and I will thank thee for the honour of it.' In this spirit George Digby, who a year before complimented Laud's book against Fisher, offered his services to the purge. So too Sir John Culpeper, later the co-author of the King's *Answer to the Nineteen Propositions*, was hot for the execution of the anti-recusancy laws, and for the rearmament of Kent, no doubt because the King was fortifying the Tower.[17]

Even at the beginning, though, there were hints of the limits of tolerance for zeal. In May 1640 the London apprentices applied the ancient art of the senseless riot to the new game of hunting the archbishop. Alderman Penington delivered in a petition in November with at least 10,000 signatures. Looking slightly ahead (it could have been predicted from past episodes), the no-ceremony Puritans turned out in like numbers at the end of November to greet the newly risen saints, Prynne and Burton. It would seem then that both Digby and Culpeper, who disliked popular agitation, brought their county petitions in their mouths, as the latter put it. It was not simply a matter of decorum.

Culpeper's came 'from those that sent me', Digby's from the 'Free-holders there present' on polling day.[18]

By and large though, 'all opposition seemed to vanish', as the Grand Remonstrance said a year later. Sometimes somersaults and juggling tricks of the mind were all that stood between unity and breakdown of the united, even popular front of the first days of November. An instructive case is the debate on the commitment of the London root-and-branch petition, introduced into the Lower House on 11 December 1640. The opposition leadership did not want to push the church settlement in December. It was a hot potato, so the petition was committed only to emerge in February 1641.

By now a few members were already having open reservations about zeal, indeed their own late enthusiasm. George Digby spoke for some others when he said he was ready 'to cry out with the loudest' against abuses in the church, though he warned against being 'led on passion . . . it is natural . . . to the multitude to fly unto extremes.' The petitioners were 'I know not what, 15,000 Londoners, all that could be got to subscribe.' Sir John Strangeways expressed the conventional worry that 'if we made a parity in the Church we must at last come to a parity in the Commonwealth.'

Alderman Penington, along with Cromwell and Nathaniel Fiennes, defended the petition he delivered in; 'mean men', he said, had as much right to sign the petition as anybody else. These three were root-and-branchers. What is much more interesting is the reaction of some of the zealots and well-intentioned who were not so certain. D'Ewes did what he always did when his zeal and his sense of propriety conflicted. He made a distinction. If episcopacy meant the bishops' 'vain aerial titles of lordship, the spoils of the crown . . . and the vast and tyrannical power which they exercise . . . as they now stand' D'Ewes was for abolition. But when D'Ewes looked at the 'spiritual function as it stood in the primitive and purest times', the question was different, 'for I should highly prize a godly preaching bishop'. The moderate Bagshaw likewise distinguished between pure episcopacy 'as it was in the primitive times' and 'in its corrupt state as it is at this day, and is so intended and meant in the London Petition'. Even as late as May, Lord Saye lectured the Upper House on the meaning of 'this hierarchical episcopacy which the world now holds forth to us'. It lends credence to Dering's apologia for his support for a Kentish root-and-branch petition in the winter, and his introduction of the main bill in May 1641. He said, 'The bill was then less than two sheets of paper, and by subjoining two more might have given us the old original episcopacy, even with the same hand that abrogated the present.' He was shortly to produce an immensely popular scheme for primitive and Grindalian episcopacy.[19]

For as long as they could, men believed what they wanted about root-and-branch. Decent, fairly conservative men found what they could in common with the more flamboyantly godly. Until they had received at least some of what they came for, they were not to be scared away by the horror stories and fear-mongering of the royalists and hard-core reactionaries. In January the King made a great show in the Lords about some 'anabaptists' discovered in Southwark. Sir Thomas Aston brought a petition from Cheshire to the Lords in February which forecast 'an extermination of nobility, gentry, and order, if not religion' if the local 'presbyterians' (independents, in point of fact) were not suppressed. Another like it from Bedfordshire is dated January in the State Papers. The future Secretary of State, Edward Nicholas, wrote or copied at about this time a scheme for using the Lords as a constitutional stopper to the flood of religious passions.[20]

By bits and pieces the legislative programme came through during the first eighteen months of the Long Parliament. The triennial bill, anticipated by the Scots, received the royal assent in February 1641. The bill was a statement of principle, despite its fascinating enforcement clauses, because it did not take effect until the next parliament. The main business of the early months was killing Strafford, which was seen as the *sine qua non* of all durable reform. Strafford's defence employed his recent elevation in the peerage to telling effect as he warned the Lords that what too-clever lawyers with 'some moth-eaten records' were doing to him, could just as well 'tear you and your posterity in pieces'. And indeed his attainder was accompanied – some would say accomplished – by threats and riots. Three peers feared they 'might be deemed to condemn him for fear of force' or acquit Strafford in fear of their lives. The King had John Lilburne (already to be seen in a good engraving, '*Aetat* 23') called to the bar of the Lords for having said that the 700 weaponless men who demanded Strafford's blood on 3 May would swell to '40 or 50,000 in arms' who would have the King if they could not get Strafford. The Lords wanted a conference with the Commons about the tumults. The Commons took their time in replying. The tumults and the army plot killed Strafford. The bill for the prevention of the dissolution of the present parliament without its own consent finished the work of the second riotous May.[21]

The price of Strafford's head was to prove dreadfully high. But not yet: the reform programme the political and judicial measures of 1641 upon which constitutional royalists were later to rely, was still in its infancy. Co-operation and good will were still necessary. Then a strange thing happened. Charles signed this legislation with something that almost could be taken for eagerness. It was almost as if the king would agree to anything the Lords and Commons produced. He made a point of saying so.[22] By midsummer Charles knew that it was unlikely that the two houses would present him with any intolerable measures for the church. The root-and-branch bill was tied up endlessly in committee in the Commons; its introduction in late May and early June drew obscure backbenchers out of their seats with ill-tempered defences of the episcopal establishment that must have been a timely warning to the leaders of the opposition. Root-and-branch apparently was brought on by the failure of the Lords to take the key, preliminary step of excluding the bishops from their temporal employments, including their seats in the Upper House.

The cause of religion was not wholly lost, however. An important ecclesiastical *avant-courier*, Denzil Holles, tried to reassure the fearful that he, and the puritan patriarch John White of Dorchester, were properly concerned with the illicit preaching of 'mechanical' men. The same press that shrilled vengeance on the prelates in November 1640 now churned out endless discoveries of separatists and schismatics. Henry Parker, our 'down-right Protestant', now reflected that he was not 'a prejudging, factious enemy to all Bishops'. Dering, Bishop Williams and Archbishop Ussher each devised practical and potentially satisfying combinations of episcopacy and presbytery. In this spirit the Upper House very cheerfully went as far as disabling bishops from all their temporal duties except their seats in the Lords. A godly, decorous retreat from the precipice of anti-Straffordian and sectarian zeal, which everybody in both houses wanted, was matched by continued concern that Laud's church be dismantled. Perhaps both sides had learnt their lesson, and the Parliament could soon be wound up. When plague broke out in August 1641, many members decided that they had had enough of parliaments for the time being. In Westminster, zeal was dead. The men of 1640 had done God's business and the king's, in which their own was included. They would have been happy to stay at home.[23]

(iii)   *Lost Innocence*

Charles had called two parliaments to find money to reduce the Scots.

The Scots, for religious and financial reasons, had a direct interest in the continuance and success of the English parliament. The Covenanting army in Newcastle had been the silent partner in the opposition's dealings. The temper of the parliaments becoming clear, it was a matter of time before Charles decided that the English remedy was worse than the Scottish disease. He began to threaten to go to Edinburgh in late May. A royal settlement with the Scots contained multiple dangers. The protection of the Covenanting army would disappear; it might even have returned as a threat. The reform programme and the personal safety of some members of the opposition would have been as insecure as in the most threatening days of Strafford. The English opposition acted directly, by raising their demands to the unacceptable level at which they remained right up to the outbreak of war. Pym suggested the parliamentary control of the King's councillors on 24 June; control of the militia and forts was mooted in the Commons on 2 and 14 August. At the same time the English opposition could not expect to delay with root-and-branch and expect the continued goodwill of the Scots. As the summer grew on some action on the church – in practice that meant removing the bishops from the Lords – became increasingly important, as a matter of security if not of principle.

On the other hand the domestic situation had also shifted. The Lords spiritual and temporal could hardly be blamed now for concluding after the events of May 1641 that their fortunes lay with the King, now that his star was rising in the north. Similar feelings in the Commons combined with the strains released by the relative, if formal, success of the reform programme. Episcopalians grew bolder and less enamoured of the Commons, going their own way if they saw 'nothing as yet to concern them from the Upper House'. The opposition leaders, the Scots breathing down one side of their neck and their fears of settlement in Edinburgh blowing down the other, found themselves increasingly committed to their necessary but unsavoury allies in the street.

All this was music to Charles's ears. If the constitutional and ecclesiastical reforms cost dearly in terms of his established policy, they also purchased public goodwill. From mid-summer the King began to acquire the moderate constitutional clothes which he had detested before, and were his habit in future. By June 1641 the Venetian ambassador wrote 'Many believe an open division may come between the Houses, and offer an opportunity to His Majesty to raise his present fortunes.'

It was still premature. The King 'will have to bide his time': the reforms were still gestating, the army plot fresh. By autumn his time had come. In fact he could delay no longer. The settlement in Edinburgh gave the Scots the radical aim of control over the king's officers. The English opposition were at once 'very jocund and cheerful' at the Scots' success, which they intended to 'take [as] a pattern' and deeply apprehensive that 'all the great offices and places' would go to Scotsmen. Charles had to check the new cause before it got out of hand.[24]

For a while he toyed with a proclamation for attendance of members at Westminster. The opposition were likely to take it for a breach of privilege, so the new Secretary of State, Nicholas, and the Lord Keeper, Littleton, discouraged the plan, for which they might have been attacked by the Commons. It was easier, and more discreet, to fan opposition in the Lords. Relations between the two houses had been deteriorating. There was a veiled skirmish in August when the Commons tried to put nine of the bishops in a *praemunire* for being on the wrong side of a division in the Upper House, an extraordinary proceeding. In September 1641 the two houses sent out contradictory instructions on religious observance. So the King began to fan divisions between the houses, while he strengthened his party in the Lords. He prepared a list of episcopal preferments and translations, which he insisted be 'expedited that they may with all possible diligence attend the Parliament'. More remarkably, he entrusted the Queen, and she poor Nicholas, with whipping the Lords. Very detailed instructions survive; this was no casual adventure. Among many instructions to have his 'servants' cross this or that matter in the Lords, is the King's revealing advice to the Digbys, when father and son expected parliamentary wrath: 'For diversion of this and other mischiefs, . . . put Bristol in mind to renew that dispute betwixt the two Houses, concerning the Parliament Protestation.'[25]

Short of success in removing the bishops and popish lords from the Upper House, the opposition could do little to break out of the pattern. They could not push through their programme of executive control until the party which temporarily benefited from the settlement in Edinburgh, the bishops and the popish lords, were removed. The Commons, in the normal course of events, could not expect to remove either. A new bill to unseat the bishops, rushed through the Commons immediately after the recess, was ignored by the Lords. The popish Lords, a term easily capable of infinite extension, went unchallenged within their own house. They also refused to join Pym in his double-

barrelled proposition to relieve Ireland without the king, and to secure
a parliamentary veto over the King's councillors. 'At the beginning
of November 1641,' wrote Sir Charles Firth, 'the leaders of the Commons found themselves brought to a standstill.' The parliamentary
way had collapsed inside Parliament.[26]

(iv) *'Daily Assaults upon the Lords': Winter 1641–2*

The opposition took the one advantage they could from the position.
The split between the houses concealed from the body of the faithful
how bitterly and narrowly the Lower House was itself divided. November letters are full of the sudden discovery of an irreconcilable split.
The Commons were harsh on William Chillingworth and even on one
of their own members, Geoffrey Palmer, who remarked on the dissension in the Lower House. At the same time the publication of the
Grand Remonstrance memorialised the division between the houses.
The importance of the Remonstrance was that it set an example; when
it told tales of the evil machinations of the bishops and popish lords
inside Parliament, it licensed or encouraged public abusiveness towards
them. The faithful were told that the malignants had a party of bishops
and popish lords in the Upper House 'as hath caused much opposition
and delay in the prosecuting of delinquents, hindered the proceedings
of divers good bills passed in the Commons House . . . What can we
the Commons do without the conjunction of the House of Lords . . . ?'
On 3 December 1641 Pym made his 'desperate motion' in reply. He
said if the Lords refused to co-operate, 'acquaint them that we, being
the representative body of the Kingdom, shall join with those Lords
who are more careful of the safety of the Kingdom, they being but
private persons, . . . to represent the same to his Majesty.' The lords
more careful of the safety of the kingdom: an apt but awkward phrase.
A more convenient one was found. 'Protestant lords' was a promising
aspirant, but since the Protestant lords were in fact the balance of power
in the Upper House, the name was doomed: the days of the 'down-
right Protestant' had passed. Not that it mattered – an even more
delightfully mindless *soubriquet* was in the air. 'They talk much,' wrote
William Montague, 'that the King is often very private with Digby and
Bristol, and that he looks but overly upon the good Lords.' Edward
Kirton, and later Clarendon, wrote of the 'good party'. They did not
mean their own. By the end of December, the rabble only admitted to
the houses 'a good man' or 'a good Lord'.

The Grand Remonstrance was an appeal to the country; both sides made sure that the country appealed to the Parliament. Royalists naturally resorted to their strongest weapon, respect for the Church and the liturgy, and produced at least eight manuscript, printed, or officially recorded texts of petitions. Dering tried to hold on to 'severe reformation' but not abolition of bishops in Kent, but faced constitutional objections from his increasingly royalist Kentish associates. Huntingdon simply rewrote parts of Aston's Cheshire petition of February 1641, and kept the rest verbatim. Chester updated its first petition to plead for the liturgy. Somerset and Gloucester each had the same things to say, in the same words. Dorset and Nottinghamshire produced mercifully short texts; Rutland insisted upon length. Nearly all protested they petitioned only because the root-and-branchers had been at it first; Aston was shortly to identify these petitions explicitly with a silent majority. None of them got inside the Commons; 'all art' and an investigative committee barred them. Three entered the Lords, Huntingdonshire by the introduction of the king's cousin, the Duke of Richmond, Somerset by the Marquis of Hertford, Cheshire by the Lord Keeper upon command of the king. The last was a calulated indiscretion because Aston had infuriated the Lords, or some of them, the previous May. None of the petitioners were thanked, probably because the good lords would have caused a scene by using their liberty of protestation.[28]

It was now the turn of the opposition, and of the supporters they were compelled to call upon. To their great good fortune the Irish rebellion re-legitimised zeal. Papists may have been murdering Protestants in Ireland. They were accused of murdering hordes more in the endless concoctions of 'certain beggarly loose scholars in alehouses', as D'Ewes called the scribbling tribe.[29] The failure to relieve 'bleeding Ireland' as well as all other grievances could be pinned on the bishops and popish lords who stood between the Commons and good King Charles. From 11 December 1641 (the anniversary of the original London root-and-branch petition) when a London petition for the exclusion of the bishops and popish lords and for a 'posture of defence' (the euphemism for taking the militia and forts out of the king's control) was submitted, until the first week of February 1642 when the Lords finally buckled under, petitions of increasing venom inundated both houses in increasing numbers. On 25 January the Lords were entertained by the texts of eight petitions.

Four events in late December and early January put victory in sight. On 27 December, twelve bishops led by John Williams, now Archbishop of York, protested they were forcibly prevented from taking their seats in the Lords by the tumults, and claimed that the proceedings of the Upper House were void until they could return with safety. The city government changed hands early in January 1642. The King lost control of London when he failed to take the Five Members, who were charged (amongst other things) with trying '(as far as in them lay) by force and terror to compel the parliament to join with them in their traitorous designs'. Finally on 11 January he abandoned London, leaving his peers to shift for themselves. On the same day armed petitioners from Buckinghamshire, put up to it by Hampden, hoped the Lords would 'co-operate with the House of Commons'.[30]

The Upper House had to decide who were their friends of the moment. The 'good Lords' aided their decisions by making semi-public protestations, where they listed themselves by name as opposed to the majority to 'discharge myself of any ill consequence that may happen thereby.' The Venetian ambassador had little doubt of the purpose of the 'good lords'; 'they would denounce [the malignant lords] to the people as enemies of the state, . . . they will unite with the Lower House for the utter destruction of the Upper.' The Commons were busy too. On 18 and 19 January in Grocers' Hall a Committee of the Whole House debated and (it seems) resolved that no members of the Commons could be raised to the Lords, except in case of descent, without consent of the Commons, and they may have been even more expansive.[31]

The flood of petitions made the implied threat of the Buckinghamshire petition increasingly clear. Petitioners to the Lords from Essex 'trembled' at the future without the relief of Ireland, London and the rest of the kingdom in safe hands, and the prelates and popish lords 'excluded your house'. On 25 January petitioners from Hertfordshire, introduced by the earl of Salisbury, noticed 'the want of compliance' of the Lords with the Commons. Curiously, considering the protestations of the good lords, the petitioners reserved a 'liberty to protest against all those, as enemies to the kingdom', who refuse to join with those members of the Lords 'whose endeavours are for the public good' and the Commons. This petition was very carefully staged, read in the Commons before being sent to the Lords. D'Ewes was shocked. In an act of great courage, Southampton and Dunsmore entered a public dissent to the giving of thanks.[32]

The leadership's connexion with the petitions was made absolutely precise that day by two petitions from Devon, both introduced by the young Earl of Bedford. A county petition recounted the usual grievances and usual remedies. Behind it lay several subordinate petitions, un-read but available, upon which it was based. One came from Tavis-tock, the other from Totnes: we might as well say that the former came from John Pym and the latter from Oliver St. John, for those were the boroughs for which they sat. The other main petition came from Exeter. Once again the 'source of all' was said to be the episcopal and popish faction in the Lords. The Exonians blamed the depression in trade on them, and warned that dearth would 'stir up many thousand persons to insolent and outrageous actions'.[33]

The Lords' education had just begun. The Commons told the Upper House that they ought to listen to four more petitions which had been submitted to the Lower House. Pym lectured them at the conference on the one voice, 'the cry of all England' as it was to be heard from London, Middlesex, Essex, and Hertfordshire. He warned that the Lords' failure to act would soon cause, by virtue of the stop of trade, 'tumults and insurrections of the meaner sort of people . . . who live for the most part on their daily gettings, . . . what they cannot buy, they will take; and from them the like necessity will quickly be derived to the farmers and husbandmen, . . . and, at this time, such tumults will be dangerous, because the kingdom is full of disbanded soldiers and officers . . . ready to head and animate the multitude . . .'.

He reminded the Lords that they knew 'what is to be done'. The Commons were happy 'to have your help and concurrence in the saving of the kingdom'; if the Lords refused the Commons 'shall be sorry, . . . that, . . . the House of Commons should be inforced to save the kingdom alone, and that the House of Peers should have no part in the honour of the preservation of it . . .'. After the conference the Duke of Richmond moved that the Lords adjourn for six months. The 'good Lords' took the opportunity to count and name themselves in a protestation over the young duke's offence. Warwick treated the Lords the next day to a petition from the seamen, who warned that if the 'persons' respons-ible for the mischiefs were not declared, 'multitudes' would take to 'that remedy . . . next at hand'. On 29 January, they came back for an answer.[34]

On 31 January, Captain Venn, member for the City who had been implicated in the disturbances before, brought into the Commons a petition from 'many thousand poor people, in and about the City of London'. They too insisted that the 'prevalency' of the bishops and popish lords was responsible for 'so great a decay and stop of trade' that they were starving. It may be remarked that they did not ask for bread.

But like Warwick's seamen, they promised not to 'rest in quietness, but . . . to lay hold on the next remedy'; likewise they wanted 'such persons who are the obstacles . . . forthwith publicly declared'. Finally they urged that the 'noble-worthies of the House of Peers, who con-cur with you in your happy votes, may be earnestly desired to join with this honourable House, to sit and vote as one entire body.' The dele-gation refused to leave the Commons until they reiterated all their points and received promises of immediate action.[35]

Said Pym, 'This is of great importance. We must go to the Lords, and if they will not join with us we must join with some of them and shew his Majesty these things.' It is what he had said two months earlier. Denzil Holles, Baron Holles of the next reign and the son of a peer, made an eloquent speech to the Lords at the conference. The Commons, he hinted, were not going to stand in the petitioners' way: 'at another time [we] should be very tender of this . . . but now consider the necessity of a multitude, a sleeping lion . . . it would but pull on the mischief sooner.'[36]

The next day, 1 February 1642, the peers voted to join in the petition to the King concerning the militia. The decision was not recorded in the Journal until 2 February; the house did not sit on the third. On 4 February petitioners from Surrey happily noted the 'concurrence' with the Commons, but told the peers to get on with excluding the bishops. They promised to defend the Lords 'so far as you shall be united' with the Lower House. The next day, Saturday 5 February, the Commons decided that it could move against the tumults that were apparently insurmountable a few days earlier: it was the same day the Lords voted to exclude the bishops. By Tuesday Kentish petitioners thanked them, promised to honour them 'so far as your Lordships shall continue to hold correspondence and concurrence with the Commons', and announced that it was now time to consider the reli-gious issue. Suffolk (9 February) reiterated the message. They said that 'thousands' who might have accompanied the petitioners 'have forborne in obedience to a late order of the House of Commons'. And so it went on. Both houses ordered the trained bands out on Shrove Tuesday when the apprentices and others 'do take more liberty to assemble themselves'.[37]

The House of Lords had been broken. The Parliamentary way had been preserved. The price could not have been higher. The King ac-quired a party. Parliament, in all but name, was a party too. Between the two were the 'neuters', whom Stephen Marshall subjected to his viperous tongue at the next fast sermon. Pym sensed the mood on 8 February when he hinted broadly that the business of the Parliament would soon be done. As for religious reform, the aim of the forces of zeal, at the real, the local level, it had hardly begun. Just as after the death of Strafford, radical reform was in a bad way. The problem was that zeal was its own worst enemy. On the one hand, almost nothing was so disastrous for the zealots as a *little* success, especially a little success in enervating but peripheral struggles. Both of the state preachers on 23 February felt forced to acknowledge the recent victory. Edmund Calamy wondered at the 'several miracles' of the past two years, which exceeded 'all the mercies that ever this nation did receive since the first reformation'; even Marshall noted (sadly) that 'all nations after any notable victory' had 'their triumphant songs'. On the other hand, the leading zealots insisted that blood was not on their hands. Victories were bad enough. Messy, reputation-damaging victories were that much worse: and apparently those were the ones which came zeal's way. So for the sake of religion *vox populi* was best forgotten. Calamy had the nerve to claim God had done all 'in a legal way, in a parliamentary way', which in a sense was true; steeling himself, the preacher added, 'without tumults'. Calamy did not dare extricate his tribe altogether from the recent struggles, for they still needed their share of the spoils – the ministers manifestly had not got what they came for. Much more cunningly, he pretended that he and his fellow parliament-pressing ministers were out of their depth in contemporary politics. Their *métier* was doom, and here was success. Would not 'all our ministers . . . be found liars, for they have prophesied the certain ruin and destruction of England'? The ministers, he hinted, could not be held accountable for their efforts, because their training gave them no clue to the outcome: England was 'a paradox to the Bible'![38]

Still the King had lost the one contest he had chosen to fight. He could no longer hide behind the divisions in parliament. Likewise the leadership of the opposition could not use the evil machinations of the malignants in Parliament to rebound shots at the King. At last, and by the backdoor, England was approaching the situation of the Scots – the fearful contest of two wills, each strong enough to fight, each gone too far along separate paths for an accommodation, each claiming an inalienable right of existence. 'The bishops being put out of the house, whom will they lay the fault upon now: when the dog is beat out of the room, where will they lay the stink?'[39] For what it was worth, the men of 1640 answered, his Majesty's evil councillors. By the end they were reduced to claiming a right to approve the King's cook. Charles chose not to see his councillors as evil. He chose not to sign the militia bill. He chose not to agree that Sir John Hotham prevented him from committing treason against himself by locking him out of Hull. He chose not to agree 'that a parliament may dispose of any thing wherein his Majesty or any subject hath a right, in such as that the kingdom may not be exposed to hazard or danger thereby'. As a man and as a king, that was his prerogative. The situation had changed so rapidly that an idea which at first had been used to weaken the King's position now became his last line of defence. Two months before the *Answer to the Nineteen Propositions*, one of his 'evil' advisers, most likely Culpeper or Bristol, put the King's case precisely. 'I hope,' he said, 'with us he shall be esteemed a third estate in Parliament.'[40]

9. England and Europe: A Common Malady?

J. H. ELLIOTT

WHEN continental statesmen looked across the Channel to the England of Charles I their reactions tended to be compounded of envy, exasperation and a certain general unease. As the Thirty Years' War moved towards its climax in the open confrontation of France and Spain, both Richelieu and Olivares redoubled their efforts to draw the English into their network of alliances or, failing this, to make sure that they gave no help or comfort to the enemy camp. Late in 1635, when Charles I hinted at the possibility of a league with the House of Austria in return for the restoration of the Palatinate to the young Prince Palatine, his proposals were treated as a matter of the highest consequence by Philip IV's Council of State in Madrid. The Count-Duke of Olivares, while foreseeing difficulties, had no hestitation in affirming England's power to be such that 'if it can be completely won to our side, there would be no counterweight in Europe to prevent Your Majesty and the Emperor from doing whatever they like.'[1]

It seems likely that inherited memories counted for at least as much as recent information in the Count-Duke's sanguine assessment of English strength. It certainly contained, like so many of his political projections, a strong element of wishful thinking. But the fact remained that England in 1635 enjoyed the almost unique benefits of peace and domestic tranquillity in the midst of a generally war-torn world. Peace in turn brought prosperity. While Englishmen in the later 1630s worried about the stagnation or depression of trade, foreigners were more likely to worry about the vigour of English commercial enterprise. To Olivares, the subjects of Charles I were 'today the masters of the world's trade, and dictate its terms as they wish'.[2]

But whether the government of Charles I possessed either the capacity or the will to translate economic power into effective and consistent political action was a question which gave rise to considerable doubts. The extraordinary tergiversations of English foreign policy during the course of his reign had given Charles the reputation in Roman Catholic courts of being an incorrigible temporiser, even when judged by the standards of heretics. There was bound too to be deep unease about the extent to which he was really the master in his own house. He might have suspended parliament, but it was well known that without parliament he lacked the money for expensive foreign enterprises. If he summoned parliament, Olivares warned, he would lose his authority and perhaps his crown, for parliament was full of Puritans, who by definition were 'republicans'.[3] In view of this diagnosis it is not surprising that, when Olivares learnt of the King's decision to call a parliament as a consequence of the Scottish revolt, he immediately feared the worst. The King was insecure because of the 'diversity of religions within his kingdoms'[4] – the most insidious of all diseases in the body politic.

The experience of sixteenth- and early seventeenth-century Europe had tended to suggest that religious uniformity was the *sine qua non* of political stability. The revolt of the Netherlands, the protracted civil wars in France and, most recently, the Bohemian rebellion, all appeared to lend weight to that venerable maxim – 'one faith, one law, one king'. Political opposition notoriously fed on religious dissent, and for the courts of Paris, Vienna and Madrid no combination was more to be feared than that between Protestant extremists and Estates. Could Charles then ever be sure of his own dominions as long as the Puritans survived?

But if, as Mr. Russell argues, there was nothing in the essence of Puritanism which made it *necessarily* an enemy of authority, any idea of a Puritan conspiracy to reduce England to a virtual republic represented no more than an ill-informed attempt to explain the present troubles of England by recourse to the presumed lessons of the continent's past. English Puritanism did in due course generate forces that were genuinely revolutionary; but if Pym and Bedford held political theories largely indistinguishable from those of the later Royalists, the mere fact of Puritan opposition would hardly, as Olivares assumed, explain the challenge of parliaments to the powers of the King.

On the other hand, continental experience clearly indicated that Protestantism and political opposition were capable of combining with lethal effect. The events of the later sixteenth century had shown how radical Protestants (and, for that matter, radical Catholics) drew from their faith a sense of moral rectitude which boded ill for princes of a differing creed. They had shown too how close-knit and dedicated religious minorities were ideally suited for organised political action when the occasion arose. The continental rulers faced with rebellion in the 1640s – in France, in Spain and in Italy – were fortunate that,

on this occasion at least, political and social revolt lacked the ammuni-
tion of religious dissent. An army commander writing from northern
Catalonia in 1639 admitted as much when he drew a parallel between
the Catalans and the Dutch, but indicated the crucial difference: 'Only
the preachers are missing, to make them lose their faith along with their
obedience.'[5]

Richelieu in the 1620s was among the last continental statesmen to
be confronted by the old alliance of a section of the political nation and
a dissenting religious minority. But this particular alliance had by now
lost much of its sting. The Huguenot movement was very much on the
defensive; there was no real solidarity between the Huguenots and the
aristocratic opponents of the cardinal; and the sons and grandsons of the
old Huguenot nobility had defected in large numbers to the church of
Rome. The combined political and religious opposition which challenged
the government of Charles I therefore looked very much like the be-
lated English version of a kind of movement which was nearly extinct
on the continent. It was not the only occasion in history when the British
Isles found themselves two or three generations behind the times.

In this instance however the time-lag may be regarded as largely
fortuitous. The organisation and activities of the Puritans in Elizabethan England reveal a sophistication of technique on a level with that
of their continental brethren; and, had Mary Tudor survived, it is not
difficult to imagine the development in England, as in the Netherlands,
of a movement of combined political and religious opposition spear-
headed by the Calvinists. But in the event Mary was succeeded on the
throne by a relatively godly princess, who possessed the arts of political
management and knew how to extract the maximum advantage from
the external danger to the national community represented by Roman
Catholic Spain.

As long as the Spanish danger persisted, Protestant dissidents would
stop short of any action which seemed to them likely to rock the boat.
To travel hopefully was itself the best guarantee that sooner or later they
would arrive. But, as Dr. Clifton points out, the situation changed in the
early seventeenth century: 'England was no longer under direct attack.'
Since the external threat had, at least for the time, subsided, there was
less cause than under Elizabeth for self-imposed restraint. Unexpec-
tedly deprived of the enemy without, this society, with all the inherited
neuroses of the recent past, found compensation in turning its attention
to the more insidious enemy within. Opposition to Charles I therefore
developed in a general climate of anti-popish fear and suspicion, at a

time when the patriotic arguments for political acquiescence were losing much of their original force.

But if the contributors to this volume are correct, there was nothing 'inevitable' about this opposition, and least of all on the religious front. The Puritans had not visibly grown more militant in the years following the death of Elizabeth, and indeed Dr. Tyacke indicates a relatively high degree of Anglican-Puritan consensus for much of the long incumbency of Archbishop Abbot. The pressures for change which destroyed this consensus came, it would seem, not from below but from above; not from the Puritan group in the country, but from the Arminian group at court. It was the activities of the Arminians which forced a redefinition of Puritanism and drove the nonconformist element into radical paths. 'The Arminians and their patron King Charles were undoubtedly the religious revolutionaries in the first instance.'

Arminianism was not, however, exclusively confined to the court; and it is tempting to speculate whether western Europe in the opening decades of the seventeenth century may not have been experiencing a general rightwards swing in religion, represented by the re-invigorated Catholicism of France and the Habsburg lands, and by the Arminian trends in the Calvinist church. If so, the possibilities of conflict – which may also in part have been a conflict of generations – were very considerable. But Charles I was perhaps more personally associated with the new religious trends than most of his contemporaries among the European princes, with the important exception of the Emperor Ferdinand II – and Ferdinand imposed *his* religious revolution on Bohemia only *after* he had crushed the resistance of its Estates. From the standpoint of the conservative Calvinist tradition the King was a dangerous innovator, whose popish proclivities imperilled the spiritual health of his subjects. If the new generation, after being led astray at the Universities, lent an ear to the siren voices of the Arminians, then the future of the nation was dark indeed.

But the innovating activities of Charles's government were by no means confined to the religious scene. No reader of this volume can fail to be struck by the constant return to a common theme – that innovation (or what passed for innovation), and even in some fields revolution, came in the first instance from the court. If this assumption is correct it could reasonably be argued that early seventeenth-century England and continental Europe were not as far apart as British historiography likes to suggest.

The tendency of modern British historians over the past few years has been to look primarily to developments in the economy and society to explain the origins of the Civil War. If this volume of essays is representative of a new historical generation, it would seem that a change of direction is under way. As might have been expected, intensive economic and social research has told us much about economic and social trends, but not so much about politics. Something was clearly missing in the fashionable interpretation of the English revolution. The later twentieth century has begun to rediscover, none too soon, what the nineteenth century took for granted – the vital importance of *government*.

By emphasising the role of government, the contributors to this volume turn the new orthodoxy on its head. In recent years we have grown accustomed to the picture of a revolutionary society and a conservative, or reactionary regime. Here, instead, we find ourselves presented with the picture of a largely conservative society and a revolutionary regime. Whatever the validity of this picture for England, it certainly makes more sense of contemporaneous events on the continent than the one it seeks to displace. Attempts to interpret the continental revolts of the 1640s by reference to a 'model' revolution in England never really managed to carry conviction. Did the bourgeois revolution succeed in England but fail in Europe because of the weakness of continental capitalism? Somehow neither the Catalan rebels nor the Frondeurs looked like very persuasive standard-bearers for a dynamic capitalist cause. The reverse model of a backwoods gentry, animated by the hostility of country for court,[6] appeared initially rather more promising, but hardly survived the Channel crossing. Neither continental court nor country – nor, for that matter, the relations between them – proved on closer examination to be quite what they ought to have been.

If however we begin not with society but the state, certain general tendencies become apparent. These tendencies are naturally concealed if the state is merely assumed to be the instrument of the governing class. But if governments are allowed to have a mind, or at least an attitude, of their own; if they aspire to achieve certain aims which are not exactly identical with those of any one social group; if they are really representative of nothing very much except themselves: then conflicts of interest between government and society are hardly a matter for surprise.

In the 1630s and 1640s this conflict of interests seems to have followed a common form. Many of the European regimes of these decades were innovating and absolutist, at least in practice if not in theory. Sometimes, as in the mind of Richelieu, the abstract entity of the state demanded unquestioning obedience; but in general the old organic community of king and people was still a widely accepted ideal. The preservation or restoration of this community therefore remained the normal aspiration of statesman and rebel alike. Yet there was no doubt that the delicate organic relationship was being exposed to heavy strains and stresses; and it seems that the immediate pressures came less from the people than the prince.

The urgent requirements of foreign policy, the pressing demands of war and defence, the fiscal benefits to be derived from extending state protection to powerful economic interests, all helped to push regimes towards a vigorous interventionism in domestic affairs. No doubt the aspirations of mid-seventeenth-century governments tended to outrun their capacity to attain their ends. Their officials were still torn between loyalty to family and hopeful clients, and to a public interest that was often no more than dimly perceived. They were struggling too to meet the requirements of their royal masters in an environment hostile to governmental action, except when local or sectional interests hoped to benefit. But the fact remained that wide areas of western Europe were now, perhaps for the first time, becoming aware of the all-pervasive presence of the central state. Royal agents were officiously busy, enforcing orders, collecting taxes, settling disputes, and recruiting, provisioning and billeting troops. Inevitably their activity sent ripples of disturbance through those tight little local communities which, taken all together, constituted the patchwork of the seventeenth-century state.

On the continent, the impact of the central government was both direct and indirect. Directly, it involved confrontations with privileged regions and privileged groups, which were now called upon to make unprecedented contributions to the Crown finances. Indirectly, the mounting scale of state expenditure, when unsupported by a comparable increase in national productivity, distorted the pattern of traditional economies, and brought serious social stress in its train. Landlords and peasants, as in Normandy in 1639, would join forces against the common enemy – the royal official whose tax demands, by impoverishing the peasantry, prevented them from paying their seigneurial dues. Yet while certain sections of the community, in both town and country, bore the full weight of governmental pressure, others were well placed to exploit the government's needs. Court favourites and officials, financiers and government contractors, big merchants with state-protected monopolies, were the new rich of these societies, living a life of opulence which stood in sharp relief to the surrounding distress.

It was then the attempt of the great continental states to mobilise their resources for war which upset the delicate social and economic balance, antagonised important interests, and precipitated revolutionary situations. The England of Charles I managed to escape the large-scale commitment to war which compelled the governments of France and Spain to improvise and innovate. But in spite of a reasonable degree of peace, the pressures upon it were much the same. The simultaneous war against France and Spain in the late 1620s exposed all the weakness of the crown's administrative and financial supports. Troops had to be levied and billeted, and the fleet kept afloat. Where could the necessary assistance be found? More dependent than most continental monarchies on taxes which required parliamentary consent, the monarchy of Charles I had less room for fiscal manoeuvre and was more liable to meet organised non-cooperation at an early stage. In these circumstances it could barely survive in peacetime, except by resort to fiscal devices which brought it increasing unpopularity, and could certainly not afford a lengthy war unless this enjoyed wide national support. As might have been predicted it was an unpopular war, fought against the Scottish vassals of the Crown, which in due course brought about its ruin.

Since the pressures on the regime of Charles I during a time of peace were rather less than those on the governments of France and Spain, even though comparable in kind, it is hardly surprising to find a correspondingly reduced urgency in the government's response. The advocates of 'thorough' at the English court shared some of the ideals of their continental counterparts. They wanted to make the royal power more effective and to mobilise more of the nation's wealth to meet the requirements of the state. But whereas the exigencies of war in France and Spain demanded, and to some extent seemed to justify, ruthless measures from ruthless men, the regime of Charles I lacked the overpowering sense of urgency which would have committed it to vigorous and consistent action. In consequence the Earl of Strafford, the one figure at court who was built in the heroic mould of Richelieu and Olivares, was not given the opportunity, until too late, to play the role for which he was cast. Whether he would have fared any better than his less purposeful colleagues is open to doubt. But the impression conveyed by this volume is of a regime which did not make the best use of its men; in which muddle alternated with occasional disconcerting bursts of energy; and which was consistent only in its unerring capacity for making the worst of every world.

No doubt the powers at Charles's disposal were much less impressive than those of the kings of France and Spain. He was more circumscribed by legal restrictions, and he lacked those vital instruments for enforcing change from above – a standing army and a local bureaucracy whose first loyalty was to the Crown. In these circumstances fiscal and administrative innovation had little chance of success without the support of the political nation. It was precisely because he knew how to obtain this support that Charles's contemporary, Gustavus Adolphus, succeeded in mobilising Sweden (a country with certain marked constitutional and political similarities to England) so effectively for its victorious wars. From the beginning, Charles's style, even more than his measures, aroused the distrust of the English political nation; and the timing could scarcely have been more unfortunate. As Englishmen looked across to the continent they saw, in one part of Europe after another, the triumph of popery and arbitrary power. 'We are the last monarchy in Christendom that retain our original rights and constitutions' claimed Sir Robert Phelips, with pardonable exaggeration, in the House of Commons in 1625.[7] Whatever happened, England must not be allowed to go the way of the rest.

The English ruling class clearly felt itself on the defensive. Surveying the activities of its government in the context of European political trends, it naturally feared the loss of ancient rights and liberties before the advancing power of the state. At least it possessed in Parliament a forum for resistance incomparably more effective than the Parlement of Paris or the Cortes of Castile. But, as the recent example of Bohemia proved, no Estates in the 1620s could count themselves entirely secure. The behaviour of the parliamentary opposition in the 1620s shows that the future of Parliament itself was believed to be at stake; and Charles's decision in 1629 to dispense with Parliament suggests that its fears were not unduly wide of the mark.

It could hardly be as obvious to contemporaries as it was to later generations that the government of Charles I was acting out of weakness rather than out of strength. This was natural as long as the spectre of Bohemian liberties haunted the House. Moreover, as Mr. Russell shows, the country gentry had no concept of the cost of government, and still less of the cost of warfare, in the 1620s. When Philip IV of Spain appealed to the Cortes of Catalonia for a subsidy in 1626 he met the same kind of amazed incomprehension. Some of the incomprehension was no doubt feigned, for perfectly respectable political reasons. But a strong impression remains that the nobles and gentry of early seventeenth-century Europe possessed very little understanding of the budgetary problems of the state.

Behind all the incomprehension, however, there lay an obstinate determination to resist change, and above all change at the behest of the king. This innate conservatism of the English governing class can hardly be seen as exceptional. On the contrary it was only to be expected of the kind of society which existed throughout western Europe at this time – a society based on privilege, property and rank. In this society, as Dr. Hill reminds us in his chapter on county government, the local community remained of paramount importance. It may well be that by this period the English nobility and gentry possessed a stronger sense of the wider community – that of the realm – than many of their continental counterparts. Regular attendance at Parliament, the growing attraction of London as a capital city, and the centralisation of education at Oxford, Cambridge and the Inns of Court, all helped to break down local barriers and create a common style of discourse, and a community of interests, in the political nation at large. This may indeed constitute an important reason for the eventual success of the English political nation in its prolonged fight to limit the powers of the Crown. But even where the sense of a national community was fairly well developed, the local community remained sacrosanct. This meant that intervention in local affairs by the central government was looked upon as an alien intrusion, which automatically called forth a conservative response.

Conservatism was also inculcated by the kind of education – historical and legalistic – which was considered appropriate for the European ruling class. The world in which this moved was dominated by law and precedent, status and contract, and it instinctively assessed the actions of the central government by reference to the past. It was true that it was prepared to accept, at least in principle, the validity of the argument from necessity, of *salus populi suprema lex*, which the governments of the 1620s and 1630s found it so expedient to invoke. But specific applications of the principle were another matter, especially when privilege and property were at stake. Law and custom, it was generally agreed, should normally determine the limits of power. It was therefore particularly disconcerting when governments tried to play the game according to the rules – as they did in the Spain of Olivares or the England of Strafford and Laud – by reviving dormant feudal obligations, and rediscovering forgotten laws. At once there were shrill cries of protest. This, it appeared, was a game which only one should play.

The defence of sectional privileges and interests should not, however, blind us to the genuine achievements of many of these aristocracies. Admittedly, 'aristocratic constitutionalism', that convenient phrase coined by Professor Michael Roberts to describe the attitude of the Swedish aristocracy,[8] conceals a multitude of injustices. But at the same time it implies a determination, whatever the motives behind it, to uphold the rule of law. This determination informed the resistance of opposition peers and gentry when faced by Charles I's demands. It is possible that the 'aristocratic constitutionalism' of this group had a more genuinely popular basis than was often to be found on the continent. Long experience of local government was likely to make the English ruling classes sensitive to shifts of mood in their own localities; and some of them, as members of parliament, had constituents whose reactions they could not entirely afford to ignore. By insisting on stringent conditions in return for subsidies, or by refusing to pay their Ship Money, they could present themselves to their local communities as staunch upholders of those 'original rights and constitutions' endangered by the power of the Crown.

Aristocratic constitutionalism presented a particular threat to innovating regimes in those societies, like England or Catalonia, where representative institutions were still vigorous, and traditional liberties well entrenched. Here political management became of critical importance if the central government were to get its way. The deficiencies of Charles I's regime in this respect are notorious. The story of the failure of personal monarchy in England – a story which also has its continental parallels – is essentially one of how the regime succeeded in alienating one section of the community after another until it was left without any visible means of support.

The growing divide between court and country, which Mr. Thomas describes, was by no means a purely English affair. Court culture was by its very nature exclusive, and the antithesis of court and country had long been a favourite literary theme. In the 1620s and 1630s a new literary generation, in England as in Spain, cultivated a style whose special delights were reserved for the few. But the appearance of this generation was perhaps less surprising than the earlier appearance of a handful of great poets and playwrights – a Shakespeare or a Lope de Vega – who could talk the language of court and country and simultaneously appeal to both. A 'breakdown of the national culture' may therefore be both too melodramatic and too parochial an interpretation of artistic developments in the England of Charles I. On the other hand, there were moments – and the 1630s were undoubtedly one such moment – when courts could do themselves serious political harm by their very style of life. The criticisms of Charles I's court theatricals echo those levelled at the court theatricals of Philip IV of Spain, held in the expensive new palace of the Buen Retiro in Madrid. In both instances, lavish court expenditure on buildings, pictures and festivities provoked strongly puritanical reactions in a society which was simultaneously being called upon to make new fiscal sacrifices.

Clearly the cultural isolation of a court might, as with the court of Charles I, be symptomatic of something deeper – of a fundamental unawareness of the country's mood. This must be regarded as an occupational hazard for seventeenth-century governments, as bureaucracies become more cumbersome, and the load of paper work increased. All over Europe the bureaucratic barriers were rising, and kings were removed one stage further from their peoples. In consequence it was all too easy for hard-pressed ministers to lose touch with reality, and to devise elaborate schemes which looked admirable when set down on paper but were administratively impossible to implement.

The over-ambitious regimes of the 1620s and 1630s ultimately brought disaster on themselves by attempting to do too much. Every new fiscal expedient created a new sense of irritation. Every breach with established custom created a deepening sense of distrust. The charmed circle of patronage was too small; the crowd of suppliants too great. Confidence was always a precious commodity for seventeenth-century monarchies, and it was all too frequently undermined by the unpredictable actions of arbitrary power. The governments of England, France and Spain all succeeded in alienating important sections of the community; and if they then attempted, as did Charles I in Scotland and Philip IV in Catalonia, to impose the assumed benefits of uniformity and centralised order on outlying kingdoms with strong national identities, they were dicing dangerously with fate.

Revolution, however, was not an inevitable response. A successful foreign policy, as Richelieu showed, could bring the monarchy a new prestige which would help it to weather domestic storms. The forum for effective opposition could, as in Castile, be weak, and powerful bonds of interest and patronage tie the governing classes to the Crown. But in the England of 1640 the monarchy was both discredited and isolated. It had broken the cardinal rules of statecraft by provoking its enemies while simultaneously alienating its natural friends. It had conjured up for itself the most dangerous of all kinds of opposition – an alliance, cemented by bonds of religion, between influential members of the political nation and the forces of popular discontent. Given these various pre-conditions the critical problem would seem to be not so much why mid-seventeenth-century England had a revolution, as why it made a greater success of its revolution than most.

LIST OF ABBREVIATIONS IN BIBLIOGRAPHY
AND REFERENCES

Barnes	T. G. Barnes, *Somerset, 1625–1640: A County's Government during the 'Personal Rule'* (Oxford 1961)
BIHR	*Bulletin of the Institute of Historical Research*
BM	British Museum
BM Add. MSS	British Museum Additional Manuscripts
BM Harl. MSS	British Museum Harleian Manuscripts
CJ	*Commons' Journals*
CSPD	*Calendar of State Papers, Domestic*
CSP Ven.	*Calendar of State Papers, Venetian*
E	British Museum, Thomason Tracts
EHR	*English Historical Review*
ECHR	*Economic History Review*
Gardiner	S. R. Gardiner, *History of England*, 10 vols (1883–4)
HMC	Historical Manuscripts Commission
Kenyon	J. P. Kenyon (ed.), *The Stuart Constitution* (Cambridge 1966)
LJ	*Lords' Journals*
P&P	*Past and Present*
PRO	Public Record Office
RO	Record Office
SP	State Papers, Public Record Office
TRHS	*Transactions of the Royal Historical Society*

Note: Place of publication is London unless otherwise stated.

Bibliography

Note: Place of publication is London unless otherwise stated.

INTRODUCTION

David Underdown, *Pride's Purge* (Oxford 1971).
Edward Hyde, Earl of Clarendon, *History of the Great Rebellion*, 6 vols (Oxford 1702).
Gardiner (*see* Abbreviations, opposite).
R. H. Tawney, 'The Rise of the Gentry', ECHR (1941).
H. R. Trevor-Roper, 'The Gentry 1540–1640', ECHR Supplement 1 (1953).
J. H. Hexter, 'Storm over the Gentry', repr. in *Reappraisals in History* (1961).
Lawrence Stone, *The Crisis of the Aristocracy, 1558–1642* (Oxford 1965).
Valerie Pearl, *London and the Puritan Revolution* (Oxford 1961).
Roger Howell, *Newcastle upon Tyne and the Puritan Revolution* (Oxford 1966).
Barnes (*see* Abbreviations, opposite).
J. H. Plumb, *The Growth of Political Stability* (1967).
Gordon Donaldson, *Scotland James V – James VII* (Edinburgh 1965).
H. J. Kearney, *Strafford in Ireland* (Manchester 1959).
Conrad Russell, 'Arguments for Religious Unity in England 1530–1650', *Journal of Ecclesiastical History* (1967).
K. V. Thomas, *Religion and the Decline of Magic* (1971).
Christopher Hill, *Economic Problems of the Church* (Oxford 1956); *Society and Puritanism in Pre-revolutionary England* (1964); 'The Many-Headed Monster', in *Essays in Honour of Garrett Mattingley*, Ed. Charles H. Carter (1966); and *Antichrist in Seventeenth Century England* (Oxford 1971).
Paul Seaver, *The Puritan Lectureships* (Oxford 1970).

I. THE GOVERNMENT: ITS ROLE AND ITS AIMS

No full-scale modern analysis of the role and aims of the early Stuart government exists. What pass for such are generally narratives derived, more or less closely, from Gardiner. But some aspects of the subject have been excellently dealt with. G. E. Aylmer, *The King's Servants: The Civil Service of Charles I, 1625–1642* (1961), fully analyses the recruitment, career patterns, fortunes and allegiances of Caroline office-holders. R. Ashton, *The Crown and the Money Market, 1603–1640* (Oxford 1960), deals with the decline of the Crown's credit-worthiness; but for Caroline finance as a whole nothing has replaced F. C. Dietz's dated *English Public Finance, 1558–1641* (1932). B. E. Supple, *Commercial Crisis and Change in England, 1600–1642* (Cambridge 1959), J. D. Gould, 'The Trade Depression of the early 1620's', ECHR, 2nd ser., vii (1954), pp. 81–8, and J. P. Cooper, 'Economic Regulation and the Cloth Industry in Seventeenth Century England', TRHS, 5th ser., xx (1970), pp. 73–99 are concerned with the the government's relations with the troubled cloth industry.

Interesting insights on the government's role, from a variety of points of view, can be found in: P. Zagorin, *The Court and the Country* (1969), Chs 1–3; C. Hill, *The Century of Revolution, 1603–1714* (Edinburgh 1961), Chs 1–6; and *Reformation to Industrial Revolution* (1967), parts i and ii; C. Wilson, *England's Apprenticeship, 1603–1763* (1965), part i; R. W. K. Hinton, 'The decline of Parliamentary

Government under Elizabeth I and the early Stuarts', *Cambridge Historical Journal*, xiii (1957), pp. 116–32; J. P. Cooper, 'Differences between English and Continental Governments in the Early Seventeenth Century' in J. S. Bromley and E. H. Kossmann (eds), *Britain and the Netherlands* (1960), pp. 62–90; and in a number of articles in F. J. Fisher (ed.), *Essays in the Economic and Social History of Tudor and Stuart England* (Cambridge 1961).

E. M. Leonard's *The Early History of English Poor Relief* (1900), is now inadequate, but there has been no full modern treatment of Caroline social policy.

Biographies of government figures are also of uneven quality. D. H. Willson, *King James VI and I* (1956), entertains with an entertaining subject, but there are no adequate studies of Charles I or Buckingham. H. R. Trevor-Roper's *Archbishop Laud, 1573–1645* (2nd edn 1962), is more stimulating than the work of the clerical hagiographers who have attacked it. Aspects of Strafford's career are excellently dealt with by H. F. Kearney, *Strafford in Ireland* (Manchester 1957); J. P. Cooper, 'The Fortunes of Thomas Wentworth, Earl of Strafford', ECHR, 2nd ser., xi (1958), pp. 227–48; and T. Ranger, Strafford in Ireland, A Revaluation', P&P, xix (1961), pp. 26–45. C. V. Wegwood in her standard biography, *Thomas Wentworth, First Earl of Strafford, A Revaluation, 1593–1641*, 2nd edn. (1961), attempts to incorporate some of the results of modern research into her earlier account, but the outcome is uneven and lacks the clarity of the first edition, which presented a coherent, even if unreal, picture of a political hero. There are no worthwhile published biographies of the important secondary figures in the government of the 1630s, Cottington, Noy, Windebank, Bankes, etc.

Collections of source material on the working of the constitution are in G. W. Prothero (ed.), *Select Statutes and Other Constitutional Documents of the Reigns of Elizabeth and James I*, 4th edn (Oxford 1913); J. R. Tanner (ed.), *Constitutional Documents of the Reign of James I* (Cambridge 1930); S. R. Gardiner (ed.), *Constitutional Documents of the Puritan Revolution*, 3rd edn (Oxford 1906); and J. P. Kenyon. The copious extracts from the patent rolls in T. Rymer and R. Sanderson (eds), *Foedera . . . ,* 20 vols (1704–32), remain a prime source of executive action. Vols xvi–xx deal with the early seventeenth century.

2. COUNTY GOVERNMENT IN CAROLINE ENGLAND 1625–1640

Without any question the best study of local government in the Caroline period is Barnes. The author is in Barnes's debt for the material used in this essay. (Although this essay has not discussed borough government one must mention Dr. Valerie Pearl's recent study, *London and the Outbreak of the Puritan Revolution: City Government and National Politics, 1625–43* (Oxford 1961). It surely must be included with Barnes's study as the best full-scale studies of local government in the period immediately before the civil war.) A shorter, but equally important study, is Joel Hurstfield's 'County Government' in *V. C. H. Wiltshire*, v (1957) although it is limited to the lieutenancy and the commission of the peace. See also Lindsay Boynton 'Billeting: The Example of the Isle of Wight', EHR (1959).

Two older studies which have held up very well are W. Notestein's *The English People on the eve of Colonization* (1954) and W. B. Willcox's, *Gloucestershire: a study in local government, 1590–1640* (New Haven 1940). Willcox limits his study to the various offices in the county but he discusses them well. Notestein presents a highly readable and compact social and administrative picture of the government of shire and parish.

For the student who wishes to get the first-hand flavour of local government in the seventeenth century there is no better introduction than the many printed Quarter Sessions records.

For a wider view, stretching beyond the outbreak of the Civil War, see Alan Everitt, *Change in the Provinces: The Seventeenth Century* (Leicester 1969), *The Local Community and the Great Rebellion* (Historical Assoc. 1969), *The County Committee of Kent in the Civil War* (Leicester 1957), and *Suffolk and the Great Rebellion: 1640–1660* (Ipswich 1961).

3. PARLIAMENT AND THE KING'S FINANCES

There is no adequate general history of royal finance during this period. F. C. Dietz, *English Public Finance 1558–1642* (1932) has not yet been superseded. The best recent work is in G. E. Aylmer, *The King's Servants* (1961), and in Robert Ashton, *The Crown and the Money Market* (Oxford 1960), and 'Deficit Finance in the Reign of James I', ECHR (1957). There is valuable information on some financial and political questions in Valerie Pearl, *London and the Puritan Revolution* (Oxford 1961). Recent work is summarised in J. P. Cooper, 'The Fall of the Stuart Monarchy', in *New Cambridge Modern History*, iv (1971), and Conrad Russell, *The Crisis of Parliaments* (Oxford 1971).

The related questions of patronage and administration have been admirably covered in J. Hurstfield, *The Queen's Wards* (1958), Penry Williams, *The Council in the Marches of Wales* (Cardiff 1958), G. E. Aylmer, *The King's Servants* (1961) and also in a section of L. Stone, *The Crisis of the Aristocracy, 1558–1642* (Oxford 1965).

On Parliamentary history, most of the best work has been done on editions of debates, of which the most notable are Elizabeth Read Foster (ed.), *Parliamentary Debates in 1610*, 2 vols (New Haven 1966), W. Notestein, F. H. Relf and H. Simpson (eds), *Commons' Debates in 1621*, 7 vols (New Haven 1935). The best modern works are D. H. Willson, *The Privy Councillors in Parliament* (New York 1940), and Clayton Roberts, *The Growth of Responsible Government* (1966). See also Robert E. Ruigh, *The Parliament of 1624* (1971). By far the best complete narrative is still Gardiner. On the political ideas of the Parliamentarians, the best book is M. A. Judson, *The Crisis of the Constitution*, now regrettably almost unobtainable.

For a pioneering example of the sort of work which is still badly needed on Parliamentary history, see Christopher Thompson 'The Origins of the Parliamentary Middle Group 1625–1629' (Alexander Prize Essay 1971), *Transactions of the Royal Historical Society* (1972). My debt to Mr. Thompson, though it will be apparent to any reader of that essay, is greater than a reading of it can indicate.

On the legal issues involved in royal finance, see W. J. Jones, *Politics and the Bench* (1972).

4. PURITANISM, ARMINIANISM AND COUNTER-REVOLUTION

C. Hill, *Society and Puritanism in Pre-Revolutionary England* (1964) and W. Haller, *The Rise of Puritanism* (New York 1938) are both in their way classics. Another interesting general study is C. H. and K. George, *The Protestant Mind of the English Reformation, 1570–1640* (Princeton 1961). J. F. H. New, *Anglican and Puritan, the Basis of their Opposition, 1558–1640* (1964) is a questionable attempt to distinguish an 'Anglican' religious tradition existing from Elizabethan days.

Important monographs are R. A. Marchant, *The Puritans and the Church Courts in the Diocese of York, 1560–1642* (1960); P. Seaver, *The Puritan Lectureships: the Politics of Religious Dissent, 1560–1662* (Stanford 1970); and S. B. Babbage, *Puritanism and Richard Bancroft* (1962). A more wide ranging study is H. R. Trevor-Roper, *Archbishop Laud, 1573–1645* (2nd edn 1962). The article by M. H. Curtis, 'The Hampton Court Conference and its Aftermath', *History*, xlvi (1961), pp. 1–16, is marred by a false antithesis between the views of King James and his bishops, many of whom were at least as sympathetic to Puritanism as himself; moreover such concessions as the king was then prepared to grant were subsequently honoured.

For two very different approaches to that adopted in the present essay the reader may consult M. Walzer, *The Revolution of the Saints, a Study in the Origin of Radical Politics* (1966) and W. Lamont, *Godly Rule* (1969).

5. FEAR OF POPERY

The best general history of English Catholicism in this period, though old and dealing only with Elizabeth's reign, is A. O. Meyer, *England and the Catholic Church under Queen Elizabeth*, republished in 1970 with a useful introduction by J. W. Bossy. The best regional study is by H. Aveling in *Northern Recusants* (1964), though J. S. Leatherbarrow in 'Lancashire Elizabethan Recusants', *Chetham Society*, cx (1947) contains a valuable discussion of the implementation of the penal laws. In 'The Extent and Character of Recusancy in Yorkshire', *Yorkshire Archaeological Journal*, xxxvii (1948–51), A. G. Dickens provides an informative guide to the numbers of English Catholics, and J. W. Bossy's study of 'The Extent and Character of Elizabethan Catholicism', P&P, xxi (1962) is the best sociological analysis.

Among biographies of priests and laity the following deserve attention: P. Caraman, *Henry Morse Priest of the Plague* (1957); William Weston's revealing *Autobiography*, edited by P. Caraman (1965); J. Wake *The Brudenells of Deane* (1953); and M. E. Finch *Five Northamptonshire Families* (Oxford 1956). Further studies can be found in the journal *Recusant History*.

Various aspects of Catholic-Protestant relations are discussed in: G. Albion, *Charles I and Rome* (1935); W. Haller, *Foxe's 'Book of Martyrs' and the Elect Nation* (1963); Carol Z. Weiner, 'The Beleaguered Isle', P&P li (1971); and R. Clifton 'The Fear of Catholicism during the English Civil War', P&P, lii (1971).

6. TWO CULTURES? COURT AND COUNTRY UNDER CHARLES I

I wish to draw particular attention to my indebtedness, for information and inspiration, to the works by Christopher Hill, H. R. Trevor-Roper, W. R. Parker, Laurence A. Sasek, L. Schucking, and Don M. Wolfe mentioned in my notes. Equally important have been C. V. Wegwood's indispensable *Poetry and Politics under the Stuarts* (Cambridge 1960); G. R. Hibbard, 'The Country House Poem of the Seventeenth Century', *Journal of the Warburg and Courtauld Institute*, xix (1956), pp. 159–74; and L. C. Knights, *Drama and Society in the Age of Jonson* (1937) – all of which stimulatingly combine historical with literary insights. Ursula Hoff, *Charles I: Patron of Artists* (1942), though I disagree with its general stance, was also useful. For Jonson, I found J. B. Bamborough, *Ben Jonson* (1970) and Stephen Orgel, *The Jonsonian Masque* (Cambridge, Mass. 1965) illuminating. A full list of the arguments published in the period for and against the stage will be found in *English Theatrical Literature 1559–1900, A Bibliography* (Society for Theatre Research 1970).

7. ECONOMIC ISSUES AND IDEOLOGIES

The political line-up:

D. Brunton and D. Penington, *Members of the Long Parliament* (1953).

C. Hill, *The Century of Revolution, 1603–1714* (Edinburgh 1961).

M. F. Keeler, *The Long Parliament 1640–1641. A Biographical Study* (Philadelphia 1954).

V. Pearl, *London and the Outbreak of the Puritan Revolution* (Oxford 1961).

P. Zagorin, *The Court and the Country. The Beginning of the English Revolution* (1969).

The economic background:

F. J. Fisher, (ed.), *Essays in the Economic and Social History of Tudor and Stuart England* (Cambridge 1961).

C. Hill, *Reformation to Industrial Revolution: British Economy and Society, 1530–1780* (1967).

M. James, *Social Problems and Policy during the Puritan Revolution, 1640–1660* (re-issue 1966).

B. E. Supple, *Commercial Crisis and Change in England, 1600–1642* (Cambridge 1964).

C. Wilson, *England's Apprenticeship, 1603–1763* (1965).

Seventeenth-century economic thought:

D. C. Coleman (ed.), *Revisions in Mercantilism* (1969).

C. Hill, *Intellectual Origins of the English Revolution* (Oxford 1965).

W. Letwin, *The Origins of Scientific Economics. English Economic Thought, 1660–1776* (1963).

C. Wilson, " 'Mercantilism': Some Vicissitudes of an Idea", ECHR, 2nd ser., x (1957).

8. POLITICS AND POLITICAL THOUGHT 1640–1642

M. A. Judson's *The Crisis of the Constitution, 1603–1645* (New Brunswick 1949, rep. 1971) remains the finest general work on political thought in the period. The common law mind, along with royalism the common denominator of moderates on both sides, was anatomised brilliantly by J. G. A. Pocock's *Ancient Constitution and the Feudal Law* (Cambridge 1957; New York 1967). F. D. Wormuth sketched the other side of the coin suggestively though rather unchronologically in *The Royal Prerogative, 1603–1649* (Ithaca 1939). I prefer William Lamont's *Marginal Prynne* (1963) to his more recent *Godly Rule* (1969). Another fine study is B. H. G. Wormald's *Clarendon* (Cambridge 1951). Gardiner is well worth reading for political thought, a point which would have saved C. C. Weston in *English Constitutional Theory and House of Lords 1556–1832* (1965) from marring a useful contribution. C. H. Firth's *House of Lords during the Civil War* (1910) is durable and pertinent. See also an article by Brian Manning, 'The Outbreak of the English Civil War' in R. H. Parry (ed.), *The English Civil War and After* (1970).

S. R. Gardiner's *Constitutional Documents of the Puritan Revolution*, 3rd edn (Oxford 1906) and Kenyon are starting points for sources, but their commentary is invaluable. J. Rushworth's *Historical Collections* and J. Nalson's *Collection* are still useful as a commentary. The editions by W. Notestein (New Haven 1923) and W. H. Coates (New Haven 1942) of parts of the *Journal of Sir Simonds D'Ewes* have made the older books more, rather than less valuable, because D'Ewes's editors have, in effect, edited the older parliamentary sources as well, in their footnotes. Because the House of Lords is a court of record, its Journal was semi-public, and full of documents inserted for the record. The CSPD is also readily to hand, and useful.

The *Harleian Miscellany* and the *Somers Tracts* have good pamphlet material for the period. The *Catalogue of the Thomason Collection*, 2 vols (1908) remains the most useful guide to the available pamphlet literature.

9. ENGLAND AND EUROPE: A COMMON MALADY?

R. B. Merriman in his *Six Contemporaneous Revolutions* (Oxford 1938) included 'The Puritan Revolution' as one of his six. 'It may not be amiss' he wrote (p. 27) 'to try to paint the picture of the English revolution, at least in its original out-lines, as envisaged from across the Channel.' But he did not carry the process very far. J. P. Cooper made an interesting attempt to discuss the 'Differences between English and Continental Governments in the Early Seventeenth Century' in J. S. Bromley and E. H. Kossmann (eds), *Britain and the Netherlands* (1960). Otherwise, attempts at comparative history have tended to get sub-merged in the debate on the 'general crisis of the seventeenth century', on which the literature is now very considerable. The best approach to this debate is through the essays reprinted in Trevor Aston, *Crisis in Europe, 1560–1660* (1965), and the first two chapters of A. D. Lublinskaya, *French Absolutism: The Crucial Phase, 1620–1629* (Cambridge 1968). For a recent contribution to this debate which places a renewed emphasis on the role of government, see the paper by Niels Steensgaard, 'The Economic and Political Crisis of the Seventeenth Century', presented to the Thirteenth International Congress of Historical Sciences (Moscow 1970).

References and Notes on Text

INTRODUCTION *Conrad Russell*

1. David Underdown, *Pride's Purge*, pp. 7–8.
2. Bedford MSS xi, iii 1290–93.
3. Gardiner, I, p. 2.
4. Jeremy Bentham, *A Fragment on Government*, p. 1.
5. *Times Educational Supplement*, 18 June 1971.
6. Joan Thirsk (ed.), *Cambridge Agrarian History*, iv (1967), p. 694.
7. M. F. Keeler, *Members of the Long Parliament* (Philadelphia 1954), 27n.
8. J. P. Cooper, 'The Counting of Manors', ECHR (1956); Eric Kerridge, *The Agrarian Problem in the Sixteenth Century and After*, pp. 19–20; Conrad Russell, 'Land Sales 1540–1640: A Note on the Evidence'; and Christopher Thompson, 'A Comment on Professor Stone's Statistics', both in ECHR (1972). I am most grateful to Mr. Thompson for allowing me to see this article before publication. See also the review of Stone's *Crisis of The Aristocracy*, by D. C. Coleman in *History* (1966). I am also very grateful to Mr. Thompson for allowing me to read several draft chapters of his thesis on the Earl of Warwick. For a persuasive rehabilitation of some of Stone's arguments, see Barry Coward, 'Disputed Inheritances: Some Difficulties of the Nobility in the Late Sixteenth and Early Seventeenth Centuries', BIHR (1971).
9. This somewhat light-hearted suggestion is based on an impressionistic survey of the MSS of Lord Keeper Coventry (Birmingham Reference Library), 'Grants and Patents', 'Grants of Offices' and 'Grants of Leases' *passim*.
10. B. A. W. Jackson (ed.), *Stratford Papers 1965–67* (Shannon 1969), pp. 229–31.
11. Barnes, pp. 294–5.
12. Wallace Notestein, *The House of Commons 1604–1610* (New Haven 1971), p. 280.
13. National Register of Archives, Sackville MSS, ON 139.
14. Birmingham Reference Library, Coventry MSS, Commissions of the Peace, Nos 70 ff.
15. *Ibid.*, Grants and Patents, No. 160.
16. Cambridge University Library MS, DD 12–20, f. 9.
17. G. R. Elton, 'A High Road to Civil War?', in Charles H. Carter (ed.), *Essays in Honour of Garrett Mattingley* (1966), 325 ff.
18. Bedford MSS cxcvii, f. 64b (Bedford's marginal notes on his copy of Pym's Parliamentary diary for 1625).
19. Barnes, p. 15.
20. Keith Thomas, p. 163.
21. C. Hill, *Society and Puritanism*, pp. 70–1.
22. Seaver, pp. 240–66.
23. Bedford MSS, xi, i, p. 100.
24. N. R. N. Tyacke, 'Arminianism in England in Religion and Politics, 1604–1640', Oxford D.Phil. Thesis (1968), p. 71.
25. C. Hill, *Antichrist in Seventeenth Century England* (Oxford 1971), p. 169.
26. H. C. Porter, *Puritanism in Tudor England* (1970) p. 92.
27. Tyacke, p. 237.

28. Stephen Marshall, *A Peace-Offering* (1641), pp. 20, 7, 37–8.

29. Jeremiah Burroughes, *Sion's Joy* (1641), pp. 57, 34, 19.

30. Huntingdon RO, Manchester MSS 32/5/17a. The identification of Fiennes as the author of this newsletter is based on handwriting.

31. CSPD 1640, cccclx, No. 40. The Earl of Essex, the Parliamentary general, paid 12s. a lb. for his tobacco, and died leaving an unpaid bill for 20 lbs. BM Add. MSS 46, 189, f. 96a.

32. Clarendon, *History* (1704), i, 145.

33. Bedford MSS, xi, i, 44.

34. CSPD 1640–1, cccclxx, No. 20, cccclxxi, No. 44 (Vane to Roe).

35. *Ibid.*, cccclxxi, Nos. 8, 42. CSP Ven, *1640–2* p. 193. (May 31, 1641) I am grateful to Mr. Michael Mendle for drawing my attention to this reference.

36. H. B. Wheatley (ed.), *Diary and Correspondence of John Evelyn* (1906), iv, pp. 120–1, 93, 91.

I. THE GOVERNMENT: ITS ROLE AND ITS AIMS

Michael Hawkins

1. Manning, in P&P, ix (April 1956), p. 47; I. Roots, *History*, li (1966), p. 92; J. P. Cooper, 'Differences between English and Continental Governments in the Early Seventeenth Century', in J. S. Bromley and E. H. Kossmann (eds.), *Britain and the Netherlands* (1960), p. 63. M. Roberts, *History*, i, (1965), p. 191n.

2. C. Hill, EHR lxxi (1956), p. 458; *Reformation to Industrial Revolution* (1968), p. 76.

3. H. R. Trevor-Roper, P&P xvi (1959), p. 61; J. H. Elliott, *ibid.*, xviii (1960), p. 25.

4. Fisher, in E. W. Ives (ed.), *The English Revolution, 1600–1660* (1968), p. 86.

5. C. H. McIlwain (ed.), *The Political Works of James I* (New York 1965), p. 22.

6. *Political Works*, p. 19.

7. *Ibid.*, pp. 61–2.

8. Kenyon, p. 103. Cf. J. W. Gough, *Fundamental Law in English Constitutional History* (Oxford 1955).

9. Kenyon, p. 55.

10. This point is amplified in Hawkins, *Wardship and Society under the early Stuarts* (in preparation).

11. This view seems to be implied in much of Dr. Christopher Hill's work: cf. especially *The Century of Revolution 1603–1714* (Edinburgh 1961), pp. 28–42; *Reformation to Industrial Revolution*, chs. 4, 5 and 6. He does however admit that monopolies could perform a useful economic function under some circumstances.

12. cf. B. E. Supple, *Commercial Crisis and Change in England, 1600–1642* (Cambridge 1959), pp. 8–13.

13. C. Wilson, *England's Apprenticeship, 1603–1763* (1965), p. 34.

14. 'Labour in the English Economy of the Seventeenth Century', repr. in E. M. Carus-Wilson (ed). *Essays in Economic History*, ii (1962), pp. 291–308.

15. Hill, *Reformation to Industrial Revolution*, p. 73. The three luxury industries quoted include, rather oddly, glass: cf. W. G. Hoskins's statement, '. . . the increased production of cheap glass, which made its use possible in ordinary houses for the first time', 'The Rebuilding of Rural England, 1570–1640', P&P, iv (1953), p. 55: and J. U. Nef's reference to the cheapness of English glass in E. M. Carus-Wilson (ed.), *op. cit.*, i (1954), pp. 101, 123.

16. C. Wilson, p. 61.

17. Supple, *op. cit.*, p. 7. J. D. Gould, EHR (1956), p. 216; J. Thirsk (ed.), *Agrarian History* (1967), pp. 819, 821.

18. Cooper, 'Economic Regulation and the Cloth Industry in Seventeenth Century England', TRHS, 5th ser., xx (1970), p. 76.

19. Supple, *op. cit.*, pp. 240, 244.

20. Cooper, 'Economic Regulation', p. 76.

21. Wilson, p. 50; Cooper, p. 74.

22. R. W. K. Hinton, 'The Decline of Parliamentary Government under Elizabeth I and the Early Stuarts', *Cambridge Historical Journal*, xiii (1957), pp. 126–7.

23. Supple, *op. cit.*, pp. 121–2 for the Adventurers' pressure.

24. Quoted by H. R. Trevor-Roper, *Archbishop Laud* (1962).

25. M. Campbell, 'Of People either too Few or too Many', in W. A. Aiken and B. D. Henning (eds), *Conflict in Stuart England* (1960), pp. 172–84.

26. W. K. Jordan, *Philanthropy in England, 1480–1660* (1959), pp. 134–5.

27. J. Thirsk (ed.), *The Agrarian History of England and Wales*, iv (Cambridge 1967), p. 213.

28. M. Beresford, 'Habitation versus Improvement': F. J. Fisher (ed.), *Essays in the Economic and Social History of Tudor and Stuart England* (Cambridge 1961), p. 50.

29. Jordan, *passim*. The doubts which have been expressed about the real value of the bequests which Jordan has analysed (given a century of inflation) do not extend to the *redirection* of charity into secular channels.

30. cf. T. Ranger, 'Strafford in Ireland: A Revaluation', P&P xix (1961), pp. 26–45.

31. A. Clarke, 'Ireland and the General Crisis', P&P, xlviii, (1970), p. 91. For Ireland generally, see H. F. Kearney, *Strafford in Ireland, 1633–41* (Manchester 1959) and A. Clarke, *The Old English in Ireland, 1625–42* (1966), besides the article cited above.

2. COUNTY GOVERNMENT IN CAROLINE ENGLAND *L. M. Hill*

1. G. E. Aylmer, *The Kings Servants; the Civil Service of Charles I* (1961), p. 7.

2. Michael Dalton, *The Countrey Justice ,containing the practice of the Justices of the Peace out of their Sessions*, 5th edn (1635). Dalton first published this work in 1618.

3. L. M. Hill, 'The Admiralty Circuit of 1591: Some Comments on the Relations between Central Government and Local Interests', in *The Historical Journal*, xiv, i (1971).

4. R. B. Pugh (ed.), *Wiltshire* in *The Victoria Histories of the Counties of England* (1957), v. The chapter on local government by Professor Joel Hurstfield on the commission of the peace and the Lord Lieutenant is a model of succinct analysis and much of the following is drawn from this chapter.

5. Barnes, p. 98.

6. M. G. Davies, *The Enforcement of English Apprenticeship, 1563–1642* (Cambridge, Mass. 1956) pp. 166–7.

7. Barnes, p. 77.

8. Barnes, p. 173.

9. Barnes, p. 179.

10. Davies, *English Apprenticeship*, p. 213.

11. Barnes, pp. 80–1.

12. G. E. Aylmer, *The Struggle for the Constitution, 1603–1688* (1963), p. 103.

13. G. E. Aylmer, *The King's Servants*, p. 65.

14. Barnes, p. 207 n.

15. CSPD 1637–8, 28.

16. CSPD, 1637–8, 258.

17. CSPD, 1638–9, 10–11.

18. Barnes, p. 233.

19. R. W. Ketton-Cremer, *Norfolk in the Civil War* (1969), p. 102.

20. M. A. Judson, *The Crises of the Constitution: An Essay in Constitutional and Political Thought in England, 1603–1645* (repr. 1971), pp. 42–3.

21. R. Ashton, *The Crown and the Money Market, 1603–1640* (Oxford 1960), xv.

3. PARLIAMENT AND THE KING'S FINANCES *Conrad Russell*

1. J. S. Roskell, 'Perspectives in English Parliamentary History', repr. in E. B. Fryde and Edward Miller (eds), *Historical Studies of the English Parliament* (Cambridge 1971), ii, p. 318.

2. BM Stowe MSS 366, f. 39a.

3. Roskell, p. 322.

4. J. N. Ball, 'The Impeachment of the Duke of Buckingham in the Parliament of 1626', in Emil Lousse (ed.), *Mélanges Antonio Marongiu* (Brussels 1968), p. 48.

5. CSPD 1625–6, xix, No. 107.

6. S. R. Gardiner (ed.), *Commons' Debates in 1625*, Camden Series (1873) (hereafter cited as *1625 Debates*) p. 114: Whitelocke's diary, Cambridge University Library MSS Dd 12–20 to 12–22 (hereafter cited as Whitelocke), f. 61. The question of lodgings for medieval members would repay further study. Medieval members were normally paid wages, and attended for short sessions.

7. C. E. Challis, 'The Circulating Medium and the Movement of Prices', in Peter H. Ramsey (ed.), *The Price Revolution in Sixteenth Century England* (1971), p. 128.

8. CSPD 1640, cccclvii, No. 9.

9. J. P. Cooper, 'The Fall of the Stuart Monarchy', in *New Cambridge Modern History*, iv (1971), p. 531.

10. Somerset RO Pym MSS No. 151; PRO E. 179/172/390. The assessment was probably on the tenant's rent of £1. 9s 6d. If so, it is a good illustration of the fact that a high entry fine and a low rent provided a good method of obtaining a low valuation for taxation. Bedford MSS., 4th Earl: miscellaneous papers: Bedford to Manchester.

11. *1625 Debates*, p. 78.

12. See J. Hurstfield, 'Political Corruption in Early Modern England', *History* (1967), pp. 16–34.

13. Coventry MSS, Grants and Patents No. 23 (grant to Harley, June 1627), No. 171, No. 129.

14. Cooper, p. 531.

15. Stowe MSS 366, f. 284b.

16. Elizabeth Read Foster (ed.), *Parliamentary Debates in 1610* (New Haven 1966), ii, p. 402.

17. CSPD, 1623–5, clxi, No. 4.

18. BM Add MSS 18, 597, f. 71b.

19. The question of the effect of the increase of the electorate on early seventeenth century politics was raised by J. H. Plumb, *The Growth of Political Stability* (1967), pp. 45–50. Remarks on this subject must remain provisional

pending the present researches of Derek Hirst on early seventeenth-century elections.

20. CSPD, 1623–5, clx, No. 89: BM Add. MS 18, 597, f. 97b, Whitelocke, ff. 40, 129.

21. BM Harl, MSS 6383, f. 105a.

22. BM Add. MSS 18, 597, ff. 72a, 93b. The appropriation could also be interpreted as an attempt by Buckingham to bribe James into abandoning his opposition to open war.

23. Stowe MS 366, f. 10a.

24. There are occasional speeches by these members which might support a different interpretation, especially by Eliot (Whitelocke f. 66) and Phelips (*1625 Debates*, p. 12). When read in full, and in the context of their other speeches on money matters, these speeches appear to be no more than polite ways of saying the king was spending too much money.

25. *1625 Debates*, p. 31.

26. *Ibid.*, p. 111: Whitelocke, f. 151.

27. Roskell, pp. 318–19; Stowe MSS 366, f. 288a.

28. Whitelocke, f. 157: Stowe MSS 366, f. 43b.

29. Stowe MSS 366, ff. 276a, 217a, 284a. See also Whitelocke, f. 28a.

30. Whitelocke, f. 66, Stowe 366, f. 276a.

31. S. M. Kingsbury (ed.), *Records of the Virginia Company* (1935), iv, pp. 39, 49–52. I would like to thank Mr. Christopher Thompson for this reference.

32. Bedford MSS, xxvii, pp. 24–6. It cannot be proved that Charles saw this document, but the similarity of many of its figures to those in Charles's 1635 balance is remarkable.

33. Whitelocke, f. 4b; Stowe MSS 366, f. 282a.

34. Stowe MSS 366, f. 199a. This attitude to the sale of titles is a sharp contrast to that of the Parliamentary leaders of 1640, who included three baronets and one holder of a bought peerage.

35. CSPD, 1640–1, cccclxvi, No. 76: CSPD, 1640, ccccliii, No. 89.

36. Huntingdon RO, Manchester MSS 36/1, ff. 3, 12. The ascription of this diary to Oliver St. John is clearly false. It is in the hand of Robert Bernard, M.P. for Huntingdon and man of affairs to the Earl of Manchester. I am grateful to Dr. Valerie Pearl for suggesting this identification to me.

37. CSPD, 1640, ccclii, Nos. 114–15.

38. BM Add. MSS 26, 637, f. 1a. (flyleaf of Bedford's copy of Pym's diary of the 1621 Parliament). Some at least of these notes were written between June and September 1628, after the Petition of Right, and before the death of Justice Doderidge.

39. This agreement with the Scots was quite explicit, and is clearly documented on the Scottish side. R. Baillie, *Letters and Journals* (1841), i, 276, 280, 297 and other refs.

40. Bedford MSS, viii, f. 41: Pym MSS, nos. 146, 237: BM Add. MSS 26, 651 ff. 11–20 (MS copy of Christopher Vernon's *Considerations for Regulating the Exchequer*, in the possession of Oliver St John); BM Stowe MSS 326, f. 73. Bedford's draft wills, Bedford Office, miscellaneous papers.

41. CSPD, 1640–1, cccclxxix, No. 89: Baillie, i 287.

42. W. Notestin (ed.), *Journal of Sir Simonds D'Ewes*, i (New Haven 1923), pp. 43–4; BM Harl. MSS 163, f. 633a.

43. BM Sloane MSS 3317, f. 21a (Hartlib's newsletter). I would like to thank Mr. Christopher Thompson for this reference. *D'Ewes* i, p. 111.

44. *Notebook of Sir John Northcote* (1877), p. 12. *D'Ewes*, i, p. 75.

45. Bedford MSS, fourth Earl, miscellaneous papers: 'The Project upon the

Clergie and Colledges': 'The Project Upon the Wardes': Christopher Vernon, in Add. MSS 26, 651, f. 17a. See also *D'Ewes*, i, p. 146.

46. BM Harl. MSS 163, f. 533a; CJ ii, p. 161; CSP Ven, 1640–2, p. 112; HMC *Montagu of Beaulieu*, p. 130; Huntingdon RO Manchester MSS 32/5/27; C. J. Sawyer and Co., *Catalogue No. 155* (Jan 1940), No. 125 (undated letter from Rous to Pym). The original of this letter does not appear to survive.

47. *D'Ewes*, i, p. 146.

48. BM Harl. MSS 163, ff. 616a–617b, 638a–640a and other refs.

49. William Bray (ed.), *Diary and Correspondence of John Evelyn* (1891), iv, p. 74.

50. Lawrence Stone (ed.), *Social Change and Revolution in England* (1965), p. 90.

4. PURITANISM, ARMINIANISM AND COUNTER-REVOLUTION
Nicholas Tyacke

1. C. Hill, *Society and Puritanism in Pre-Revolutionary England* (1964); W. Haller, *The Rise of Puritanism* (New York 1938).

2. A. Clark (ed.), *Register of the University of Oxford* (1887–9), ii pt. 1 pp. 194–217; G. Abbot, *A Sermon preached at Westminster* (1608), pp. 19–20.

3. H. C. Porter, *Reformation and Reaction in Tudor Cambridge* (Cambridge 1958), pp. 365–75; P. Collinson, 'The "nott conformytye" of the young John Whitgift', *Journal of Ecclesiastical History*, xv (1964), pp. 192–200; A. F. Scott Pearson, *Thomas Cartwright and Elizabethan Puritanism, 1535–1603* (Cambridge 1925), pp. 22–3, 396.

4. J. Ayre (ed.), *The Sermons of Edwin Sandys* (Cambridge 1842) pp. 223, 448; R. A. Marchant, *The Puritans and the Church Courts in the Diocese of York, 1560–1642* (1960), pp. 18–21; L. Carlson (ed.), *The Writings of Henry Barrow, 1590–1591* (1966), p. 62.

5. S. Benefield, *A Sermon preached at Wotton Under Edge* (Oxford 1613); S. Gardiner, *A Dialogue* (1605), sigs. E3v, B4r; W. Scott (ed.), *Somers Tracts* (1809), ii, pp. 307–8, 311.

6. C. Hill, *Puritanism and Revolution* (1958), pp. 216, 238; R. Abbot, *A Defence of the Reformed Catholic of W. Perkins* (1611); F. Rous, *Testis Veritatis* (1626), pp. 2–3; C. H. McIlwain (ed.), *The Political Works of James I* (Cambridge, Mass. 1918), p. 274; W. P. Baildon (ed.), *Les Reportes . . . in Camera Stellata, 1593 to 1609* (1894), p. 191; Kenyon, p. 41.

7. L. Andrewes, *Responsio* (1610), p. 123; T. G. Crippen (ed.), 'Of the Name of Puritans', *Trans. Congregational Hist. Soc.*, vi (1913–15), p. 83; E. Arber (ed.), *A Transcript of Registers of the Company of Stationers, 1554–1640* (1875–94), iii.

8. H. Foley, *Records of the English Province of the Society of Jesus* (1877–83), i, p. 70; M. Tierney (ed.), *Dodd's Church History* (1839–43) iv, pp. 179–80; HMC, *Salisbury* xviii, p. 21; A. G. R. Smith, *The Government of Elizabethan England* (1967), p. 65; P. Collinson, *The Elizabethan Puritan Movement* (1967), p. 159.

9. R. Bancroft, *Dangerous Positions and Proceedings . . . under pretence of Reformation* (1593); M. Knappen (ed.), *Two Elizabethan Diaries* (Chicago 1933); p. 32; T. Rogers, *The Faith, Doctrine, and Religion professed and protected in . . . England* (Cambridge 1607/8); Elizabeth Read Foster (ed.), *Proceedings in Parliament, 1610* (New Haven 1966), ii, p. 78; G. Goodman, *The Court of James I* (1839), ii pp. 160–1; P. Hembry, *The Bishops of Bath and Wells* (1967), p. 211; *The Works of [King] James* (1616), sig. e. For much of the information in this

and succeeding paragraphs, see my forthcoming book *The Rise of English Arminianism*, which is to be published by Oxford University Press.

10. P. Seaver, *The Puritan Lectureships . . . 1560–1662* (Stanford 1970), pp. 224–9; R. A. Marchant, p. 43.

11. Manchester MSS (formerly at PRO), Hughes to Nathaniel Rich, 19 May 1617; L. Hughes, *A Plain and True Relation of . . . the Summer Islands* (1621); C. Hill, *Puritanism and Revolution*, p. 146; I. Morgan, *Prince Charles's Puritan Chaplain* (1957); W. Notestein (ed.), *Commons' Debates 1621* (New Haven 1935), iv, p. 63.

12. W. Notestein (ed.), *Commons Debates for 1629* (Minneapolis 1921), p. 100.

13. J. Sansom (ed.), *The Works of John Cosin* (Oxford 1843–55), ii, pp. 61–4.

14. *Ibid.*, p. 74; Kenyon, pp. 154–5; S. R. Gardiner, *The Constitutional Documents of the Puritan Revolution, 1625–1660* (repr. Oxford 1962), p. 76.

15. Kenyon, pp. 153–4; S. R Gardiner (ed.), *Debates in the House of Commons for 1625* (Camden Soc., N.S. vi, 1873), p. 49.

16. *Commons Debates for 1629*, pp. 12–15, 27.

17. BM Add. MSS 25, 285. I owe my knowledge of this volume to Dr. V. Pearl.

18. Bedford MSS xi, 96, 100, 158, 248, 1236, 1293; W. Fiennes, Viscount Saye, *Two Speeches* (1641), pp. 13–14; N. Fiennes, *A Speech . . . concerning Bishops* (1641); R. Greville, Lord Brooke, *A Discourse opening the Nature of . . . Episcopacy* (1641). E. Clinton, *Countess of Lincoln's Nurserie* (1622), p. 17; *Complete Peerage* (1929), vii, pp. 696–7; I. Morgan, p. 43; D. Underdown, *Pride's Purge* (Oxford 1971), p. 20.

19. S. R. Gardiner, pp. 103–5; I. M. Calder, *Activities of the Puritan Faction . . . 1625–1633* (1957), p. xxii.

20. R. Howell, *Newcastle-upon-Tyne and the Puritan Revolution* (Oxford 1966), p. 112; CSPD 1631–3, p. 571.

21. R. F. Williams (ed.), *Court and Times of Charles I* (1848), i, p. 347; G. Abbot, *An Exposition on the Prophet Jonah* (1613), pp. 436–7; *The Sermons of Edwin Sandys*, p. 199.

22. *The Geneva Bible* (facsimile of first edition, Wisconsin 1969).

23. R. Abbot, *Antichristi Demonstratio* (1603), pp. 92–3; S. Marshall, *Copy of a Letter* (1643), pp. 11, 20; H. R. Trevor-Roper (ed.), *Essays in British History* (1965), p. 89.

24. M. C. Kitshoff, 'Aspects of Arminianism in Scotland', unpublished M.Th. thesis (St. Andrews 1968).

25. Kenyon, pp. 167–8, 172, 198; W. A. Shaw, *A History of the English Church . . . 1640–60* (1900), i, pp. 65–76

26. G. F. T. Jones, *Saw-Pit Wharton* (Sydney 1967), p. 50; Dr. Williams's Library, MSS Modern Folios 12.7; BM Add. MSS 5247, and Harl. MSS 986; *Old Parliamentary History* (1760–3), xi, p. 435.

5. FEAR OF POPERY *Robin Clifton*

1. The House of Commons' *Protestation* of 3 May 1641, in S. R. Gardiner (ed.), *Constitutional Documents of the Puritan Revolution 1625–60* (Oxford 1927), pp. 155–6.

2. A. B. Hinds (ed.), CSP Ven. 1643–47 (1926), No. 61; *Special Passages*, E 105 No. 10, No. 43, p. 353; G. Ormerod (ed.), *Tracts relating to Military Proceedings in Lancashire during the Civil War* (Chetham Society, O.S., 1844), ii, p. 3; *Perfect Diurnal*, BM Burney 15, No. 42, (n.p. 28 Mar 1643); *Ibid.*, BM Burney 18, No. 38, p. 302.

3. *Two Proclamations by the King . . .*, E 112 No. 22 (17 Aug. 1642); *The True*

Copie of a Letter Imparting divers passages of high and dangerous consequence,
E 124 No. 15, p. 5 (25 Oct. 1642); 'The Private Correspondence between King
Charles I and his Secretary of State Sir Edward Nicholas', in W. Bray (ed.),
*Memoirs Illustrative of the Life and Writings of John Evelyn . . . and the Private
Correspondence between King Charles I and Sir Edward Nicholas*, 2 vols (1818),
ii, Pt. 2, p. 46.

4. E. Hyde, *The History of the Rebellion and Civil Wars in England*, ed. W. D.
Macray, 6 vols (Oxford 1888), ii, p. 276n.

5. W. Perkins, *Lectures upon the three first chapters of Revelation . . . in which
is proved that Rome is Babylon* (1604), p. 369.

6. R. Sibbes, *Complete Works*, ed. A. B. Grosart, 7 vols (1864), ii, p. 42.

7. *Sermons, or Homilies, appointed to be read in Churches* (1817), 'A Sermon of
Good Works', pp. 49–52; 'A Sermon on Idolatry', pp. 169–70, 226–8.

8. Sibbes, *Works*, iv, p. 357.

9. J. Gee, *The Foot out of the Snare* . . . (1624), pp. 13, 27; J. Wadsworth,
The English-Spanish Pilgrim . . . (1629), p. 80; R. Sheldon, *The Motives of
Richard Sheldon Pr. for his just voluntary and free renouncing of Communion with
the Bishop of Rome* (1612), pp. 77–8; H. Yaxlee, *Morbus et Antidotus. The disease
with the antidote* (1630), pp. 13–21; T. Abernethie, *Abjuration of Popery, by
Thomas Abernethie: Sometime Jesuite* (Edinburgh 1638), p. 22.

10. *Sermons or Homilies*, p. 104.

11. See esp. P. Toon (ed.), *Puritans, the Millennium, and the Future of Israel*
(1970) on this subject.

12. W. Perkins, *Lectures upon the three first chapters of Revelation . . .* , p. 371.

13. L. Stone, *The Crisis of the Aristocracy* (Oxford 1965), pp. 741–2; C.
Butler, *Historical Memoirs respecting English Irish and Scotish Catholics from
the Reformation*, 4 vols (1819–21), i, pp. 296–8.

14. P. Caraman (ed.), *The Autobiography of John Gerard* (1951), pp. xvii–
xviii; P. Caraman, *Henry Morse, Priest of the Plague* (1957), p. 7; T. G. Law,
*A Historical Sketch of the Conflicts between Jesuits and Seculars in the Reign of
Queen Elizabeth* (1889), p. 105.

15. A. G. Dickens, 'The First Stage of Romanist Recusancy in Yorkshire
1560–90', *Yorkshire Archaeological Journal*, xxxv (1940–3), pp. 157–81; D.
Mathew, *Catholicism in England 1535–1935* (1936), pp. 55–8; P. Caraman,
Henry Morse, pp. 141–2; A. C. Wood, *Nottinghamshire in the Civil War* (Oxford
1937), p. 187; B. H. Cunnington (ed.), *The Records of Wiltshire . . . extracts
from the Quarter Sessions . . . Rolls* (Devizes 1932), p. xv; BM Harl. MSS 787,
Dell Papers, f. 21 *verso*, Archbishop of Canterbury's Report for his Diocese
1637.

16. F. X. Walker, 'The Implementation of the Elizabethan Penal Statutes
against Recusants 1581–1603' (University of London Ph.D. Thesis, 1961),
pp. 49, 51, 111–12, 136–7; LJ (12 July 1641), iv, p. 309n.

17. A. G. Dickens, 'The Extent and Character of recusancy in Yorkshire
1604', *Yorks. Arch. Journ.*, xxxvii (1948–51), pp. 24–8; G. Albion, *Charles I and
the Court of Rome* (1938), p. 13 and n.2; F. O. Blundell, *Old Catholic Lancashire*,
3 vols (1925), iii, pp. 133–4; 'Registers of Dunbenhalgh and St. Mary's Enfield,
in the Township of Clayton-le-Moore, County Lancaster', *Catholic Record
Society*, xxxvi (1936), p. 217; G. Anstruther, *Vaux of Harrowden* (Newport,
Mon. 1953), p. 113.

18. G. Albion, *Charles I and . . . Rome*, pp. 7–8, 251–2, 262 n.1; C. J. Ryan,
'The Jacobean Oath of Allegiance and English Lay Catholics', *The Catholic
Historical Review*, xviii (1942), p. 174.

19. J. Gillow, *Biographical Dictionary of English Catholics*, 5 vols (1883), ii,

p. 108; Tierney-Dodd, *Church History*, iv, p. 76n; H. Foley, *Records of the English Province of the Society of Jesus*, 8 vols (1875–83), iv, pp. 391–2; R. Challoner, *Memoirs of Missionary Priests and other Catholics* . . . *1579–1684*, 2 vols (Manchester 1803), ii passim; SP 16/10/21, Deputy-Lieutenants of Staffordshire to the Privy Council 24 Nov. 1625.

20. E. Hyde, *State Papers collected by Edward, Earl of Clarendon*, 3 vols (Oxford 1767–86), i, p. 355, for Charles saying that the majority of English Catholics would take the Oath 'were they not terrified by an over-awing power' For Charles's discussions over the Oath see *ibid.*, i, pp. 169–70, 180, 184, 188–96, 207, 271–3; and Albion, *Charles I and Rome*, chs. x, xi passim.

21. Albion, *Charles I and Rome*, p. 164 (for Henrietta Maria's remark); Speech to the Second Parliament of the Protectorate, 17 Sept. 1656, T. Carlyle (ed.), *Oliver Cromwell's Letters and Speeches*, 3 vols (1857), iii, p. 167; G. Sitwell, 'Leander Jones' Mission to England 1634–35', *Recusant History*, v, (1959–60), pp. 141–2; *Clarendon State Papers*, i, pp. 91–2; Albion, *Charles I and Rome*, pp. 12–13; *Ibid.*, pp. 136–7, 179; A. G. Lee, *The Son of Leicester* (1964), pp. 169–72, 197–8.

22. *The Downfall of Dagon, or the taking down of the Cheapside Cross*, E 100 No. 21 (2 May 1643). For the reference to disease and infection see HMC 4th Report, House of Lords MSS, p. 97, a 'Petition of artificers of London and Westminster' to the House of Commons 16 Aug. 1641.

23. BM Harl. MSS 164, f. 880 (30 Aug. 1641), Sir Simonds D'Ewes's Parliamentary Diary.

24. BM Add. MSS 34218, Fane Papers, f. 10 *verso;* J. O. Halliwell (ed.), *The Autobiography and Correspondence of Sir Simonds D'Ewes*, 2 vols (1845), ii, pp. 353–4.

25. SP, 14/81/54, i–iv; BM Landsdowne MSS 82, f. 103; J. Bruce (ed.), *Verney Papers* (Camden Soc.), lvi, pp. 119–20.

26. *Buckinghamshire* in *The Victoria Histories of the Counties of England* (1905–27), i, p. 319 and n.; *The Winthrop Papers* (Collections of the Massachusetts Historical Society, 4th ser., 1893), iv, p. 92; D. Laing (ed.), *The Letters and Journals of Robert Baillie D. D.*, 3 vols (Edinburgh 1841), i, p. 198.

27. Gardiner, ix, pp. 133–6; SP 16/458/12, 13.

28. Gardiner, ix p. 128; SP, 16/455/4, 457/58, 460/5, 40, 48, 46, 50, 56, 463/27; HMC, 9th Report, p. 499; *ibid.*, 12th Report, Rutland MSS, app. iv p. 522; T. T. Lewis (ed.), *The Letters of Lady Brilliana Harley* (Camden Soc. 1854), lviii, p. 95; Westminster Cathedral MSS, xxix, f. 340.

29. SP, 16/467/90.39; HMC, MSS in Various Collections, ii, Buxton MSS, p. 258; for London Petition, see SP, 16/648/29.

30. W. Notestein (ed.), *The Journal of Sir Simonds D'Ewes* (New Haven 1923), pp. 31 n. 4, 36, 25; CJ, ii, p. 26

31. CSP Ven. 1640–42, Nos 185, 191; Gardiner, ix, p. 364.

32. H. Stocks and W. Stevenson, *Records of the Borough of Leicester* . . . 1603–88, 3 vols (Cambridge 1923), iii, p. 322; HMC, 10th Report, Corporation of Bridgnorth MSS, app. iii, p. 433–4; *ibid.*, 11th Report, Corporation of Bridgnorth MSS, app. vii, p. 147; *ibid.*, 14th Report Portland MSS, app. ii, p. 81–2.

33. HMC, 5th Report, House of Lords MSS, p. 7; *ibid.*, 13th Report, Portland MSS, app. i, p. 28–9; W. H. Coates (ed.), *The Journal of Sir Simonds D'Ewes* (New Haven 1942) p. 300 and n. 19.

34. SP, 16/468/57, 100, 485/95; F. R. Raines (ed.), *The Stanley Papers Part III* (Chetham Soc. 1867), lxvi, p. lxviii.

35. *Perfect Diurnal*, BM Burney 12 (28 Feb.–7 Mar. 1642), pp. 5–6; *Diurnal Occurrences*, E 201 (28 Feb.–7 Mar. 1642), pp. 5–6; *A Bloody Plot Practised by*

some Papists, E 134, No. 8 (18 Jan. 1642); Bloody Newes from Norwich . . . , E 179
No. 10 (Nov. 1641); Coates, D'Ewes' Journal, pp. 12 on. 9, 222–3; CJ, ii, p. 328.

36. LJ, iv, pp. 426, 417–18; Coates, D'Ewes' Journal, pp. 125, 146; N. Wallington, Historical Notices of events occurring chiefly in the Reign of Charles I, 2 vols
(1869), ii, pp. 42–4; SP, 16/488/68; Exceeding Good Newes . . . E 135 No. 2
(Feb. 1642); CJ, ii, pp. 372–3; R. C. Anderson (ed.), The Book of Examinations
and Depositions Part IV, 1622–44 (Southampton Record Soc., 1936), xvi, p. 30.

37. Examinations and Depositions (Southampton Record Soc.), xvi, pp. 42–3;
Terrible Newes . . . , E 112 No. 3 (Aug. 1642), p. 5.

38. BM Harl. MSS 163, ff. 682 verso, 685; M. Foley, Records of the Society of
Jesus, ii, pp. 425–6; F. Peck, Desiderata Curiosa, 2 vols (1779), ii, pp. 474–5.

39. J. Harland, 'The Lancashire Lieutenancy under the Tudors and Stuarts'
(Chetham Soc. 1850), i, pp. 278, 298; A Discourse of the Warr in Lancashire
(Chetham Soc. 1864), lxii, pp. 19, 21.

40. For examples see G. F. Nuttall, Visible Saints (Oxford 1957), p. 113;
T. Smith, A Gag for the Quakers (1659); and R. Clifton, 'The Popular Fear of
Catholics during the English Revolution', P&P, lii (1971), pp. 33–4.

41. Hyde, History of the Rebellion, i, pp. 399–400, 409n; E. Ludlow, The
Memoirs of Edmund Ludlow, 2 vols (Bern 1698) i, p. 17; Baillie, Letters and
Journals, i, p. 397.

42. For examples of contemporary attitudes, see nn. 1–3; for the Elect Nation
view in 1641, see John Milton, Of Reformation in England, and Thomas Goodwin,
A Glimpse of Sion's Glory (1641), printed in A. S. P. Woodhouse (ed.), Puritanism
and Liberty (1966), pp. 233–41.

43. M. V. Hay, The Blairs Papers 1603–1660 (Edinburgh 1929), pp. 32–4,
79–80.

44. For meetings see Hyde, History of the Rebellion, i, p. 327; BM Harl. MSS
164, f. 324 verso; CJ ii, pp. 372–3, 411, 579; SP, 16/457/21, 467/41; HMC, 5th
Report, House of Lords MSS, p. 13; ibid., 14th Report, app. ii, Portland MSS,
p. 69; Harley Letters (Camden Soc.), lviii, p. 105; Coates, D'Ewes' Journal, pp.
146, 300; Strange Newes from Staffordshire, E 149 No. 25 (4 June 1642). For the
purchase of arms see LJ, iv, pp. 564–5, 576, 579, 581, 583, 596; CJ, ii, pp. 372–3;
SP, 16/467/104, 488/68; BM Add. MSS 11045, f. 151; HMC, 5th Report, House
of Lords MSS, p. 7; ibid., 9th Report, Pole-Gell MSS, app. ii, p. 391. For food
purchases see HMC, 5th Report, House of Lords MSS, p. 13; ibid., 14th Report,
iii, Portland MSS, p. 67.

45. BM Lansdowne MSS 82, Burghley Papers, f. 103; and above nn. 37–9.

6. TWO CULTURES? COURT AND COUNTRY UNDER CHARLES I

P. W. Thomas

1. Concerning the complex nature of Puritanism see Christopher Hill's
Society and Puritanism in Pre-Revolutionary England (1964; repr. 1969).

2. The last point is from The Order of the Causes of Salvation and Damnation
(1598; repr. 1606); the dig at long hair from An Exposition of Christs Sermon on
the Mount (1608); the other phrases occur in The Whole Treatise of the Cases
of Conscience (1606). He expounds the proper use of images in A Warning Against
the Idolatry of the Last Times (1601). All these were published in Perkins's
Cambridge.

3. The denunciation occurs in Sonnet LXVI of Greville's sequence Caelica;
the pragmatic note is struck in his Treatise of Humane Learning. Joan Rees,
Fulke Greville, Lord Brooke 1554–1628 A Critical Biography gives a useful
account: see especially her Chapter 8, 'Humanist and Calvinist'.

4. See L. B. Waller, *Fletcher, Beaumont and Company, Entertainers to the Jacobean Gentry* (New York 1947) and Clifford Leach, *The Fletcher Plays* (1952) who (pp. 11–12) quotes Coleridge. Dryden's tribute appeared in his *Essay of Dramatick Poesie* (1668).

5. Quoted by Ursula Hoff, *Charles I, Patron of Artists* (1942), p. 17.

6. See C. H. Herford and P. and E. Simpson's edition of *Ben Jonson*, vi (1938), p. 501.

7. For these and Dorset's comments, see S. R. Gardiner (ed.), *Documents Relating to the Proceedings against William Prynne, in 1634 and 1637*, (Camden Soc., NS, xviii, 1877), pp. 24, 90.

8. For Suckling, see O. L. Dick (ed.), *John Aubrey's Brief Lives* (1949) and the Introduction in Thomas Clayton (ed.), *The Works of Sir John Suckling* (Oxford 1971).

9. The Petition is reprinted in Appendix C of Don M. Wolfe (ed.), *Complete Prose Works of John Milton, Vol. I: 1624–1642* (New Haven 1953). Wolfe's Introduction to this volume contains a useful account of the reformist movement in the decades prior to the Civil War.

10. Butler's piece was published in 1682; *Anti-Britanicus* was a three-part pamphlet published in Oxford on 4, 11, 18 April 1645; Cleveland's dig is from *The Character of a London Diurnall* (1645).

11. *Mercurius Britanicus*, No. 64, 30 December – 6 January 1645; the jibe at Jones is in No. 24, 4–11 January, 1644.

12. John Allibond to Peter Heylin, SP 16/448/79.

13. The phrases are from, respectively, the *Hue and Cry after Sir John Presbyter* (1649); *Hudibras* (1663); and *The Hind and the Panther* (1687).

14. Cited by Christopher Hill, *Society and Puritanism in Pre-Revolutionary England* (1964; rep. 1969), p. 28.

15. *The Litany of John Bastwick* (1637).

16. See *Poems of Anne Bradstreet*, edited with an Introduction by Robert Hutchinson (New York 1969).

17. See W. R. Parker's splendid two-volume *Milton: A Biography* (Oxford 1968).

18. The quotations are from *The Reason of Church Government* (1642) and *Paradise Regained* (1671) respectively.

19. Parker, *op. cit.*, p. 142.

20. See William and Melville Haller 'The Puritan Art of Love', *Huntington Library Quarterly* (1941–2), pp. 235–272 and L. Schucking, *The Puritan Family* (1929, rep. 1969).

21. Milton's phrase in *Eikonoklastes*.

22. Christopher Hill's *The Century of Revolution 1603–1714* (1961, rep. 1969) and *Puritanism and Revolution* (1958, rep. 1969), display the richness of the scene; Cromwell's encouragement of able and progressive men is illustrated by H. R. Trevor-Roper's 'Scotland and the Puritan Revolution' and 'Three Foreigners' in *Religion, the Reformation and Social Change* (1967). A sensible, measured account of the Puritan contribution to letters is given by Laurence A. Sasek, *The Literary Temper of the English Puritans* (Baton Rouge 1961).

23. See H. R. Trevor-Roper, 'Oliver Cromwell and his Parliaments', *op. cit.*

24. *Preface to the Fables* (1700).

7. ECONOMIC ISSUES AND IDEOLOGIES *Penelope Corfield*

I would like to thank Professor F. J. Fisher and Peter Clark for criticising early drafts of this essay.

1. B. Schofield (ed.), *The Knyvett Letters, 1620–1644* (1949), p. 107.

2. W. Letwin, *The Origins of Scientific Economics. English Economic Thought, 1660–1776* (1963), pp. 207–221.

3. E. Burke, *Reflections on the Revolution in France*, edited by C. C. O'Brien (1968), p. 170

4. Most writers now accept that the Tudor economy was not a planned one. See C. Hill, *Reformation to Industrial Revolution: British Economy and Society, 1530–1780* (1967), p. 73. For an alternative view however, see L. Stone, *The Crisis of the Aristocracy, 1558–1641* (Oxford 1965), p. 425.

5. J. Thirsk (ed.), *The Agrarian History of England and Wales, Vol. IV: 1540–1640* (Cambridge 1967), pp. 200–55, 593–696. For a different emphasis, which discounts the social hardship, see E. Kerridge, *Agrarian Problems in the Sixteenth Century and After* (1969), *passim*, especially pp. 119–33.

6. Hill, 65–9. See also F. J. Fisher, 'Tawney's Century' in F. J. Fisher (ed.), *Essays in the Economic and Social History of Tudor and Stuart England* (Cambridge 1961), pp. 1–14.

7. E. Hobsbawm, 'The General Crisis of the European Economy in the Seventeenth Century', P&P, No. 5 (1954), pp. 33–53, and No. 6 (1954), pp. 44–65. The controversy over these articles has centred round their political analysis rather than their economic data. See also C. Wilson, *England's Apprenticeship, 1603–1763* (1965), p. 75.

8. B. E. Supple, *Commercial Crisis and Change in England, 1600–42* (Cambridge 1964), pp. 1–20, 125–31.

9. See R. Ashton, 'Charles I and the City' in F. J. Fisher (ed.), *op. cit.*, 138–63, and also V. Pearl, *London and the Outbreak of the Puritan Revolution* (Oxford 1961), especially pp. 99–101 and 207–8.

10. See Kerridge, 112–18. See also M. Beresford, 'Habitation versus Improvement: the Debate on Enclosure by Agreement', in F. J. Fisher (ed.), 48–55. For Pym, see J. Rushworth (ed.), *Historical Collections*, iii, i, 23.

11. For the debate on enclosures, see Beresford, pp. 40–69, and J. Kent, 'Social Attitudes of Members of Parliament, 1590–1624' (unpublished Ph.D. thesis, University of London 1971), pp. 171–243. For Raleigh, see C. Hill, *Intellectual Origins of the English Revolution* (Oxford 1965), pp. 165–6, and for Hartlib, see C. Webster (ed.), *Samuel Hartlib and the Advancement of Learning* (Cambridge 1970), p. 82, and his note on *Macaria*, P&P No. 56 (1972), pp. 34–48.

12. J. Selden, *Table Talk* (1887), p. 121.

13. M. James, *Social Problems and Policy during the Puritan Revolution, 1640–1660* (re-issue 1966), p. 97.

14. Supple, pp. 117–18, 244, and also T. G. Barnes, pp. 172–89.

15. CSPD, 1637–8, pp. 103–4.

16. S. and B. Webb, 'The Assize of Bread', *Economic Journal* (1904), pp. 196–218. See also E. P. Thompson, 'The Moral Economy of the English Crowd in the Eighteenth Century', P&P No. 50 (1971), pp. 89–94.

17. E. Hyde, *History of the Rebellion and Civil Wars in England* (Oxford 1888), i, p. 85.

18. C. Hill, *Society and Puritanism in Pre-revolutionary England* (1964), p. 490. For the controversy over the companies, see James, *op. cit.*, pp. 135–8, and 193–223.

19. E. W. Ives, 'Social Change and the Law', in E. W. Ives (ed.), *The English Revolution, 1600–1660* (1968), pp. 117–20.

20. See D. O. Wagner, 'Coke and the Rise of Economic Liberalism', ECHR, 1st ser. vi (1935), pp. 30–44; B. Malament, 'The "Economic Liberalism" of Sir Edward Coke', *The Yale Law Journal*, lxxvi (1967), pp. 1321–58, and C. Hill, *Intellectual Origins*, pp. 233–43.

21. See A. Friis, *Alderman Cockayne's Project and the Cloth Trade: The Commercial Policy of England in its Main Aspects, 1600–25* (Copenhagen 1927), *passim*, and Supple, pp. 35–51.

22. Wilson, p. 115.

23. Hill, *Intellectual Origins*, pp. 234–5. See also J. P. Cooper, 'Economic Regulation and the Cloth Industry in Seventeenth Century England', TRHS, 5th ser., xx (1970), pp. 73–99.

24. S. A. Strong (ed.), *A Catalogue of Letters and Other Historical Documents exhibited in the Library at Welbeck* (1903), p. 204.

25. James, p. 147.

26. A. P. Newton, *The Colonising Activities of the English Puritans. The Last Phase of the Elizabethan Struggle with Spain* (New Haven 1914), pp. 314–18.

27. F. Bacon, *Essayes or Counsels Civill and Morall* (1897), pp. 52–3, 112. See also Hill, *Intellectual Origins*, pp. 96–100.

28. W. Knowler (ed.), *The Earl of Strafforde's Letters and Dispatches* (1739, i, p. 93 and ii, pp. 19–20.

29. Gardiner, x, p. 206.

30. P. Zagorin, *The Court and the Country. The Beginning of the English Revolution* (1969), pp. 119–55.

31. Hyde, iv, p. 179.

32. T. Hobbes, *Behemoth, or the Long Parliament*, edited by F. Tönnies (1969), pp. 3–4.

8. POLITICS AND POLITICAL THOUGHT 1640–1642
M. J. Mendle

1. Kenyon, p. 206.

2. J. G. A. Pocock, *The Ancient Constitution and the Feudal Law* (Cambridge 1957). *Argument of Nicholas Fuller* (1641) E 156 No. 19, p. 14.

3. Henry Parker, *Case of Shipmoney* (1640), E 204 No. 4, p. 4.

4. Sir John Finch in *State Trials*, iii col. 1225. See also *ibid.*, col. 174 and cols. 1184–5.

5. Wilson, cited in L. Stone (ed.), *Social Change and Revolution in England, 1540–1640* (1966), p. 117. Sir T. Aston, *Remonstrance Against Presbytery* (1641), sig. B4 recto. N. Wallington, *Historical Notices . . . of the Reign of Charles I*, edited by R. Webb (1869), ii, p. 14. W. Coates (ed.), *D'Ewes*, pp. xxiv, 356 n. 4.

6. Sir B. Rudyerd, E 196 No. 2 p. 1.

7. HMC *Ormonde*, New Ser. ii, pp. 378–9. Lucy Hutchinson called these public constitutional debates 'but the prologue to the ensuing tragedy', *Memoirs of the Life of Colonel Hutchinson* (1908), p. 76. C. C. Weston, *English Constitutional Theory and the House of Lords* (1965).

8. Pym in Kenyon, p. 198 and E 198 No. 35, p. 5. Grimston, E 198 No. 5, p. 5.

9. BM Harl. MSS 4931, f. 47. D. Gardiner (ed.), *Oxinden Letters* (1933), i, p. 163. S. R. Gardiner, ix, pp. 106–7.

10. Saye in *Winthrop Papers*, iv (Boston, Mass. 1944), p. 267. BM Harl. MSS 4931, f. 47. CSP Ven., 1636–1639, pp. 536, 548. L. P. Smith (ed.), *Life and Letters of Sir Henry Wotton* (Oxford 1907), ii, p. 407. See also BM Harl. MSS 1219, ff. 1–2.

11. Bagshaw, E 196 No. 31, p. 3. Saye, E 198 No. 16, p. 8. Parker, p. 35.

12. Henry Parker, *Altar Dispute* (1641), E 140 No. 19, sig. A2 verso. [John Corbet], *Epistle Congratulatory of Lysimachus Nicanor* (1640), E 203 No. 7,

pp. 10–11; see also p. 4. Edward Arber (ed.), *Transcript of the Register of the Company of Stationers* (1877), iv, p. 474, licensed by Windebank 19 February 1639/40.

13. *A Sermon . . . 1 September 1640*, E 157 No. 4, pp. 12, 37–8. D.N.B. *sub* Downing, Calybute. Cf. Henry Parker, *Discourse concerning Puritans*, E 204 No. 3, p. 44.

14. Parker, *Shipmoney*, p. 20; *Observations upon Some of His Majesties Late Answers and Expresses* (1642), pp. 19, 25.

15. Kenyon, p. 21.

16. So Sir Edward Dering in E 196, No. 20, pp. 11–12; BM 3274 No. 2, p. 12; and CSPD 1641–1643, pp. 294–5. Evidently Dering edited the phrase out of the expanded version given in his *Collection of Speeches* (1642) E 197, No. 1. See also W. Notestein (ed.), *Journal of Sir Simonds D'Ewes* (New Haven 1923), p. 149, n.18.

17. Rudyerd, E 196 No. 2, p. 3. Rous BM Add. MSS 6411, ff. 38b–41b, *inter alia*. Phelips, in Notestein and Relf (eds), *Commons Debates for 1629* (1921), pp. 176–8. Throckmorton, in Sir John Neale, *Elizabeth and her Parliaments* (1957), ii, p. 151. Parker, *Discourse*, p. 58. Digby, E 196 No. 6, p. 9. Culpeper, E 196 No. 8, p. 3.

18. See generally V. Pearl, *London and the Outbreak of the Puritan Revolution* (Oxford 1961) to which I am here and elsewhere heavily indebted. Digby and Culpeper as in n. 17 *supra*, p. 2 and p. 1, respectively.

19. Digby, E 196 No. 30, pp. 8, 15–16. D'Ewes (Notestein), pp. 339–40. Bagshaw, E 196 No. 31, pp. 1–2. Saye, E 198 No. 16, p. 1. Dering, *Collection of Speeches*, *op. cit.*, p. 3. See n. 24 *infra*.

20. CSPD, 1640–1, pp. 418, 445–6, 484. Sir T. Aston, *Collection of Sundry Petitions*, E 150 No. 28, pp. 1–4. LJ, iv, p. 174. BM Harl. MSS 6424, ff. 6a–7a.

21. Strafford quoted in C. V. Wedgwood, *Thomas Wentworth, First Earl of Strafford, 1593–1641: A Revaluation* (1964), p. 361. BM Harl. MSS 6424, ff. 58a–59b. J. O. Halliwell (ed.), *Autobiography and Correspondence of Sir Simonds D'Ewes, Bart. . . .* (1845), ii, p. 268.

22. CSPD, 1641–1643, p. 44.

23. BM Harl. MSS 163, f. 276a. Henry Parker, *The Question Concerning the Divine Right of Episcopacy Truly Stated* (1641), E 162 No. 4, sig. A2 verso. The final version of Dering's scheme is outlined in his *Collection of Speeches*, *op. cit.*, pp. 155–61. An earlier version made the rounds anonymously and under misleading titles; I hope to elaborate on this elsewhere. Ussher's scheme was not printed until 1656. See E 897 No. 1, E 894 No. 3 and *Reliquiae Baxterianae* (1696) for texts and controversy over them. *The Bishop of Armagh's Direction* (1642), E 153 No. 8 was repudiated by Ussher. It is probably correctly ascribed to Ephrain Udall. See D.N.B. *sub* Udall, Ephraim and CJ, ii, p. 81. Williams's scheme in HMC, *Fourth Report* (1874), p. 81.

24. D'Ewes, *Autobiography and Correspondence, op. cit.* ii, pp. 270–1. CSP Ven., 1640–1642, pp. 161, 164. William Bray (ed.), *Diary and Correspondence of John Evelyn* (1906), iv, pp. 95, 97.

25. Evelyn, *Diary and Correspondence, op. cit.*, iv, pp. 84–5, 91, 110, 112, 128–9, 136–7, 139, BM Harl. MSS 6424, ff. 88b–89a. LJ, iv, pp. 338, 345. CJ, ii, pp. 245.

26. C. H. Firth, *The House of Lords during the Civil War* (1910), p. 99.

27. W. Coates (ed.), *Diary of Sir Simonds D'Ewes* (New Haven 1942), p. 228. HMC *Buccleuch*, i, pp. 286–8. CSPD, 1641–1643, pp. 194, 215. Clarendon, *History of the Rebellion* (1888), i, p. 485. Cf. CSP Clar., i, p. 221, and for commentary *D'Ewes* (Coates), p. 216 n. 11. Bramston cited in Firth, *House of Lords, op. cit.*,

p. 104. The account in *Persecutio Undecima* (1647), pp. 64–7 is particularly valuable for this time, and has provided the subheading.

28. For Kent, see A. M. Everitt, *Community of Kent and the Great Rebellion* (Leicester 1966), pp. 89–91 and sources there cited. For all the rest, except Rutland, sufficient annotation and valuable comment in *D'Ewes* (Coates), pp. 290–1 n. 3; see also pp. 165–6. For Rutland, BM Egerton MSS 2986, pp. 253–7; Aston, *Collection of Sundry Petitions*, sig. A2 verso. LJ, iv, pp. 467, 469, 482.

29. BM Harl. MSS 162, f. 351b.

30. LJ, iv, pp. 500–501, 506. Bulstrode Whitelocke, *Memorials of English Affairs* (Oxford 1853) i, p. 156. Wallington, ii, p. 1 and n. The petitioners denied the connection: BM Harl. MSS 162, f. 314b.

31. LJ, iv, pp. 490, 533, 543. CSP Ven., 1640–1642, p. 289. Sir R. Verney, *Notes of Proceedings in the Long Parliament* (Camden Series) edited by John Bruce (1845), pp. 147–9. BM Harl. MSS 162, f. 335. Harl. MSS 480, ff. 36a–37b. *A Continuation of the True Diurnal of Passages*, No. 2, BM Burney 12 No. 6. *A True Diurnal of the Passages*, No. 2, BM LR 263, b. 38.

32. LJ, iv, pp. 535–6; BM Harl. MSS 162, f. 347b.

33. LJ, iv, pp. 536–7; HMC *Fourth Report* (1874), p. 114; HMC *Fifth Report* (1876), pp. 4–5.

34. LJ, iv, pp. 537–44, 549.

35. BM Harl. MSS 480, f. 81b. Harl. MSS 162, f. 360b. BM 669 No. 54, f. 4. Clarendon, *History*, i, pp. 549–50, does justice to the episode of 'this horrible petition'.

36. BM Add. MSS 14827, f. 23b. LJ, iv, p. 559. HMC *Mss. of the House of Lords*, *Addenda* XI (New Ser.), pp. 306–7.

37. LJ, iv, pp. 559–72, *passim.*, 595, 599. BM Add. MSS 14827, f. 25a.

38. Stephen Marshall, *Meroz Cursed* (1642), p. 1. Edmund Calamy, *God's Free Mercy to England* (1642), pp. 4, 7, 39.

39. Sir F. Pollock (ed.), *Table Talk of John Selden* (1927), p. 18.

40. Kenyon, p. 243. *Plea for Moderation* (1642), E 143 No. 7 sig. B2 recto. This very important pamphlet is anonymous. The grounds for attribution are too involved for discussion here.

9. ENGLAND AND EUROPE: A COMMON MALADY?

J. H. Elliott

1. A(rchivo) G(eneral de) S(imancas), Est(ado), leg(ajo) 2520. *Voto* of Olivares in the Council of State, 8 December 1635.

2. AGS Est. leg. 2521. El Conde-Duque sobre despachos de Inglaterra, 3 January 1637.

3. *Ibid.*

4. AGS Est. leg. 2521. *Voto* of Olivares in Council of State, 6 March 1640.

5. J. H. Elliott, *The Revolt of the Catalans* (Cambridge 1963), p. 368.

6. See H. R. Trevor-Roper, 'The General Crisis of the Seventeenth Century', in Trevor Aston, *Crisis in Europe, 1560–1660* (1965), pp. 59–95, and the resulting controversy.

7. Quoted by M. A. Judson, *The Crisis of the Constitution* (New Brunswick, 1949, rep. 1971), p. 221.

8. 'On Aristocratic Constitutionalism in Swedish History' (Creighton Lecture for 1965, repr. in Michael Roberts, *Essays in Swedish History* (1967)).

Notes on Contributors

Conrad Russell is Professor of History at Yale University. He was formerly Reader in History at Bedford College, University of London. His publications include *The Crisis of Parliaments: History of England 1509–1660* in the Shorter Oxford History of the Modern World and *Parliaments and English Politics 1621–29*.

ROBIN CLIFTON, Lecturer in History, University of Warwick, formerly research student at Balliol College, Oxford. Has in preparation a history of the 1685 rebellion, and is working on relations between Catholics and Protestants in 17th century England.

PENELOPE CORFIELD, Lecturer in History, Bedford College, University of London. Formerly a student at St. Hilda's College, Oxford, and at the London School of Economics and Political Science.

J. H. ELLIOTT, Fellow of the Institute of Advanced Studies, Princeton, New Jersey, U.S.A. Formerly Professor of History, King's College, University of London and Lecturer in History, University of Cambridge. Author of *The Revolt of the Catalans; Imperial Spain; Europe Divided, 1559–1598*; and *The Old World and the New*. At present working on the career and politics of the Count-Duke of Olivares.

MICHAEL J. HAWKINS, Reader in History in the School of English and American Studies, University of Sussex. Author of 'Sales of Wards in Somerset, 1603–1641', *Somerset Record Society*, lxvii, and has in preparation volumes on *Wardship and Society in Early Stuart England* and *The Personal Rule of Charles I*. His research intersts include the relationship between literature and social change in the period 1580–1640, and the professions as avenues of social mobility in early modern England.

L. M. HILL, Assistant Professor of History, University of California at Irvine, California. Graduate of Kenyon College, Gambier, Ohio; Research Fellow at the Institute of Historical Research, London. Has in preparation a biography of Sir Julius Caesar, and has published an edition of the latter's *The Ancient State, Authoritie, and Proceedings of the Court of Requests*. His research interests also include the Exchequer in the early 17th century.

M. J. MENDLE, Instructor, School of Liberal Arts, Brooklyn College of the City University of New York. Undergraduate at the College of Letters, Wesleyan University; Woodrow Wilson National Fellow, 1966–67. Has in preparation a study of political thought, 1640–1642.

P. W. THOMAS, Lecturer in English, University College, Cardiff. Graduate of Jesus College, Oxford. Author of *Sir John Berkenhead*, a study of the leading Royalist journalist. Has in preparation an edition of the plays and poems of Sir Thomas Salusbury, and an edition of the Newsbooks of 1640–1653 for the *English Revolution* reprint series.

NICHOLAS TYACKE, Lecturer in History, University College, University of London. Undergraduate at Balliol College, Oxford.

Index